EXODUS TO
NORTH KOREA

ASIAN VOICES

A Subseries of Asian/Pacific/Perspectives

Series Editor: Mark Selden

Identity and Resistance in Okinawa
By Matthew Alden
Tales of Tibet: Sky Burials, Prayer Wheels, and Wind Horses
edited and translated by Herbert Batt, foreword by Tsering Shakya
Voicing Concerns: Contemporary Chinese Critical Inquiry
edited by Gloria Davies, conclusion by Geremie Barmé
Peasants, Rebels, Women, and Outcastes: The Underside of Modern Japan
by Mikiso Hane
Comfort Woman: A Filipina's Story of Prostitution and Slavery under the Japanese Military
by Maria Rosa Henson, introduction by Yuki Tanaka
Japan's Past, Japan's Future: One Historian's Odyssey
by Ienaga Saburÿ, translated and introduced by Richard H. Minear
Sisters and Lovers: Women and Desire in Bali
by Megan Jennaway
Moral Politics in a South Chinese Village: Responsibility, Reciprocity, and Resistance
by Hok Bun Ku
Queer Japan from the Pacific War to the Internet Age
by Mark McLelland
Behind the Silence: Chinese Voices on Abortion
by Nie Jing-Bao
Rowing the Eternal Sea: The Life of a Minamata Fisherman
by Oiwa Keibo, narrated by Ogata Masato, translated by Karen Colligan-Taylor
Growing Up Untouchable in India: A Dalit Autobiography
by Vasant Moon, translated by Gail Omvedt, introduction by Eleanor Zelliot
Exodus to North Korea: Shadows from Japan's Cold War
By Tessa Morris-Suzuki
Red Is Not the Only Color: Contemporary Chinese Fiction on Love and Sex between Women, Collected Stories
edited by Patricia Sieber
Sweet and Sour: Life-Worlds of Taipei Women Entrepreneurs
by Scott Simon
Dear General MacArthur: Letters from the Japanese during the American Occupation
by Sodei Rinjirÿ, edited by John Junkerman, translated by Shizue Matsuda, foreword by John W. Dower
A Thousand Miles of Dreams: The Journeys of Two Chinese Sisters
By Sasha Su-Ling Welland
Unbroken Spirits: Nineteen Years in South Korea's Gulag
by Suh Sung, translated by Jean Inglis, foreword by James Palais

EXODUS TO NORTH KOREA

Shadows from Japan's Cold War

TESSA MORRIS-SUZUKI

ROWMAN & LITTLEFIELD PUBLISHERS, INC.
Lanham • Boulder • New York • Toronto • Plymouth, UK

ROWMAN & LITTLEFIELD PUBLISHERS, INC.

Published in the United States of America
by Rowman & Littlefield Publishers, Inc.
A wholly owned subsidiary of The Rowman & Littlefield Publishing Group, Inc.
4501 Forbes Boulevard, Suite 200, Lanham, Maryland 20706
www.rowmanlittlefield.com

Estover Road, Plymouth PL6 7PY, United Kingdom

British Library Cataloging in Publication Information Available

Library of Congress Cataloging-in-Publication Data

Morris-Suzuki, Tessa.
    Exodus to North Korea : shadows from Japan's cold war / Tessa Morris-Suzuki.
        p. cm. — (Asian voices)
    Includes bibliographical references and index.
    ISBN-13: 978-0-7425-5441-2 (cloth : alk. paper)
    ISBN-10: 0-7425-5441-4 (cloth : alk. paper)
    ISBN-13: 978-0-7425-5442-9 (pbk. : alk. paper)
    ISBN-10: 0-7425-5442-2 (pbk. : alk. paper)
    1. Return migration—Korea (North) 2. Repatriation—Korea (North) 3.
Koreans—Japan—History. 4. Korea (North)—Foreign relations—Japan. 5.
Japan—Foreign relations—Korea (North) 6. Cold War. I. Title.
JV8757.5.M67 2006
325'.2520519309045—dc22

                                                                        2006030281

Printed in the United States of America

∞™ The paper used in this publication meets the minimum requirements of
American National Standard for Information Sciences—Permanence of Paper for
Printed Library Materials, ANSI/NISO Z39.48-1992.

We travel like other people, but we return to nowhere . . .

(Mahmoud Darwish, "We Travel like Other People"
from the collection of poems *Victims of a Map*)

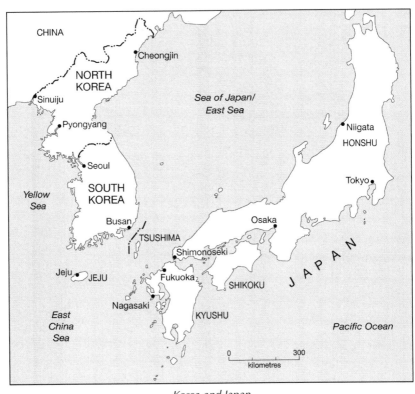

Korea and Japan

CONTENTS

Part IV: Accord

Part V: Arrivals

ACKNOWLEDGMENTS

So many people contributed to the making of this book that it would be impossible for me to thank them all individually. However, first and foremost, my thanks go to the "returnees" and others who shared their stories with me—above all to "Taniguchi Hiroko," Yi Yang-Soo, Oh Su-Ryong, and "Yamada Kumiko." I am particularly grateful to Yi Yang-Soo for helping me obtain other important information related to the repatriation project, including material recently declassified by the South Korean government.

Access to the valuable resources held by the International Committee of the Red Cross (ICRC) was greatly assisted by the kindness and expertise of the staff of the ICRC Archives, particularly Fabrizio Bensi. In Japan, Australia, the United States, and elsewhere, Pak Jeong-Jin, Hyun Moo-Am, Andrei Lankov, Sara Berndt, Curtis Gayle, Dane Alston, Hea-Jin Park and Leonid Petrov gave generous assistance in locating other archival sources. The task of sorting and managing the large mass of documents related to this story would have been impossible without the superb organizational skills of Christine Winter, and my research was helped and supported by Karashima Masato, Jen Badstuebner, Tokunaga Risa, Steven Jarvis, and Matsuda Hiroko. I am also most grateful to Ishimaru Jirô of Asia Press for his valuable help, particularly in arranging interviews with returnees, to Chang Myeong-Su for his comments and information, and to Tim Amos for introducing me to the poems of Mahmoud Darwish.

Versions of the manuscript were read by Robin Fletcher, Neville Fletcher, and Maxine McArthur, who provided wise advice and encouragement. My warm thanks also go to my companions on parts of this journey through Cold War history, particularly to Kang Sang-Jung and family,

Han Heung-Cheol, Hayashi Rumi, Koh Sun-Hui, and to Hiroshi, Patrick, and all my family for their patience and support. Last but not least, my thanks go to Mark Selden, inspirer of so much East Asian research and writing, and to Susan McEachern and Alden Perkins of Rowman & Littlefield for editorial advice and help.

The interpretations, understandings, and misunderstandings in the text that follows are, of course, my own alone.

NOTE ON NAMES AND ROMANIZATION

The names of Japanese, Korean, and Chinese people mentioned in this book are given in the normal East Asian order—surname first (except in quotations where the order is reversed). In romanizing Korean personal and place names, I have generally followed the romanization system approved by the South Korean government, for example, Busan (pronounced "Pusan"), Jeju (pronounced "Cheju"), and Gyeongsang (pronounced "Kyeongsang"). However, I have made exceptions where institutions or individuals express a preference for a different romanization, or where an alternative romanization has become standard usage (such as "*Chongryun*" rather than "*Chongryeon*," and "Kim" rather than "Gim").

I

DEPARTURES

1

MORNING SUN

1959

The train comes out of the long tunnel into a dark world of snow.

Beyond the fogged windows of the carriages, the night unfolds for mile after mile, its blackness concealing mountains and forests. Just occasionally, the light from a farmhouse reveals a patch of frozen earth, the branches of a pine tree, or a bamboo bent by the first snowfalls.

But inside the carriages, everything is noise and color; and as each station comes into view, the sea of frozen darkness outside gives way to a momentary island of light. At all the main stops along the line, it seems as though something between a carnival and a political demonstration is in progress. The platforms are crammed with people, singing, cheering, waving flags. Amid the crowds, vendors carry trays laden with rice-balls and roasted chestnuts. Young women in smart gray slacks—the ubiquitous fashion of the late 1950s—run from carriage to carriage, serving tea to the passengers whose laughing, excited faces peer out from the windows.

And around the perimeter of each station stand row upon row of police, their presence testifying to the fact that this is no ordinary train journey.

The first carriage has been turned into a mobile doctor's office where men and women in Red Cross uniforms attend to a steady stream of passengers suffering from coughs, colds, aches, and pains. As the train reaches Takasaki around 1:00 a.m., two of the passengers give brief speeches of thanks to the medical staff. The speeches are in Japanese, but the greetings and conversations in the carriages and on the platforms take place in a mixture of languages and accents—Japanese and Korean, the rhythms of village speech, and the cadences of the professional classes—for this diverse band of more than three hundred travelers includes teachers and engineers, prosperous families, as well as those escaping lives of poverty.

The passengers are almost all Korean, but most have lived in Japan for decades; many have lived here all their lives. Old men and women speak with the pronunciation of the southern provinces of Korea from which they came—some in the dialect of Jeju, Korea's southernmost island, but many members of the younger generation, born in Japan and possessing no memory of ancestral villages, speak Korean only haltingly and with Japanese accents.

Through the excitement and the laughter run currents of anxiety and sadness. Some passengers sit hunched in corners, trying to snatch a little sleep or wiping away quiet tears. One of those whose expression shows unease as well as hope as she journeys toward Niigata is "Shin Jong-Hae," a round-faced thirteen-year-old with long hair tucked behind her ears. Most teenagers are traveling with parents, brothers, and sisters, but she has set off on this journey in the company of the woman next door, Mrs. Pak, and her small children.

Shin Jong-Hae's mother is dead, and her father's whereabouts are unknown, although there are rumors that he is living in North Korea, where he has become an officer in the army of the Democratic People's Republic. Since her mother's death, Jong-Hae had lived with her eldest sister and brother-in-law not far from Tokyo, but now her sister is in the hospital, pregnant and suffering from tuberculosis. Her younger sister is also ill with the same disease.

Her harassed brother-in-law is traveling with Jong-Hae, but only as far as the port of Niigata. There he plans to say goodbye, entrusting her to the care of Mrs. Pak, who has promised to look after her on the journey into a new life.

Shortly before dawn, the snow thins as the train pulls out onto the wide, flat coastal plain whose paddy fields yield Japan's best rice, the raw material for its best *sake*. At Nagaoka, volunteers come around with wooden boxes packed with rice, pickles, and fish for the passengers' breakfast. Around eight in the morning, they finally reach the terminus, and the passengers, laden with hand baggage and bleary eyed with fatigue, struggle out from the warm carriages onto Niigata Station, where an icy morning wind whips in from that stretch of sea that in Japanese is called the Sea of Japan and in Korean is called *Donghae*—the East Sea.

Niigata, on this morning of Friday, 18 December 1959, is a city gripped with a strange mood of tension and excitement. The route to the converted U.S. army base, now adorned with the symbols of the Red Cross—where the passengers from the night train will spend the last three days of their life in Japan—is lined with the expressionless figures of policemen. Six hundred police have been drafted to guard more than nine hundred people, who are gathering in Niigata today from all parts of the country in preparation for departure from Japan.

The security cordon is not designed to protect the passengers from the citizens of Niigata, for most of the citizens welcome both the arrival and the departure of the travelers, as they have welcomed the thousand or so who passed through the city a week earlier, and will welcome the tens of thousands of others who will flow like a river along the same route over the coming years. But the city is abuzz with rumors of protests and possible sabotage by agents of the South Korean Syngman Rhee regime. In some places, members of the South Korean–affiliated Residents' League (*Mindan*) have been dragged by police from the railway tracks, where they lay down in an effort to stop the trains bringing departing Koreans to Niigata. Press reports even speak of plans by groups of South Korean agents to plant bombs in the Red Cross Center.

The tension extends beyond the bounds of the city, beyond the shores of Japan.

In South Korea, the military is said to have been placed on high alert. Along the eastern seaboard of the Asian continent, Soviet warships are engaged in unusual maneuvers.

But the passengers who have just arrived on the overnight train from Tokyo have more immediate and mundane concerns. Guided by group leaders from the General Association of Korean Residents in Japan (*Chongryun*) and officials from the Japan Red Cross Society, they spread themselves out in the dormitories of the Red Cross Center, locate blankets and pillows, find their way to the bathrooms and cafeteria, and line up in the center's shop to buy cameras, toothbrushes, transistor radios, and seasickness pills. As the day wears on, other groups arrive from Hokkaido in the north and from Kyoto, Osaka, Hiroshima, and Yamaguchi in the west. Long-lost acquaintances recognize and greet one another with cries of astonished delight; strangers exchange life stories in this sudden moment of camaraderie; children make new friends.

The three and a half days in the Red Cross Center are a time of suspended animation. One life has come to an end. The travelers have sold or given away the possessions they cannot take with them. They have packed up their remaining belongings and said goodbye to the neighbors, relatives, and friends with whom they have spent most of their lives. Sometimes the partings were bitter, for the decision to leave is fiercely contested, and has the power to tear families apart. Always, the farewells have been emotional. This is a one-way journey. There will be no return.

But the new life still lies beyond the gray-green horizon, in a place hardly any of the travelers have ever seen; a place where very few have any family, friends, or acquaintances; a place known only from photographs and encouraging phrases. The photographs they have seen show gleaming white apartment buildings rising from the ruins of a war-ravaged land or plump cows in newly built barns. "In the Republic, people eat white rice every day. . . . In the Republic, our children will get a university education," they are told. The Republic in question is the Democratic People's Republic of Korea—North Korea. In their bodies, these people are leaving for a profoundly unfamiliar world; in their hearts and minds, they are going home to the dream of a future reunited Korea.

The dormitories of the Red Cross Center are adorned with North Korean flags, the youngsters sing "The Song of General Kim Il-Sung," and the older women wear their best *chima jeogori*, the beautiful national dress of their homeland. But the transistor radios, when switched on to check that they are working, emit brief blasts of big band jazz and Bing Crosby's "White Christmas," and the mood and motives of the returnees are far too complicated to be captured by ideological slogans. Each individual story has its own particular twists and nuances.

Mr. Kang from Kawaguchi, who left Niigata for North Korea the week before, told one of the eager reporters clustered around the Red Cross Center, "I can't feed my family in Japan. My missus is dead, and I've got three kids. At least over there we'll get enough to eat."

But Mr. Koh, who has been living in Tokyo after arriving in Japan as an illegal immigrant, has loftier aspirations. He studied film and fine arts at college in Tokyo. As a Korean in Japan, he feels that his future is limited, and his creative impulses as a documentary filmmaker cannot find a proper outlet: "After I've gone home to Korea, I'm hoping to collaborate on documentaries with Japanese producers."

Saturday and Sunday, the last two days before departure, are taken up with a final round of bureaucratic processes. Identities have to be rechecked, emigration cards issued. Among the flocks of officials, one energetic, middle-aged Red Cross official moves with a particularly purposeful stride, viewing the scene around him with an almost proprietary gaze.

His name is Inoue Masutarô, and the deference with which he is treated makes it clear that he is a figure of importance.

The travelers who encounter him, however, have not the slightest inkling just how great an influence the smiling Mr. Inoue has had upon their destiny.

On these final days, a particularly important rite of passage remains to be completed. One of the low white barracks that make up the Red Cross Center contains a row of small offices, renamed "the Special Rooms." At the entrance to the corridor that leads to these offices, the departing travelers wait to be summoned, one family group at a time, for an encounter with the Special Room officials.

There is something strange about these rooms. Marks on the jambs show where the doors have recently been removed from their hinges. Now the entrances stand open, and the voices of those within drift out into the corridors—the firm, defiant voices of the ideologically committed, the softer murmurs of the less self-assured. But the speakers remain unseen, shielded from prying eyes by flowered screens that have carefully been placed across the gaps created by the absent doors.

Some of the travelers have been forewarned about these rooms and know what to expect and what to say. Inside each room sit three or four people, including a European, a Japanese official, and an interpreter. Every family member is asked a few simple questions: name and (in the case of children) age. Then comes the crucial question: Do you really wish to leave Japan and live the rest of your life in the Democratic People's Republic of Korea?

If they had been asked this question six months earlier, many of the people who pass through the Special Rooms would surely have hesitated, weighing hopes against doubts. But now the months of debate and self-questioning are over. Having come this far, it would be extraordinarily difficult to go back, and the process runs smoothly and efficiently.

Smoothly, that is, until Shin Jong-Hae enters the Special Room in the company of the Pak family.

Suddenly there is official consternation. Why is this thirteen-year-old traveling with a family to whom she is unrelated? Where are her parents? Have her relatives given permission for her to leave Japan? Jong-Hae's brother-in-law is summoned and taken into a separate room for questioning. Hesitantly, reluctantly, he describes his family's plight. He can no longer afford to care for Jong-Hae, and this seems the best way to ensure that she has some sort of future. Who knows—maybe she will even be able to find her lost father in the Republic.

Figure 1.1.   Returnees leave the Red Cross Center by bus for the port of Niigata (© ICRC)

The officials frown and suck their teeth in consternation. Jong-Hae, her brother-in-law, and the Paks are left waiting in a state of rising anxiety while hasty telephone calls are made to Tokyo and higher authorities are consulted.

Meanwhile, another emergency is unfolding. A twenty-one-year-old woman, who arrived at the center heavily pregnant, has begun to feel the first unmistakable pangs of childbirth, and her anxious young husband rushes her to the center's infirmary. Around 1:30 on the morning of 21 December, the day they are due to depart for North Korea, the couple's first child, a boy, is born. The birth goes smoothly, and the proud parents insist that they and their new baby are ready to leave on the repatriation ship later that day. But the doctors are less certain. Inoue Masutarô, roused early from sleep, is dispatched to negotiate with the ship's Russian medical staff, who are nervous about accepting this last-minute addition to their passenger list.

On Monday, 21 December the occupants of the Niigata Red Cross Center are up before first light, packing bags and tidying the dormitories. At this last moment, it becomes a matter of pride to leave everything in order when they depart. This is the shortest day of the year: dawn, when it comes, reveals a bleak scene of scudding, sleet-laden clouds. The weather forecast warns of gales at sea.

A fleet of four buses ferries the travelers in groups to the harbor along a route specially planted with a row of willow trees in honor of the occasion. The trees look spindly and frail in the winter wind. Two large Soviet passenger ships, the *Kryl'ion* and *Tobol'sk*, lie alongside the dock, their white sides newly painted with the sign of the Red Cross and adorned with banners in Korean reading, "A fervent welcome to our compatriots from Japan on their return home!"

The dock is crammed with family, well wishers, and the officials who will gather up the travelers' departure cards as they board the ships. On the buildings all around, the community association *Chongryun* has set up loudspeakers that blare out greetings, messages of encouragement, and promises of a bright future in the Socialist Fatherland. The wintry sea is churned to the color of jade as the beat of the ships' engines begins to accompany the sounds of the loudspeakers and the clamour of cheers, laughter, and weeping on the dock.

After some persuasion by Mr. Inoue, the ship's medical staff has finally agreed to accept the newborn baby, and his proud parents carry him up the gangplank and, carefully, down into the lower decks of the repatriation ship. Below deck, the narrow corridors smell of engine fumes, clogged drains, and sour cabbage. But the family has its own cabin, and there is a clinic staffed with admiring, friendly Russian staff.

The parents have named their baby Jo-Il—"Jo" for the first syllable of *Joseon* (Korea) and "Il" for the first syllable of *Ilbon* (Japan).

The characters, as it happens, also spell the words "Morning Sun." He is their hope for the future, the light at the start of their new life. His name embodies their belief that, in making this journey, they are bridging the gap between the foreign land where they have lived their lives and the unknown homeland to which they are returning.

But the officials at the Red Cross Center have received word from Tokyo that they must not allow the departure of minors who are unaccompanied by relatives and have refused to issue exit documents to Shin Jong-Hae. She is left behind with her brother-in-law, sobbing as she says her farewells to the Pak family in the sleet that now begins to blow across the city of Niigata.

Around half past three in the afternoon, with a long, low parting note from their foghorns, first the *Kryl'ion* and then the *Tobol'sk* pull away from the dock, and head toward the harbor mouth and out into the turbulent sea beyond.

Her real name was not Shin Jong-Hae, but everything else about her story is as close to the truth as I can determine—all meticulously recorded in the documents of the time. I do not know what happened to her in the end. The records show that she became a momentary focus of public controversy. The community association *Chongryun* protested to the Red Cross when she was refused permission to leave for North Korea, and local government officials made hasty efforts to find another family who could accompany her on a later repatriation ship. Most likely, she left Japan sometime in 1960, in the company of people she knew and trusted less well than the Pak family. Perhaps, in North Korea, she managed to find her father; but then again, perhaps not.

Maybe, after all, she remained in Japan and still lives there today, glad of having escaped the fates that befell many others with whom she had traveled to Niigata.

I wonder whether she is still alive, whether she might some day even read the words I am writing, and recognize her story in them. If she does, no doubt she will shake her head in places, remembering things differently from the way that I have told them here. I have tried to reconstruct the story with care, and very much of it—from the slacks worn by the young women who served tea on the railway stations to the goods sold by the shop in the Niigata Red Cross Center—can be retrieved from the written record.

But I am a foreigner, telling this story from a place far removed in space and time. I do not know how many of the 976 people who left Japan on the *Kryl'ion* and *Tobol'sk* on 21 December 1959 are still alive. But I know that each person who remembers that day has a unique memory of events and that none remembers the story precisely in the way I have told it here.

And what of the baby Jo-Il? Did he live long enough for his name, with its Japanese echoes, to become an embarrassment and to be concealed or changed? Or does he still bear that name proudly today?

The Cold War, in all the world except the Korean Peninsula, has been over for many years. But in Korea it has survived, mutating into a strange and frightening node of tension in the twenty-first century's so-called global war on terror. North Korea—the most feared corner of George W. Bush's "Axis of Evil"—remains a mystery to the outside world. Our television screens show us only grim ranks of marching troops; the masklike smiles of dancers and gymnasts who, with terrifying perfection, perform mass displays of devotion to the Dear Leader; or blurry shots of orphaned children or starving farmers who have crept across the border into China. Looking at those faces, I keep thinking that Jo-Il may be among them. In the very week when I started to write this book, if he is still alive, somewhere Jo-Il was celebrating his forty-fifth birthday.

This book is about an accidental journey. It is a journey in search of the stories of people like Shin Jong-Hae and Jo-Il;

of the 357 people who traveled from Shinagawa Station in Tokyo to the port of Niigata on the night of 17 December 1959;

of the 976 people who left Niigata for the North Korean port of Cheongjin on 21 December 1959;

of the 51,978 people who left Japan for North Korea by the same route between December 1959 and the end of 1960;

of the 93,340 people who, between the start of the repatriation movement in December 1959 and its termination in 1984, migrated from Japan to begin new lives in North Korea.

I embarked on a quest for their stories almost by chance, when an unexpected encounter with a mass of newly declassified documents on the topic made me realize just what an extraordinary and disturbing history this is. Since then, the attempt to retrace the repatriation story has become a kind of personal odyssey. Along the way, I have had the privilege of meeting some of those who passed through the Red Cross Center in Niigata during the 1960s and 1970s on their journey in search of a better life, and have heard the stories both of those who boarded the repatriation ships and one who, at the very last moment, was turned back and remained in Japan.

Oh Su-Ryong, then a young man in his twenties, described how he arrived in Niigata in February 1962, traveling in hopes that North Korean society would provide him with the education he had missed in Japan. Yi Yang-Soo, then a ten-year-old boy, set off on the same journey the previous year accompanied by his mother. "Yamada Kumiko," a Japanese woman now in her seventies, told me how she left around the same time with her Korean husband and his extended family. "Taniguchi Hiroko" recalled the dilemmas of being a teenager forced to leave her school, her friends, and her dreams for the future when her Korean-born father became chronically ill, and her family decided to move to North Korea in search of welfare and medical care.

As I started to research this neglected corner of history, I was astonished to realize how many of my friends in Japan had acquaintances or relatives who had migrated to North Korea on the repatriation ships. It was not only the lives of the 93,340 "returnees" that were transformed by the repatriation, but also the lives of the hundreds of thousands of relatives and friends whom they left behind.

Their stories matter because they matter—each one of them, that multitude of individuals whose lives came to be tangled in the key events of colonialism, decolonization, and Cold War. But the significance of this story—long ignored in Japan itself and almost totally unknown to the rest of the world—also goes beyond their individual fates.

It is a tale of intrigue, deception, and betrayal whose web extends to the governments of Japan and North Korea, to the Kremlin and the White House, and to one of the world's most revered humanitarian institutions, the international Red Cross movement.

The "return" of those 93,340 people—86,603 ethnic Koreans, together with 6,731 Japanese and six Chinese spouses or dependents—to North Korea between 1959 and 1984 is not the only example of a voluntary mass migration from capitalist to communist camps during the Cold War. In 1960, at the very time when the repatriation to North Korea was in full swing, some ninety-four thousand people of Chinese ancestry were repatriated from Indonesia to the People's Republic of China—just part of a process in which perhaps as many as half a million overseas Chinese (mostly from Southeast Asia) returned to post-Revolutionary China, in time to encounter the height of the Great Leap famine that took tens of millions of lives.

Yet the circumstances of the Korean repatriation seem particularly extraordinary. The Koreans who left Japan were forsaking life in Asia's richest country just when it was entering the period of its 1960s economic miracle. More remarkably still, almost all of those returning (like some 97 percent of all Koreans in Japan) in fact originated from South Korea. Most were going to places they had never seen before, where they had no friends or relatives. And yet they chose to leave the country where most had lived for decades, in search of new lives in the Democratic People's Republic of Korea (DPRK).

Why did they go? Equally important, what happened to them when they got there? The second question is particularly difficult to answer, for the governments and nongovernmental organizations that devoted immense time and energy to planning and organizing their departure seem to have lost interest in them almost the moment they sailed out of Niigata Harbor. Many of those who were repatriated to North Korea stayed in contact with friends and relatives in Japan and elsewhere for several years. Some stay in contact still and have over time settled into North Korean society, made careers, and brought up families there.

But in other cases, contact suddenly ceased some months or years after their repatriation. Many of the returnees, we now know, endured discrimination and persecution in their new home. An unknown number disappeared into concentration camps, never to be seen again. In the past few years, a handful of survivors of the forgotten tragedy have begun to trickle across the border into China, and around one hundred—among them Ms. Yamada, whose story we will hear more about later—have, very quietly and without fanfare, been allowed to return to Japan by a Japanese government who would surely prefer the whole incident to sink into oblivion.

The repatriation of Koreans from Japan to North Korea was not just a bizarre footnote to the twentieth-century history of Northeast Asia. It was an event that lay at the hub of Asia's Cold War. It was a defining moment in the Japan–North Korea relationship, although one rarely publicized. It became a key to the troubled postwar relationship between Japan and the Republic of Korea (ROK)—South Korea. The plan also took shape at a crucial moment in Japan-U.S. relations, when the two countries were in the midst of discussing the contentious renewal of their Mutual Security Treaty, a fact that influenced the Eisenhower government's approach to the repatriation issue. Behind the scenes, the Soviet Union became a central player in the scheme, which Nikita Khrushchev used to further his vision of the USSR's world role. In a more indirect way, the repatriation thus also became a factor in the shaping of superpower relations at a critical moment of the Cold War. In retracing the journey of repatriation, I have found myself rediscovering the history of the Cold War from an entirely new angle. I have also come to see the current crisis on the Korean Peninsula—the endgame of the Cold War—in a new light.

This book is at the same time an attempt to reflect on one of the unresolved questions of history: What happens when the small stories of personal lives and the grand stories of global politics intersect? How far are we, as individuals, free to choose the courses of our lives, and how far are we the playthings of historical forces too large for us even too see, let alone control?

In one sense, Shin Jong-Hae, the baby Jo-Il and his parents, the would-be student Mr. Oh, the schoolboy Yi Yang-Soo, the young wife Ms. Yamada, and the teenager Ms. Taniguchi were (as we shall see) all the unwitting objects of the most cynical of political machinations. The intrigues and manipulation that surrounded them were all the more remarkable because they were carried out not just by politicians on both sides of the Cold War divide, but also by "humanitarian" nongovernmental groups who were supposed to be protecting the interests of the Korean minority in Japan. The repatriation, indeed, was perhaps the strangest and most disturbing episode in the postwar history of the Red Cross movement.

And yet these people were never merely the pawns of Cold War politics. Although they could not know the full extent of the power games in which their lives had become enmeshed, most Koreans who chose to return from Japan to North Korea did exercise a choice, and many exercised it shrewdly, with an awareness of the limited options open to them and an intense determination to make the most of those options.

Meanwhile, the individuals who spun the webs of political intrigue surrounding the return process were themselves not absolute masters of their own destinies. Their motives were as complex as those of the returnees. They too saw only part of the picture. The multiple, overlapping, contradictory conspiracies in which they indulged (sometimes with a self-conscious air of melodrama) often had less practical effect than they would have liked to believe.

Above all, this story is one that continues to reverberate in the current crises of international politics in Northeast Asia. The relationship between North Korea and its neighbors remains one of the most dangerous points of friction in the twenty-first-century world. Discovering a point where big histories and little histories intersect can provide human insights that help make sense of that relationship. In remembering Shin Jong-Hae and Jo-Il, in encountering others who made similar journeys, I hope to make visible the human faces, so long obscured by the rhetoric of the Cold War, as they are still obscured by the rhetoric of power, fear, and ideology today.

2

HOSTAGES TO HISTORY

2002

Early on the morning of 17 September 2002, a plane took off from Tokyo's Haneda Airport carrying Japanese Prime Minister Koizumi Junichirô, a handful of his senior foreign policy advisors, and thirty journalists. The jet flew west over the mountainous central spine of the island of Honshu and out across the expanse of sea that separates Japan from the Asian mainland. Over forty years after the departure of the first repatriation ships from the Japanese port of Niigata to North Korea, Japan's political leader was finally making the same journey, though by a different route and in very different circumstances.

Just after 9:00 a.m., Koizumi's plane dipped through the clouds and landed on the gray and empty expanse of Pyongyang's international airport. As the Japanese prime minister stepped onto the tarmac, the North Korean government's second-in-command, Kim Yeong-Nam, hurried forward to greet him. It was the first time in fifty-seven years—since the end of the Pacific War and the division of the Korean Peninsula—that a Japanese prime minister had visited Japan's neighbor and former colony, the Democratic People's Republic of Korea.

Koizumi's visit to Pyongyang caught the world by surprise. Two years earlier, in the summer of 2000, South Korean President Kim Dae-Jung had made a highly publicized trip to Pyongyang for a summit meeting that raised hopes of Korean reunification, an end to the last remaining fault line of the Cold War. But President Kim was a reformer famous for his "Sunshine Policy" toward the impoverished and Stalinist North. Prime Minister

Koizumi, on the contrary, was the head of a government known for an abiding hostility to North Korea. He was also a staunch ally of U.S. President George W. Bush, whose State of the Union address earlier that year had labeled North Korea a member of the "Axis of Evil" and an archenemy in America's war on terror.

Since the momentary sunshine of the June 2000 summit between Kim Dae-Jung and North Korean leader Kim Jong-Il, the shadows of conflict had again gathered over Northeast Asia. Bush's Axis of Evil speech produced an angry response from the volatile North Korean leadership, and earlier progress toward easing U.S.–North Korea tensions was sharply reversed. By the autumn of 2002, tensions in Northeast Asia were rising, and there was even talk of war—a terrifying prospect that, observers predicted, would leave millions dead and make the horrors of the conflict in Iraq pale into insignificance by comparison.

Against this background, Koizumi's visit to Pyongyang was brief and tense. Japanese officials had planned the protocol with care. The contrast with the two Kims' Summit of 2000 was striking. On that occasion, Kim Jong-Il, an erratic and reclusive figure long seen by the outside world as at least half-mad, had surprised journalists by his relaxed demeanor and witty conversation. This time, the two leaders met in a sparsely furnished room in the Hall of Flowers—the guesthouse for foreign dignitaries on the banks of Pyongyang's Daedong River—well away from the eyes and ears of the media. The official photograph of Kim Jong-Il greeting Koizumi shows the two stern-faced leaders shaking hands from as far apart as physically possible, literally keeping each other at arm's length.

The results of their meeting, though, seemed at first to exceed even the most wildly optimistic expectations. Koizumi and Kim Jong-Il concluded their two and a half hours of discussions by signing the Pyongyang Declaration, an announcement that their two countries would take steps to "settle the unfortunate past between them" and move towards the establishment of diplomatic relations. Most remarkable of all was North Korea's agreement to abandon its long-standing insistence that Japan pay compensation for the effects of its thirty-five years of colonial rule in Korea (from 1910 to 1945). In return, the Japanese prime minister expressed "deep remorse and heartfelt apology" for the colonial past, and Japan promised to provide substantial (though unspecified) sums of aid to North Korea.

The Pyongyang Declaration also included one other important sentence, not widely noticed by the world's media: Both sides agreed that they would "sincerely discuss the issue of the status of Korean residents in Japan."

But even as Koizumi and his retinue headed back to Tokyo on the after-noon of that day—even as Japan's newspapers competed to rush special is-sues on the summit into print—the Pyongyang accord was beginning to unravel.

For Japan, the greatest stumbling block to improved relations with North Korea was the mysterious disappearance of at least a dozen Japanese citizens during the 1970s and 1980s. Over the past few years, the Japanese media had reported growing suspicions that some or all of those who van-ished had been kidnapped and spirited across the border by North Korean agents. During his meeting with Koizumi, Kim Jong-Il confirmed that these suspicions were correct.

According to Kim's astonishing admission, thirteen Japanese had been kidnapped by overenthusiastic "elements of a special agency of state," ap-parently in the belief that they could be used to train North Korea's spies or that their identities could be assumed by North Korean agents engaged in clandestine missions abroad. Of the thirteen, five were still living in North Korea and eight (according to Pyongyang officials) had died.

The saddest story of all was that of Yokota Megumi, who had been just a child when she was snatched off the street by North Korean agents as she made her way home from junior high school in the city of Niigata. Ac-cording to the official account, she had grown up, married, and had a daughter in North Korea, but had suffered from depression and committed suicide in a Pyongyang mental hospital in 1993.

The North Korean leader's apology for the "adventurism" of the kid-nappers did nothing to mollify the Japanese public, which was outraged at the news. All the outside world's worst fears about the behavior of this rogue state had been confirmed. The fury of the Japanese media and pub-lic was intensified by the highly implausible explanations offered by the North Korean government about the responsibility for the kidnappings and about the circumstances surrounding the deaths of the (allegedly) deceased kidnap victims. Relatives in Japan refused to believe that they were dead and have continued ever since to insist that North Korea is still holding them for its own nefarious purposes. Victims' support groups claim that many more missing people have also been kidnapped by North Korea and that the Kim Jong-Il regime may still be holding scores of Japanese people captive.

As for the five survivors, Japanese and North Korean officials agreed that they would be allowed to make a two-week visit to Japan to be re-united with their families, after which they were to return to North Korea to decide their long-term future. But when the bewildered-looking victims set foot on Japanese soil just over a month later, their arrival sparked a wave of national emotion. Their families and supporters refused to allow them to return to North Korea, fearing that they might disappear again. Caught up in this wave of public feeling, the Japanese government agreed that they should remain permanently in Japan. The response from North Korea was to accuse Japan of violating its agreements about the return of the kidnap victims.

Meanwhile, the Japanese media's chorus of fear and loathing toward the North Korean regime drowned out the Pyongyang Declaration's remaining promises of détente. Schemes for increased Japanese aid to North Korea were abandoned amid mutual recriminations between the two nations. So too were promises by both countries to reexamine the status of Koreans in Japan.

Revelations about the kidnappings left many Koreans in Japan feeling ashamed and embarrassed. Schools run by the North Korean–affiliated General Association of Korean Residents in Japan (*Chongryun*) became the targets of abusive messages and threats of violence. At the height of the public outcry surrounding the kidnappings, a little-known Japanese ultranationalist group staged a series of attacks on buildings owned by Korean groups seen as linked to the North, planting firebombs or firing guns into the buildings' facades. In the year following the summit, relations between Japan and the Democratic People's Republic of Korea reached a new nadir.

But the five surviving kidnap victims were not the only people returning from North Korea to Japan around this time. There were also others who arrived with much less fanfare—most of them nervously avoiding the harsh light of publicity. They reached Japan after convoluted and often terrifying journeys. They had crossed frozen rivers under cover of darkness, hidden in the houses of strangers, entrusted their fates to shadowy guides and brokers. They had lived in constant fear of betrayal and arrest, violence and death. Even after they reached Japan, their lives remained full of uncertainty. They were afraid of discovery and retribution by the long arm of the North Korean state, and were desperately anxious about the plight of family left behind in North Korea. Many were nervous, too, about the likely reactions of Japanese neighbors and workmates if their pasts were revealed.

These were survivors of the repatriations that had begun with such public celebration in December 1959. Decades after their "homecoming" to North Korea, a handful of former returnees were coming home again, this time to Japan. And once again, it was a homecoming fraught with ironies.

One of the people making this journey to Japan not long before the Pyongyang Summit was Yamada Kumiko, a small, round-faced Japanese woman with soft brown eyes and a warm smile. She looks like everyone's favorite grandmother. Yamada-san had grown up in a provincial town in Japan, married the son of Korean immigrants, and left on a ship from Niigata in the early days of the repatriation scheme. Her eldest daughter was a toddler and Yamada-san was expecting her second baby when they boarded the repatriation ship. Now the daughter who traveled with her to North Korea is entering middle age.

A little while before Koizumi's visit, mother and daughter had slipped across the border from Korea to China.

It was not the first time Yamada Kumiko had crossed the border. As food shortages in North Korea turned into famines from the end of the 1980s onward, more and more people have been driven to make the dangerous journey to and fro across the narrow river that marks Korea's northern border, in a desperate search for goods to sell on the black market. Crossings often take place at night under the cover of darkness, which is made all the more profound by North Korea's chronic energy shortage: it is a darkness devoid of streetlights, empty of car headlamps, under a black sky untainted by the neon glow of cities. Border guards or police are bribed to look the other way. The icy northeast Asian winter is the best period for these crossings. As Yamada Kumiko explains, "It's easier to cross the river when it's frozen, but you have to pay people on both sides of the border, and if that doesn't work out, you're likely to get arrested at any moment."

Yamada-san first made a clandestine border crossing in search of some way to feed her family.

"Around that time," Yamada-san recalls, "it was really easy to get cigarettes in China, and people said, 'If you take Korean pork across to China, you can get cigarettes.' So I went and bought up these cigarettes and brought them back across the frozen river, dragging them over the ice. I'd had a word with the policeman at the border, so that was all right. But the scary part was that I still had to walk a long way to get home from the border. If I'd come across any police on the way, it would have been a disaster. I was with my younger daughter, and we had this little kind of hand cart. Well, we got back home OK and buried the cigarettes in the hole in the ground that we used for storing *kimchi* pickles. Then I'd take out about ten packs at a time, and go to the market to sell them. You can't do it during the daytime. It's got to be at night. There are lots of people who earn a living like that."

I listened to her story some three years after her return, sitting at a table in her little apartment in a quiet Japanese suburb, while Yamada-san served tea in cups shaped like cute cartoon animals (mine was a green frog) and apologized profusely for her lack of proper refreshments to offer a guest. The contrast between the setting and the story she was telling about her remarkable life was unsettlingly surreal.

When she crossed the border out of North Korea for the last time, Yamada-san says, "I never imagined in my wildest dreams that we would end up coming back to Japan. But once I got across, an acquaintance in China said to me, 'How about it? How about going to Japan to work for a couple of years?' 'Could I really do that?' I asked. 'Sure,' said my Chinese friend.

"Well, I'd heard these stories about people in China who are human traffickers—you know, they catch people and sell them. I really started wondering if my Chinese friend could be one of those people. I didn't know what to do. I was of two minds whether to go back to North Korea or to try to get to Japan. But there are some Japanese people in that part of China too, and I was put in touch with one of them. This Japanese person said they could get a copy of my family registration papers from Japan. I waited about a month, and sure enough, my daughter's and my documents arrived from Japan."

Soon after, Yamada-san and her daughter traveled to Beijing and boarded a flight to Japan. They left behind family and friends to whom they had said no farewells when they crossed the river, believing that they would see them again in a matter of days or, at the most, weeks.

Yamada-san laughs a little ruefully as she remembers the bewildering experience of the journey back to Japan. "You can imagine—I'd never been on a plane before. When we went over to North Korea it was by ship, and that was ages ago. Everything was so strange—the food on the plane and all that. I had no idea what to do, and I was really scared that I was going to do something embarrassing and make a fool of myself."

Returning to Japan was an equally disorienting experience. Even for Yamada Kumiko, Japanese by birth and upbringing, arriving in Tokyo was like landing on another planet. The city looked as extraordinary to her as it did to her daughter, whose whole life had been spent in North Korea.

"We got on a train from Narita Airport into Tokyo," She says. "That train was so fast! I'd never been on anything like it before. When I looked out of the window, the houses were all completely different from what I re-membered. I thought, 'Japan's really changed.' It was forty years, after all. . . . And the advertisements! There were all these neon signs with weird words on them. Not so much English words, but, you know, *katakana*.★ I could read the script, but I had no idea what they meant."

The Japanese that she had barely spoken in decades was rusty on her tongue. The food in the cafeteria where they ate their first dinner was a mystery too. It was only when they arrived at the apartment that welfare officials had prepared for their arrival, and saw the two white futons spread out waiting for them on the straw *tatami* mats, that finally Yamada Kumiko thought, "It's true. We really are back in Japan."

But in 2002, my path and Yamada-san's had not yet crossed. When she returned from North Korea, and when Prime Minister Koizumi traveled to Pyongyang, I was profoundly ignorant about the story of the repatriations to North Korea. Even though one of my main interests is the history of Japan's frontiers and those who cross them, I had seen only a few passing references to the fact that some North Koreans in Japan had returned home in the 1960s and 1970s, and until very recently I had thought little of it.

I grew up in Britain while these events were taking place, but I was utterly unaware of any of them. The great landmarks of the Cold War—the Suez crisis and the Hungarian invasion—were the first political events I can remember, strange names without clear meaning that became embedded in my childhood memories. I was a latecomer to the study of East Asia—before taking a teaching job in Japan and later migrating to Australia, I had studied Russian as an undergraduate and spent a month in the Cold War Soviet Union. The events taking place in Japan and Korea during those years were a world away.

Leafing back through the diaries that I keep intermittently, I notice that, in the week in 2002 when Koizumi went to Pyongyang and when Yamada-san and her daughter were nervously settling into the strange patterns of life in Japan, the southern spring had finally arrived in my hometown of Canberra. A raucous flock of white cockatoos had descended on the balcony outside my office on the university campus, destroying my potted oleander bush, so I bought a tub of flowering hyacinths to replace them, and some bean and tomato seedlings to plant in our garden at home.

Meanwhile, I was following events in North Korea and Japan with amazed curiosity, reading every article I could find in the newspapers. The Pyongyang Declaration seemed important, and not only because of the

---

★The Japanese phonetic script used for writing foreign words and many brand names.

implications of its success or failure for the future of the East Asian region. It also contained that single fleeting reference to "the status of Korean residents in Japan."

During the period of Japanese colonial rule from 1910 to 1945, hundreds of thousands of Koreans crossed the waters to the colonial power. Some were brought over forcibly to work in mines and factories; others came in relatively fortunate circumstances, as students enrolling in Japanese colleges or merchants plying their trade in the cities of the colonial mother country. Many more arrived in Japan in response to social and economic pressures: fleeing rural poverty, searching for an income on construction sites, in textile mills, in restaurant kitchens, and in tiny back-alley factories.

In September 2002, I had just embarked on a research project about a particular part of their history.

The day 15 August 1945 is remembered in Japan as *Haisen no Hi* (the Day of Defeat in War). On that searing summer's noon Emperor Hirohito, making a public radio broadcast for the first time, asked the people of Japan to "endure the unendurable" and announced the nation's surrender to the Allied powers. In Korea, it is known as *Gwangbokjeol* (the Day of the Return of the Light), the dawn that followed the long night of Japanese colonialism. At the time of the Day of Defeat and the Return of the Light, more than two million Koreans were living in Japan, while an even greater number had migrated to China, Manchuria, and the Soviet Union.

Immediately after Hirohito's surrender broadcasts, tens of thousands of Koreans in Japan headed for port cities, seeking any transport that would take them home. From late 1945 onward, an official repatriation program was implemented, and in all, over a million people returned to the southern half of the Korean Peninsula. A further 351 Koreans were also repatriated to the North before deteriorating relations between the two halves of the divided peninsula put an end to repatriations to North Korea. Meanwhile, growing political tensions and poverty in Korea were making return difficult for many people, and eventually over six hundred thousand Koreans remained in Japan and became the country's largest foreign minority.

Colonialism, discrimination, violence, the division of the peninsula, and the Korean War have all cast their shadows over the history of *Zainichi* Koreans—Koreans in Japan. They have struggled, failed, succeeded, faced prejudice and discrimination, intermarried. Some have maintained a strong sense of ethnic pride; others have assimilated or sought out their own delicate balance between the cross-currents of multiple identities. Today, Japan's Korean minority has a fourth and fifth generation. Most *Zainichi*

Koreans speak little or no Korean; most have no memories of life in Korea. They are permanent residents, but hundreds of thousands remain foreigners under Japanese law, unable to vote and required (like other foreigners) to carry their alien registration cards with them at all times.

The history of the *Zainichi* Korean community is well known in Japan and has been the subject of academic books, novels, and (more recently) several movies. My research, though, concerned a less familiar part of the story.

Exploring the Australian archives, I came to realize that the Allies, who occupied Japan after its defeat, had played a central and rather disturbing role in determining the destiny of the Korean minority in Japan. The United States provided the largest contingent of troops in occupied Japan, but they worked alongside the British Commonwealth Occupation Force (BCOF), a multiethnic force that included British, Australian, New Zealander, and Indian troops serving (as one writer has put it) under a common flag in "the last gasp of an Empire that would never be seen again." Among the force's main roles from 1946 to the end of occupation in 1952 was assisting the return of displaced people (both Japanese and Koreans) to their homes. Another mission was to patrol the straits between Japan and Korea, helping the Japanese police control movement back and forth between the two countries.

The British, Australian, and other troops who arrived in a war-devastated Japan had little knowledge about Japanese history and culture, but they did their best to learn. Young men and women, some of them fresh from the battlefields of the Pacific War, gazed with curiosity, but also with some sympathy, on the alien people they had conquered. Few, however, had much useful information about the Koreans. Recognizing the vital importance of knowing your enemy, Allied forces had trained experts in the Japanese language, but there had seemed no necessity to learn Korean. The occupation troops in Japan were told to treat Koreans as liberated people, but nobody really seemed sure what that meant, and in any case, everyone assumed that they would all soon go home.

As the Cold War began to creep across Asia, however, something strange started to happen. While shiploads of Koreans were returning to South Korea from Japan, the Allied authorities became aware that small boats were trying to make the perilous journey in the opposite direction— smuggling groups of people back into Japan. Some of these boat people were hoping to find family members from whom they had become separated after the war. Others were fleeing economic hardship and political disturbances in Korea.

In the tense environment leading up to the outbreak of the Korean War, Japan's Allied occupiers grew more and more uneasy at this uncontrolled movement of people back and forth across the water between Japan and the continent. Unable to distinguish between people seeking their families or returning to homes in Japan, people engaged in smuggling, and those working for left-wing political organizations, the occupation authorities ended up regarding them all with deep suspicion, and when an outbreak of cholera added to their concerns, they closed the border.

Husbands and wives, parents and children who happened to be on opposite sides of the divide found themselves separated by an invisible line in the sea that they could no longer cross without breaking the law.

The occupation forces were instructed, if necessary, to fire on unauthorized vessels trying to cross the border between Korea and Japan. I do not know whether any boats carrying these migrants were in fact sunk, but it is clear that air patrols from the coasts of Kyushu and Honshu forced many leaky and overloaded boats back out to sea and to an uncertain fate. Those who were arrested were shipped to detention camps—initially to a camp near the port of Sasebo, and later to the notorious Ômura Detention Center near Nagasaki, where they were held until they could be deported to South Korea. But tens of thousands managed to make it past the coastguards and reach cities like Osaka or Yokohama, where some still live today.

The Geneva-based International Committee of the Red Cross (ICRC) was responsible for conducting inspections of Ômura Detention Center. So a chance trip to Europe, some eighteen months into my research project, seemed like a good opportunity to see if their archives contained descriptions of the center as it was in the 1950s.

I was also hoping that Red Cross documents might shed some light on a question that had begun to intrigue me. In the course of my research, I had visited the beautiful, mountainous island of Tsushima, the part of Japan nearest to Korea. Tsushima served as the entry point for many boatpeople crossing the border from the southern part of Korea, and I had hoped that I might find Korean people who had lived on the island since the postwar years and would be able to share their memories of those times. But my hopes were disappointed.

Almost all the Korean population of Tsushima, it turned out, had left the island after volunteering for repatriation to North Korea in the 1960s and 1970s. Many had never been heard from again. As I traveled around Japan collecting material for my project, again and again I encountered similar stories.

The ICRC, I learned, had supervised the repatriations. So before leaving Australia for the trip to Europe, I emailed the committee's archives to ask whether they had any material on these topics. The reply was prompt and friendly:

"For the moment," wrote the archivist, "only the ICRC's general archives up to 1950 are open to the public. A process of declassification of our general archives from 1951 to 1965 (so including the question of the repatriation of Korean residents in Japan to North Korea) is in progress, and these archives will soon be public."

By the time I got to Europe in June, the process of declassification had just been completed.

3

GENEVA: CITY OF DREAMS

2004

I can pinpoint the day, in fact, almost the hour, when the repatriation story took over my life. It was Monday, 7 June 2004, a glorious early summer's day in Geneva. I had arrived in the city by plane from Heathrow the afternoon before. Friends of mine were currently in Germany, and I had suggested that we meet in Geneva while I was there, but their train would not arrive until evening. Before they arrived, on that Sunday afternoon, I set out for a walk along the shores of Lake Leman toward the building where I would be doing research during my stay in Geneva.

I had last been in the city over ten years earlier, in the midst of a cold and dreary winter. Seeing it again in summer, I was overwhelmed by its beauty. In Mon Repos Park, young people were sitting hand in hand, dangling bare feet over the translucent waters of the lake, and looking out toward the peak of Mont Blanc—a wisp of snow, impossibly high in the sky on the distant horizon. Families had spread picnic blankets between the flower beds, and tiny striped squirrels darted through the deep shadow of the trees.

The building I was looking for stood on a bluff above the lake and from a distance resembled a French chateau. Long, shuttered windows pierced the rampart of white walls. The square central turret was topped by an imposing upward sweep of gray tiles. The letters and insignia that surmounted the turret told me I had reached my destination: CICR—*Comité International de la Croix-Rouge* (the International Committee of the Red Cross).

Because it was Sunday, the main ICRC building was closed and deserted, but next door a modern glass and steel annex offered an inviting es-

Firgure 3.1.   The International Committee of the Red Cross, Geneva (Author's photograph)

cape from the glare of the sun. This was the International Museum of the Red Cross, and the story told within its walls was to prove crucial to understanding some of the tragic ironies of the repatriation to North Korea.

Inside, a flight of steps led down into the basement, into a postmodern maze whose flickering screens, dimly lit photographs, and fragments of text offered glimpses of the history of one of the world's oldest and most curious experiments in humanitarianism.

Words engraved in glass recalled the ancient human yearning for kindness, mercy, and the relief of suffering. Video presentations captured fragments of the horrors of modern mass warfare: the 1859 Battle of Solferino, whose miseries impelled a young Geneva businessman named Henry Dunant to plead for better treatment of wounded soldiers. Solemn nineteenth-century photographs depicted the faces of the founding fathers: Dunant himself; Gustave Moynier, the philanthropic lawyer who mobilized the Geneva Public Welfare Society to respond to Dunant's appeal; the doctor Théodore Maunoir; and the others who joined them in 1863 to form the International Committee for the Relief of the Wounded, later renamed the International Committee of the Red Cross.

The huge global venture of the Red Cross started as the initiative of this little group of Genevese philanthropists; and astonishingly, even in the twenty-first century it retains strong elements of its parochial origins as a philanthropic project of the Geneva Public Welfare Society. The ICRC's multinational professional staff may fill the mock chateau next door, but the committee itself is, still today, a small group of charitably minded Swiss citizens, selected by personal invitation. And though the invitations are no longer limited to citizens of Geneva, the names of the city's humanitarian dynasties run like litanies through the history of the Red Cross: Dunants, Maunoirs, and Boissiers recur generation after generation.

Their photographs, looking out from the video screens, seemed almost to compose a collective self-image of Geneva itself, the city of Calvin and of Jean-Jacques Rousseau, of solid bourgeois morals, uneasy consciences, and utopian dreams. A chronology displayed on the museum's walls recalled the treaties and conventions to which the city has given its name:

> the 1864 Geneva Convention for the amelioration of the condition of wounded soldiers on the battlefield;
>
> the 1925 Geneva Protocol on the use of chemical and biological weapons;
>
> the two new Geneva Conventions of 1929, which strengthened protection of the war wounded and prisoners of war;
>
> the four Geneva Conventions of 1949, which—inspired by the horrors of the Second World War—once again reinforced the power of international law to protect the wounded and prisoners of war, and extended its scope to cover the protection of civilian detainees.

All of them products of the Red Cross movement, the conventions reflect the impassioned hope that human beings might learn from the disasters wrought by national and ethnic hatreds, war, and tyranny.

The name of Geneva has become synonymous with the possibility of a better world—a world ruled by reason and justice. In that summer of 2004, I could not help also feeling that it was a world imperiled by the shadows of suicide bombers and by the haunting orange-clad figures of shackled prisoners, indefinitely incarcerated behind the barbed wire enclosures of Guantanamo in the name of democracy.

The museum's maps traced the worldwide growth of the movement as one country after another set up its own national Red Cross or Red Crescent society: Turkey as early as 1868; the United States in 1881; Japan in 1887;

Korea in 1905 (although this disappeared with the advent of Japanese colonialism, to be recreated in divided form after the Pacific War). Now, 181 countries possess a national Red Cross society.

Upstairs in the bookshop, I bought a pamphlet setting out the fundamental principles of the Red Cross, developed over decades and formally codified in the 1950s by Jean Pictet: humanity, impartiality, neutrality, independence, voluntary service, unity, universality. Each country, I discovered, may have only one Red Cross Society, which is expected to raise its own funds and assist the welfare work of the national government, while remaining independent of politics—a testing commandment in any age and particularly at the height of the Cold War.

As I leafed through this pamphlet, I began to realize that the International Committee has the power to define overarching values and principles and to grant or deny accreditation to national societies. But it has very little power to command obedience to its principles or to discipline those who transgress them. This, I later realized, helped to explain the disquieting documents that were to about to confront me in the archives next door.

My friends Kang Sang-Jung and his wife Mariko arrived in Geneva late that evening, and it was only on the following morning that we were able to sit down for a long talk over coffee and croissants in the restaurant of our hotel.

Kang Sang-Jung, who is a professor of politics at the University of Tokyo, was spending six months on sabbatical in Germany. We chatted about my research and about his autobiography, which had been published in Japan a couple of months earlier. The two topics are connected. Kang Sang-Jung is a second-generation member of the Korean community in Japan whose autobiography movingly describes how his father arrived in Japan as a penniless teenager in search of work in the 1930s, and how his mother traveled alone from Korea to join her betrothed in the year when Japan attacked Pearl Harbor. Like many colonial migrants to Japan, Kang's father traveled the country, shifting from one low-paid, casual job to another. During the war, he was a laborer in an armaments factory in Tokyo, and at the time of Japan's defeat, he moved to the southern city of Kumamoto in Kyushu, where other members of the family were also living.

Kang, the youngest of three sons (one of whom had died in infancy during the war), was born in an impoverished Korean settlement in Kumamoto in 1950. During his childhood, Koreans in Japan were barred from all forms of public employment and found it virtually impossible to obtain positions in large Japanese companies.

In the Korean community where he lived as a small child, he recalls, people "supported themselves by keeping pigs and making 'moonshine'— illicit liquor. . . . The civil war in their homeland had torn away the hopes of the adults of the settlement, and destroyed their dreams of liberation. They had nowhere to go, and their lives vacillated between sorrow and anger. The atmosphere in the settlement was constantly seething like a pressure cooker."

Yet, he says, "For some reason, the grownups always treated me with kindness, and I received great affection. At least as far as I am concerned, the place conjures up only fond memories."

Around the middle of the 1950s, however, Kang's parents (who, like many Koreans at that time, lived under a Japanese name) moved out of the settlement and into a small house in the center of Kumamoto, where they set up their own little family business collecting and recycling garbage.

Soon after, the movement for repatriation to North Korea began. At first, departure for North Korea was just spoken about as a remote possibility, but in August 1958 a mass campaign emerged, coordinated by the North Korean affiliated association *Chongryun* (the General Association of Korean Residents in Japan). The next month, the North Korean leader Kim Il-Sung and Foreign Minister Nam Il issued a statement welcoming *Zainichi* Koreans to the Socialist Fatherland and offering them free transport, homes, jobs, education, and welfare.

Suddenly, mainstream and community newspapers and magazines in Japan were full of headlines proclaiming, "Return of Compatriots from Japan Welcomed: Livelihood to Be Completely Guaranteed," and "No Unemployment for Returnees: Housing Ready to Receive 50,000 People."

For those who had few prospects in Japan, it was an attractive proposition. In February 1959 the Japanese government, ostensibly responding to pressure both from the North Korean government and from the *Zainichi* Korean community, agreed "for humanitarian reasons" to give exit permits to those who wanted to take up the North Korean offer. An official committee was set up to work with the Japan Red Cross Society in processing applications for repatriation, and at the same time the Japanese government called in the International Committee of the Red Cross to verify that all those leaving Japan were really departing of their own free will.

Little by little, the population of communities like the one where Kang Sang-Jung had been born dwindled, as one family after another packed their bags and left for North Korea. His parents were among those who chose not to leave. From relatives in South Korea, they had heard disturbing stories about political and social conditions in the North. And besides, they were afraid that if they went to the North, they might never again be able to visit the family's ancestral graves in the far south of the peninsula. But gradually the friends, neighbors, and playmates of Kang's early years disappeared.

Yet even for someone whose own life had been so closely touched by the repatriation movement, there were many puzzling questions that remained unanswered. Why had so many people chosen to move to North Korea? And why had the Democratic People's Republic of Korea—a desperately poor country struggling to recover from the devastation of the Korean War—agreed to receive such a flood of immigrants on such apparently generous terms? Had the Japanese government's decision to allow the repatriation really been purely humanitarian, or had Japan's leaders quietly rejoiced to send off people whom they regarded as members of an undesirable and troublesome minority? What had been the role of the International Red Cross in all this?

"So what do you think you're going to find in the archives?" asked Mariko-san as we finished breakfast.

"I have no idea," I said. "It might just be a few a pages of letters. But anyhow, it's a beautiful day. If there's nothing much there, we could just go sightseeing instead."

The headquarters of the International Committee of the Red Cross was in fact designed not as a chateau but as a hotel, and its large, dimly lit reception area still retains some of the original atmosphere. The floor is paved with brown mosaic, and an imposing staircase leads from the central hallway to the floors above. Even the man at the reception desk, with his somber dress, lugubrious face, and formal manner, might have been a concierge from the better class of Edwardian hotels. He asked me to sign the visitors' book and wait while an official came to guide me to the sanctum where the committee's records are held.

But the archivist, when he appeared, proved to be vivacious, welcoming, and friendly. He took me down to the basement reading room, placed in front of me the massive tome of the archive's printed catalogue, and helped me find the section dealing with repatriations from Japan to North Korea. The list of files went on for pages. Hardly knowing where to start, I selected a few files at random and summoned them up from the stacks.

There, in neatly ordered gray cardboard boxes, were mountains of telegrams, reports, carbon copies of letters, and hand-scrawled memos, most of them written in French or English, exchanged almost fifty years ago. The writers and recipients were people I had never heard of, but some names reappeared so often that they soon became familiar. In the rhythms of their written prose, I even began to think I could hear their voices echoing faintly across half a century.

Leopold Boissier, president of the International Committee of the Red Cross, writes cautious, diplomatic messages, soothing ruffled egos and proposing compromise solutions. Shimazu Tadatsugu, president of the Japan Red Cross Society, signs his letters with an elegant flowing hand, quite unlike the spiky European script of his colleague Inoue Masutarô, whose letters generally run to several pages of closely typed text. Ri Byeong-Nam (generally referred to in the ICRC records as Li Byung Nam), secretary-general of the North Korean Red Cross, meanwhile, seems to communicate entirely in terse telegrams laden with "strenuous protests" about one issue or another and (as often as not) demanding "immediate replies."

The archive was a treasure trove indeed—there were long and detailed reports from the Ômura Detention Center, and thousands of pages of correspondence relating to the repatriation. The problem would be to extract a meaningful story from this overwhelming mass of evidence in the few days that I had allowed myself for research in Geneva.

And by the time I had been in the archives for half an hour or so, I also began to experience another growing realization: There was something wrong with these documents.

The story emerging here did not fit the sketchy outlines of this history as I knew it. The dates were too early, and the letters were coming from the wrong places.

In 1956 (according the official accounts), there had been a small demonstration in support of repatriation by Koreans in Japan, and this had attracted the concern of the International Committee of the Red Cross. However, it was only in 1958 that a mass repatriation movement had broken out within the Korean community, with the strong support the North Korean government. Throughout, the Japanese government and Red Cross were supposed to have been mere onlookers—responding to the demands of others, and not becoming deeply involved in the process until 1959, when the pleas of Koreans for return to their homeland became too insistent to ignore.

But the mountain of letters on the files began well before the first demonstrations by *Zainichi* Koreans, and many of them came from the Japanese authorities.

As early as September 1955 (the records showed), an envoy from the Japan Red Cross Society raised the problem of Koreans in Japan with the ICRC, foreshadowing further discussions about a possible repatriation. By the spring of 1956, Japanese officials were already speaking of a "return" of sixty thousand people, and the Japanese Red Cross was busy contacting shipping lines in a highly confidential search for boats to carry them to North Korea.

The language of the letters was confusing, too. Phrases about "humanitarianism," "the welfare of the Koreans," and the "deep desire of North Koreans in Japan to return home" were interspersed with jolting descriptions by the Japanese Red Cross of Koreans in Japan as being "very violent" and "acting as a fifth column" in Japanese society. One report by a Japanese Red Cross official advised Geneva that "Japan has had no experience hitherto of being embarrassed by the question of minority and lacks knowledge how to handle it."

What was going on here? The more I read, the more bewildering things became. At one moment, the Japanese Red Cross officials were deep in secret negotiations with Soviet diplomats; the next, they were receiving off-the-record briefings from the Japanese intelligence services. Meanwhile, the North Korean government and the North Korean Red Cross Society remained perversely reticent, leaving little trace of their thoughts or actions. I read until my eyes began to blur and my head ached, but still I couldn't make sense of it.

And yet by early on the afternoon of that Monday, the story had begun to matter very much. Because among the highly confidential missives, the secret meetings, and the growing evidence of deceit in high places were just a handful of letters that reminded me what it was all about: English translations of letters sent by returnees soon after their arrival.

The slightly clumsy language into which they had been rendered could not conceal the desperate mixture of suffering, anxiety, and hope in those messages to friends and family—messages that had been dispatched from North Korea to Japan via China and Hong Kong, opened en route by Chinese censors, passed on to the Red Cross, typed out in English, and finally filed into boxes in a basement in Geneva to be read by a bewildered researcher from Australia in the twenty-first century, as the dream of a socialist Korea finally crumbled into bitter dust.

Some letters were starkly practical:

Four of us are suffering from something wrong with intestines, and our work is to go to the hospital every day. Medicine is also not so good. M. has stayed away from work since 2nd of this month. Mother lost her weight about 4 kilograms. I think it is because of food.

Others clung firmly to optimism amid the hardships:

I have never been more proud and pleased to be a Korean in these 40 years of my life than when I saw my fatherland in front of my eyes. . . . Our nation . . . had such a diligent people who constantly build for tomorrow without haste and hurry. For a long time we were under pressure of foreign countries and lived miserably. Therefore I could not help being so proud and pleased to be a Korean at that moment. . . .

Onjo, where I have been stationed is located in the northeast end of Korea. It is so remote that you will have a hard time to find it on the map. On the edge of a wood the Tumen river is running placidly and outside the cold Siberian wind is blowing with a peculiar plaintive tone. . . . As this place is a remote farm village, we sometimes feel inconvenient to get daily necessities as compared with Japan, from where we returned only recently. However, we do not feel it as a pain, for we know that this problem will be settled at the time of completion of the second 5-year-plan. Anyway I can foresee a progress in our living standard.

And then there were the reports on "Mr. Yoon," a returnee who bore the scars of a recent industrial accident and who entered the Special Room in Niigata on 13 January 1960. Mr. Yoon seems to have given the Red Cross more trouble than any other returnee, not only because he was torn by doubts whether to stay or leave, but more particularly because he refused to speak.

At first, the officials thought that he was dumb. Gradually, however, they realized that he was capable of speaking but was determined to write all his answers to questions for fear that his words would be misused by others. Because he insisted on writing everything, he is the only returnee whose exchanges with officials in the Red Cross Center in Niigata remain verbatim on the record in Geneva.

When I read his words on this first occasion, I found them difficult to understand. It was only gradually over the next few months, as I began to piece the story together, that they started to make sense. There were a couple of lines that caught my attention immediately and have stayed with me like a haunting refrain ever since. Mr. Yoon wrote these words the day before he left Japan for North Korea and gave them to a representative of the International Committee of the Red Cross, who translated them into English. The first sentence is underlined in the original:

<u>*My rights have been disregarded.*</u> *The reason that I write is that there is no other way to express my mind more clearly and correctly—and surely you will understand.*

I did *not* understand, but I knew that I had to try.

Realizing that I had no hope of reading all the files in the few days that I had allowed for research in Geneva, I rushed to a department store in the center of town and bought a digital camera, with which I frantically photographed what seemed to be the most important documents. Even so, by the end of the week, when I was due to leave for Japan, I had looked at no more than a fraction of the material on repatriation in the archives.

On the flight from Geneva to Heathrow and on to Tokyo's Narita Airport, I kept wondering about the documents that I had been reading. Until then, I had not studied the repatriation process closely. Perhaps there were books that could provide an explanation for the puzzling mass of correspondence I had found? Perhaps there were experts in Japan who could explain the story to me? On the long bus trip from Narita to the crowded Tokyo district of Roppongi where I was staying, slipping back and forth between sleep and waking, I found Mr. Yoon's words circling through my mind like a cry in the dark. He must have insisted on writing those lines because he hoped that they would be read by someone who would respond. But there was little sign that anyone had done so; and now, more than forty years later, it was difficult to grasp what he had been trying to say.

My rights have been disregarded. . . . There is no other way to express my mind. . . . Surely you will understand . . .

In Tokyo, I scoured the bookshops, libraries, and computer databases for material on the repatriation movement. Everywhere, I encountered the face of North Korean leader Kim Jong-Il, often set against backdrops bristling with missiles and other weaponry, staring out at me from the dust jackets of bestsellers. The vividly colored titles told their own story: *Kidnap: the Crimes of North Korea*; *The Misery of the North Korean "Paradise."*

Yet just across the aisles were mountains of magazines featuring the faces and love lives of Korean movie idols like Bae Yong-Joon (star of the massively popular TV series *Winter Sonata*). For in the midst of the crisis with North Korea, Japan had been swept by a South Korea craze. Korean films and TV dramas dominated the nation's screens; Korean singers topped the music charts; supermarkets offered alluring displays of pepper-red *kimchi* (Korean pickles), unthinkable ten years earlier.

This was not merely froth and trivia. Positive attitudes, it seems, are breaking down the old prejudices; the realities of a multiethnic Japan are gradually being acknowledged. Young *Zainichi* Koreans no longer have to struggle as the older generation did. Though some institutional barriers remain for those who keep their Korean nationality, many of the cruder forms of discrimination have disappeared, and a growing number of young people are now choosing to become naturalized Japanese citizens. Even Japan's richest man, communications tycoon Son Masayoshi, is a naturalized Japanese of Korean ancestry.

The South Korea craze and the passionate public interest in the North Korean kidnapping story had also stirred uneasy memories of the repatriation of *Zainichi* Koreans to North Korea. These memories were still muted and fragmentary, tucked away (for the most part) in academic publications or small-circulation, serious journals. But research on the subject was clearly increasing. A researcher at Meiji University, Kawashima Takane, had begun to use Japan's new Freedom of Information Law to obtain long-secret official documents on the subject. Eminent Korea experts such as Takasaki Sôji were publishing articles on the repatriation in a leading monthly magazine.

In one bookstore I found another intriguing book on the topic that had recently been published by Chang Myeong-Su, a former official of the North Korean–affiliated community association *Chongryun*. Chang, who lives in Niigata, had as a young man been very actively involved in the repatriation movement. At the height of the movement, he had spent much of his time in the Red Cross Center in Niigata, helping returnees pack their belongings, exchange money, and prepare for the journey to North Korea. But as time went on, he found that stories began to circulate of arrests or disappearances of those whom he had helped to return to the DPRK. Efforts to alert other members of the *Chongryun* to the problem were met with bland indifference, and eventually Chang resigned in protest and became a fierce critic both of *Chongryun* and of the North Korea regime.

The central message of Chang Myeong-Su's book was simple and startling. The repatriation, he claimed, had been an act of ethnic cleansing carried out on behalf of a racist Japanese establishment by none other than that supposed standard-bearer of humanitarianism, the Japanese Red Cross. The language and conclusions seemed extreme, but some of Chang's hypotheses about specific actions by Red Cross officials certainly appeared to fit the information I had seen in Geneva.

Back in Canberra, in the grip of a cold southern-hemisphere winter, I discussed the repatriation story with my colleague Andrei Lankov, a scholar of Russian origin and an expert on North Korean history.

Andrei's reaction caught me by surprise. I had been expecting that he might shed some light on the North Korean side of the story, but his immediate response, instead, was to point me in the direction of the Soviet Union. In tones of some excitement, he recalled how some years earlier, reading material on North Korea in the archives of the former Soviet

Union, he had noticed references to the USSR's involvement in the repatriation of Koreans from Japan. The USSR, he was convinced, had played some central and hidden role in the story.

But Andrei's next comment was discouraging. Having opened the archives to the public, the new Russian state had evidently discovered that they contained too many uncomfortable secrets, and restricted access to them again. There was now apparently little hope of rediscovering the documents that he had seen, and since they were not directly related to his research topic, Andrei himself had not taken notes on them.

I felt fascinated and frustrated. Something that had begun as a small story was growing larger and larger before my eyes, and yet the Soviet connection seemed tantalizingly impossible to pursue. Meanwhile, however, I had reorganized my research plans and dipped deep into my dwindling fieldwork funds to make a second, longer visit to the Geneva archives, where I managed to work my way through most of the repatriation material.

As the year drew to a close, I sat in my office trying to plan the next year's research. But by that time, I was beginning to realize that I could no longer control, or even predict, the itinerary of the journey on which I had embarked. This story was like a giant jigsaw puzzle whose pieces had been scattered across many countries. As I tried to assemble one corner of the puzzle, the blanks in other corners became all the more perplexing.

Here and there, I began to glimpse motifs: the survival into the Cold War era of imperial institutions and colonial prejudices; the global dreams of the Great Powers; the way that humanitarian rules and institutions at times became playthings in the battles of the Cold War ideologies. But I still had no idea where many of the missing pieces lay or whether the puzzle would ever be complete. This sense of uncertainty was disquieting, but also in a strange way exhilarating.

I gave up trying to plan and decided to follow this story wherever its meandering course took me.

I erased the tidy schedule that I had drawn up on the whiteboard of my office wall, realizing that I was cast adrift on the currents of Cold War history.

II

BORDERLINES

4

ACROSS THE EAST SEA

That deceptively simple phrase "North Koreans" causes much confusion. In the Cold War world, fluid politics were all too often frozen into the patterns of glacial geography.

Everything I have heard about the repatriation suggests that the great majority of "returnees" actually came not from the north but from the extreme south of Korea—the southeastern region of Gyeongsang and the island of Jeju.

Who then were the North Koreans in Japan who "wished to return to their homeland," these tens of thousands who would ultimately board the ships in Niigata? In the official documents of the time, they remain largely faceless, ciphers in statistical tables, names devoid of personal histories. If so many of them came from the south of the peninsula originally, what turned them into North Koreans, and what did they really want?

In Tokyo I have begun to come across a few of their stories.

One of these stories is captured in a remarkable documentary film by Japanese director Haramura Masaki. It tells the life history of Yang I-Heon, now an elderly woman living in the Japanese city of Osaka, a determined and courageous woman—a survivor.

Yang I-Heon was born in 1916 in a coastal village on the Korean island of Jeju, a place famous for its *Haenyeo* (women of the sea)—female divers who reach great depths beneath the sea surface in search of shellfish. Yang grew up to be a diver, and like many others, migrated to Japan in search of work at the start of the Pacific War. In the final year of the war, when allied bombing raids flattened many Japanese cities, she returned to her home island where, after a brief relationship with a local man, she had a baby. Soon after, however, violence engulfed the island. Her village was burnt down, and she was forced to flee again to Japan, leaving her little daughter behind with relatives. In Japan she married a fellow migrant from Korea and had six children.

Yang I-Heon's husband was a political activist who spent much of his time developing ethnic schools for Koreans in Japan. It was she who supported the family, traveling around the country in the summer months to dive for abalone and other prized sea creatures. Her work, captured on film footage from the 1960s, was extraordinarily hard and dangerous.

Perhaps it was the hardship of their mother's existence that persuaded three of her sons to join the repatriation to North Korea.

In the film, we see footage of scenes on Niigata docks in the 1960s as her youngest son departs. Yang I-Heon's face as she waves goodbye expresses the agonized choice of a mother who can hardly bear to part from her children, and yet who has been persuaded to believe that this was the only way to secure their future.

The final section of the film records Yang's journey to North Korea for a brief reunion with her sons. These scenes were filmed not long after Koizumi's 2002 visit to Pyongyang and the return of the five Japanese kidnap victims. Solid black ranks of riot police guard the Niigata docks, from which the *Mangyeong Bong*, the only ferry to link Japan and North Korea, departs. Behind these lines stand a mass of Japanese demonstrators, waving placards and venting their fury at this symbol of the feared rogue state across the waters.

Slowly, Yang I-Heon, a small bent figure, makes her way up the gangplank, on her way to what will probably be her last meeting with her sons.

What impelled people like Ms. Yang to set out on their circuitous journeys? And how was it that people like Ms. Yang's sons come to be labeled North Koreans and "returned" to North Korea? Why did they choose a path in life that has left their family scattered across three countries: South Korea, Japan, and North Korea?

To make sense of these conundrums, I need to see the place where their journeys began. And so, almost exactly a year after my first visit to the International Committee of the Red Cross in Geneva, I sit looking out of the window of Japan Airlines flight 957 from Tokyo's Narita Airport, watching the South Korean city of Busan emerge from the summer haze below.

The last time I visited Busan was back in 1974, when South Korea was under the iron grip of the Park Chung-Hee dictatorship. Martial law was in force and hundreds of opponents of the Park regime languished in the country's overcrowded prisons.

My vague impressions of Busan from that time are of a grim port city with huddles of grimy redbrick buildings straggling up the lower slopes of its steep hillsides. Now, looking out of the plane's window, I am reminded of the sight of Hong Kong from the air. Towering white apartment blocks balance on the perilously thin strips of land between the sea and the rugged mountains. On the ground, it soon becomes obvious that Busan, like South Korea as a whole, has been transformed beyond all recognition since the 1970s. Near the station, a Babel of signs in Russian and English, Tagalog and Chinese compete to lure customers to cafés and souvenir shops. The avenues of the city center are lined with smart boutiques, and giant electronic hoardings advertise this year's Busan International Film Festival.

Of all Korea's major cities, this is the nearest to Japan. Halfway up the rugged peak of Yongdusan, which rises sheer out of the consumer paradise of downtown Busan, stand two monuments that symbolize the city's ambiguous relationship with the country across the water.

The first is a massive bronze statue of Admiral Yi Sun-Sin, Korea's greatest military hero and the man who in the last decade of the sixteenth century repulsed the tide of Japanese warlord Toyotomi Hideyoshi's abortive but devastating attempted invasion of Korea. Hideyoshi's ultimate, delusory aim was to conquer the great Chinese empire, but his incursion into Korea gouged a lasting scar through the centuries of peaceful relations that had linked Japan to the Korean Peninsula. It also fed an enduring Korean nationalism whose tangible force has left the country's parks and public spaces dotted with statues of Admiral Yi, clad in scaly armor that seems (judging by the expression on his face) to be causing him considerable discomfort.

The other monument on Yongdusan is a more modest, illustrated signboard marking the site of the *Waegwan*—the Japanese Quarter. After the defeat of Hideyoshi's forces, Japan and Korea both turned inward, closing their ports and imposing strict controls on contacts with the outside world. For over two hundred years, from the early seventeenth to the middle of the nineteenth century, the only Japanese people allowed to travel to Korea were merchants and emissaries from Japan's island domain of Tsushima, hundreds of whom inhabited the walled Japanese Quarter in Busan.

Japan's beautiful, mountainous island of Tsushima itself is, indeed, much nearer to Busan than any Japanese city. It is the only part of Japan that can be seen from the Asian mainland; on a clear day, its faint outlines are visible from the peak of Yongdusan, floating like a mirage on the furthermost edge of the world.

Busan's role as a gateway to Japan survived the coming of the modern era, the demise of the *Waegwan*, and Japan's second great incursion into Korea. In the second half of the nineteenth century, as Japan embarked on a massive program of industrialization and modernization, Korea's Yi dynasty struggled to adapt to the pressures of an age of global empire building. The strategic position of the Korean Peninsula made it a target of the rival ambitions of China, Russia, the Western imperial powers, and the newly emerging imperial power to the east, Japan. By 1905 Japan, fresh from an astonishing military victory over Russia, was ready to expand its power into the Asian continent and forced the Korean king to submit to a humiliating arrangement that turned Korea into a protectorate of Japan. Five years later, Korea was formally annexed as a Japanese colony, and the last of the Yi kings lost his throne.

In colonial times, migrants from all the surrounding regions of Korea—from the countryside of the Gyeongsang region and from Jeju Island to the south—would gather in the port of Busan in search of boats to take them to the Japanese cities of Shimonoseki, Osaka, and beyond.

Busan was also the port through which many eventually headed home. And among those who made that return journey is one of my two traveling companions, Han Heung-Cheol. We are on our way to Jeju Island, but first, he wants to guide us around Busan Harbor and the district of Yeongdo, where he lived as a teenager after his return from Japan.

Han Heung-Cheol's father was one of the tens of thousands of Jeju islanders who migrated to Japan in search of work in the middle of the twentieth century. During colonial times, he had repeatedly crossed back and forth on the ferry that linked Korea and Japan, and in the postwar period, when life on Jeju was very bleak, he migrated to the booming Japanese city of Osaka, where he found work in a Korean restaurant and where he met and married a fellow Jeju islander whose parents had moved to Japan before the war. Heung-Cheol, now in his late thirties, was born in Osaka and lived there until his was thirteen, when his family returned to Korea.

They came to this city and lived for a while on Yeongdo, a large island in Busan Harbor, where many migrants from Jeju have congregated and where Han Heung-Cheol's grandfather, a sailor, had settled with other members of their extended family.

Tall, bespectacled, and soft-spoken, Han Heung-Cheol has a warm smile and is given to sudden bursts of infectious enthusiasm for the places and things we see along our way.

My other companion on this journey of discovery is Hayashi Rumi, a small, vivacious Japanese woman who works for a publishing company. Hayashi-san is in Korea for several months, learning the language and developing exchanges with Korean publishing firms; but she, like me, is a stranger to these parts, constantly puzzled and enthralled by the sights and sounds we encounter on our meandering walk around the streets of Yeongdo and in our travels around the island of Jeju.

Han Heung-Cheol leads us first through the backstreets and into the heart of the community, the market. Its long narrow aisles are lined with stalls selling clothes, shoes, mountains of fruit, giant green watermelons, and pyramids of variegated mushrooms and fungi. We pause to gaze at tanks full of live fish, huge arrays of medicinal roots and herbs, and across the way, the row of flattened pigs heads, each with a beatific smile on its face, as though its owner in death had gone straight to pig heaven.

If Yeongdo market seems an exotic wonder to Hayashi Rumi and myself, we three travelers are a source of wonder to the market people of Yeongdo. Foreign visitors are not unusual, but a Westerner, a Japanese woman, and a bilingual Korean all walking around the market together speaking Japanese—that is quite a novelty.

The woman at a stall selling socks and cotton slippers greets us with a few words of Japanese.

"Where are you from?" she asks. A small plump woman in her sixties with tightly permed gray hair, she has taken a break from work and is sitting on the ground next to the neighboring shoe stall, meditatively rubbing one ankle as she chats to her friend. When we tell her about our journey, she volunteers her story—a story like thousands of others to be heard all over the city.

"I was born in Japan," she says. "My parents went there to get work before the war. We used to live in Wakayama."

"Do you remember Japan well?" I ask (via Han Heung-Cheol, who patiently interprets for us throughout the journey).

"Oh yes," she says, "What I remember most are the bombing raids. It was wartime, you see. We children used to have these little black suits. When we heard the American planes come, we were supposed to put them on and run into the air-raid shelters. But then the war ended and we came back home."

"Did you come straight back here to Busan?"

"No. We got on a boat and it took us to . . . What was it called? I don't remember now. Somewhere further north. Then we had to find our own way south by train. It was a hard journey."

There were many hard journeys and further hardships waiting to greet the travelers when they arrived home. The sock seller and her family were among over a million Koreans who streamed back across the East Sea—in little fishing boats, rickety ferries, or the occupation authorities' "liberty ships"—over the course of the months that followed Japan's defeat in war.

But the end of that war was not the end of the migrations, for on the Korean Peninsula, new storms of conflict were brewing, and their first waves were about to break on the rocky shores of Jeju Island.

Unknown to the people of Korea, five days before Emperor Hirohito's surrender broadcast, thousands of miles away in Washington, D.C., a decision had been made about the postwar destiny of their country.

Throughout the Pacific War, the Soviet Union, engaged in a life-and-death struggle with Nazi Germany, had maintained a neutrality pact with Japan. But with Hitler defeated, three days after the atomic bombing of Hiroshima, the USSR revoked the pact, and its troops began to sweep into the northern reaches of Japan's continental empire. Before U.S. forces could reach the south of the Korean Peninsula, Soviet forces had already begun to enter the north.

The U.S. government, alarmed by these developments, was determined to prevent a wholesale Soviet takeover of Korea. On the night of 10 August 1945, a committee of U.S. military and civilian officials met in Washington to decide on a strategy. Joseph Stalin and Harry Truman had already agreed that Korea should be jointly occupied by the U.S. and the USSR, and a quick decision was needed on the way in which the country would be divided between the occupying powers.

At around midnight, officers Dean Rusk and Charles H. Bonesteel were given a map of Korea and sent into a separate room to work out an appropriate dividing line between Soviet and U.S. zones. According to Rusk's account of the event, he and Bonesteel wanted the line to follow the existing administrative boundaries, so that it would cause as little political disruption as possible. But they had been given just thirty minutes to complete the task, and their only map was a small-scale map of East Asia. It was Bonesteel who pointed out that the thirty-eighth parallel divided Korea neatly in two, while leaving the capital, Seoul, in the southern (U.S.) zone. So the thirty-eighth parallel was suggested as the dividing line, and (rather to the surprise of the U.S. government) the Soviet Union promptly accepted the proposal.

The line worked very satisfactorily on the map and in the committee rooms of Washington and Moscow. But unfortunately it did not correspond to anything on the ground: not to provincial or city boundaries, nor to the divisions of region, culture, or accent.

Above all, it did not correspond to the line between the political Right and Left. That line wove and coiled and twisted all over the country. It ran through the middle of villages, between the houses of neighbors, and down the center of the tables where families gathered for meals. It ran also through the middle of the Korean community in Japan and straight through the dreams of those whose visions of a free Korea fitted the ideologies of neither of the two new Cold War camps.

Ideological divisions existed in every country at the end of the Pacific War, but in Korea their social impact was made far worse by that straight line on the map. As governments on both sides of the divide struggled to make the line between Left and Right and the line between North and South coincide, political dissenters on both sides were transformed into aliens in their own land. Critics of the regime in the South became "North Korean agents;" critics of the regime in the North became "South Korean spies."

And that was how Koreans, both in Korea and in Japan, became (to borrow the words of Palestinian poet Mahmoud Darwish) "victims of a map."

I start thinking of Mahmoud Darwish's words two days after our visit to Yeongdo market, as I sit in a taxi with Han Heung-Cheol and Hayashi Rumi, heading south along the highway that cuts across the center of Jeju Island. We flew from Busan to Jeju the previous day and have hired a taxi to see the island. The taxi driver, Mr. Koh, speaks fluent, rapid-fire Japanese and turns out (perhaps predictably) to be a former migrant to Japan. He went there, he tells us, as a young man in the 1960s and spent many years working in factories to earn the money that would buy his freedom from the ancestral bonds of farm labor.

On either side of the highway stretch fields enclosed by drystone walls, made of the purplish-brown basalt from which the island is formed. Here and there are orchards of citrus trees surrounded by protective rows of tall pine trees, and beyond them the vivid green of the forest stretches toward the distant peak of Mount Halla, whose volcanic cone rises to a height of almost two thousand meters in the very center of the island. The day is warm, the air softened by a faint mist blowing in off the sea.

The lush abundance of Jeju's landscape is deceptive. Rain falls frequently, but the volcanic soil does not retain the water, which runs off straight into the ocean. A dry spell rapidly produces drought, and for centuries, the islanders labored hard to wrest crops of barley, millet, and beans

from the merciless basalt soil. When Mr. Koh was child, his village held little but the prospect of a life of backbreaking farmwork. The natural hardships of the land were intensified by the pressures of colonization: good
farmland was confiscated and handed over to the Japanese military or private companies and large Japanese fishing fleets appeared in the waters off
Jeju, exhausting the riches of the fishing grounds and the shellfish beds
where the island's diving women earned their living.

"There was nothing but a few cows and horses in our village," says Mr.
Koh. "When my big brother went away to school in the city, my father
would walk thirty kilometers there and back to visit him."

It was the search for something beyond the harsh horizons of that village world that sucked Mr. Koh, Han Heung-Cheol's grandparents and father, and a stream of other Jeju people into the industrial maw of Osaka and
other expanding Japanese cities. At the peak of Korean prewar emigration in
the mid 1930s, about one-quarter of all Jeju islanders were living in Japan.

On the southern side of the island, the road winds down toward a stretch of
coast that, for a moment, reminds me of the Mediterranean. We park the
car and walk out on the cliffs, to the point where a steep flight of wooden
steps leads down to a pebbly beach. Below, a couple of brightly striped para-
sols and a blue awning have been set up on the beach, and for a moment I
expect to see sunbathers or families eating their picnics. The sturdy female
figures hanging up wetsuits to dry catch me by surprise. They are divers, elderly women most of them, still plying their trade with cheerful disregard for
the troops of tourists and gaggles of children on school outings who stream
past them onto the beach.

Following the flow of people, we walk down the steps and across the
beach to the foot of the Jeongbang Falls, a great torrent of water that plunges
more than twenty meters from the cliff top into the sea below. When we arrive, the area around the foot of the falls is crowded with laughing, shrieking
schoolchildren. But as the school party departs the beach empties, and all that
can be heard is the ceaseless roar of water onto rocks.

We take off our shoes and socks and dip our feet in the icy current
where salt and fresh water meet. The water is very clear. I reach through its
surface, pick out a heavy, brown pebble of worn basalt, and slip it into my
backpack to take home.

It is on this return journey that Mr. Koh begins to tell another story about
the olden days. Told in an unexpected rush of words, his reminiscences are
at first difficult to understand.

"I remember when they turned our village into a castle," he says. "They built a huge stone wall right round the village. It was two, three meters high. The rebels and the police were fighting outside, you see, and the wall was to keep them out. The police used to come at night, all of a sudden. They'd say, 'Run and hide! Run and hide!' Sometimes they'd say things like, 'Hide until two o'clock in the morning. After that, our operations will be over, and it will be safe to come out.' It was really stupid. No one in our village had a watch or a clock. How were we supposed to know when it was two o'clock in the morning?"

He pauses for a moment and adds, "They were like animals, those police. More like animals than human beings. I saw them beating people. I was, oh, about nine years old at the time, I guess."

Listening to him speak, I begin to realize that we are hearing about a force beyond mere poverty. This was the force that drove Yang I-Heon the diving woman to flee from the island, leaving her baby daughter behind, the force that pushed thousands of others onto boats bound for Japan, and that, in the end, transformed so many Jeju islanders into North Koreans. But Mr. Koh's words do not really begin to make sense until the following day, when we go for another excursion around Jeju Island in the company of Oh Seung-Kook, the head of the 4/3 Research Center.

5

TO THE FIELD OF
DANCING CHILDREN

Like "9/11" in the rest of the world, in Jeju the term "4/3" (*sa-sam*) needs no further explanation. It is engraved on living memory: 3 April 1948. Yet until recently, it was not an easy topic to talk about. In the 1980s and early 1990s, the authorities twice sent Oh Seung-Kook to prison in an unsuccessful attempt to curb his curiosity about the events of 4/3. Today, however, his Research Center flourishes; South Korea's central government has recently published an exhaustive report on the history of 4/3, and the president himself, Roh Moo-Hyun, has visited the island to bow his head in apology on behalf of the government of the Republic of Korea for the events that occurred in 1948 and thereafter.

We met Mr. Oh on our first day in Jeju. He is a stocky, ebullient man who talks with passion and much gesticulation about the history of the island and is eager to share its story with others. That is why he has volunteered to leave his office for the afternoon, to show us some of the history that lies just beneath the surface of Jeju's green landscape. The route we take heads south again, but this time to the southwest corner of the island. We leave the main road behind and wind our way through a maze of stonewalled fields. On either side, the landscape stretches flat to the sky. Far away to the south, the single limestone peak of Sanbangsan stands stark on the horizon. Most of the fields have been recently tilled, and here and there, groups of people in cotton hats are harvesting the potato crop. This is Jeju's best farmland—the only wide plain on the island.

In colonial times, Mr. Oh explains, the Japanese government confiscated the land from the farmers and turned it into one of the largest military bases in Korea. During the early 1940s, when fighting spread throughout the Pacific, the base grew and grew as the Japanese military prepared for the feared Allied attack on the heartland of their empire.

But in the end, the American typhoon of steel swept past Jeju to land instead on the southern Japanese island of Okinawa. Blessing their merciful escape from the horrors of war, the Jeju islanders welcomed the liberation and watched the colonizing army pack its bags and depart. Many of the Japanese soldiers, says Mr. Oh, were in tears as they boarded the ships for Japan.

At last Jeju's people, like the people of Korea as a whole, seemed free to determine their own destiny. Local committees were quickly set up in towns and villages all over the island. Colonial collaborators were dismissed from their posts, and new police and officials began to be trained.

Their hopes were short-lived.

The Soviet forces in the north of the country "restructured" the committees that local people had created in eager anticipation of independence, ensuring that Communist members gained the upper hand. Meanwhile in the South, the U.S. forces saw the local committees in their half of the peninsula as poorly organized and dangerously left wing and refused to recognize their authority. Instead, they created a government under the leadership of Syngman Rhee (Yi Seung-Man), a nationalist leader who had been living in the United States for more than thirty years. For reasons of order and efficiency, they left many of the existing bureaucratic structures created under Japanese colonial rule intact.

So less than two years after Japan's surrender, Jeju islanders found themselves back under the control of policemen and officials brought in from outside the island—many of them Korean officials from other parts of the country who had built careers in collaboration with the Japanese colonial administration.

"They call it 4/3," says Mr. Oh, "but things really started on 1 March 1947. That's the anniversary of the big independence movement which took place in colonial times. On that day, a huge crowd of demonstrators gathered outside the site of the old administrative headquarters—right where your hotel is today. About thirty thousand people took part. Some of them supported the left-wing South Korean Workers Party, which was popular in Jeju then, but the demand that they all shared was a united country. There was talk of separate elections in South Korea, you see, and it seemed that the division of the country might become permanent. Their slogan was 'united independence.' They used to say, 'Let's stop eating western candy and achieve united independence.'"

In a divided Korea, a movement like this was almost inevitably identified by the authorities as a Soviet or North Korean conspiracy. As the size of the demonstration swelled, the police appear to have panicked; they fired on the demonstrators, killing six people. A fierce purge of left-wingers on the island followed. People suspected of instigating the protests were rounded up, detained without trial, and often beaten and tortured. Events steadily escalated until April of the following year when, says Mr. Oh, "The radical left-wing leaders on Jeju were driven into a corner. They became convinced that they were going to be killed anyway, and they decided to go down fighting."

About 300 to 400 of the most radical young men gathered on the forested slopes of Mount Halla, and on 3 April 1948 they launched an attack, killing a number of right-wing leaders and police who had collaborated with the Japanese in colonial times. That was the beginning of the event that in Korean history is known as "the 4/3 Incident," but that might better be described (as it was by some observers at the time) as Jeju's civil war, a prelude to the even greater and more devastating civil war that was to engulf the nation two years later. As in all civil wars, terrible things were done by both sides, but there was little doubt at the time, and there is none today, that most of the violence was perpetrated by the South Korean police and military and by militia battalions brought to Jeju by the authorities from other parts of Korea.

What was happening in Jeju in 1948 was not a secret, even if few outsiders grasped the magnitude of the violence. There were even sporadic reports in the mainstream western media of the day. Allan Raymond, a journalist with the *New York Herald Tribune*, was one of those who visited Jeju in 1948. He interviewed two staunchly anti-Communist Catholic missionaries—one Australian and the other Irish—who were among the very few foreigners left on the island. They told him, "All this turmoil fits into the Russian pattern, but the police are making Leftists. If you have taken a beating from one of those policemen, you are naturally a rebel against him. Who wouldn't be?"

Raymond also talked to General William F. Dean, chief of the U.S. Military Government in Korea. For of course, while this was happening, Korea was still under American military occupation, although the United States was soon hoping to hand over control to a South Korean government headed by Syngman Rhee. Dean told the U.S. reporter that "police brutality and terrorism of Rightist political bands were indeed causes of the island struggle, but that the part which the Communist party was playing should not be underestimated." He reassured the journalist that he had ordered the removal of the police chief, and that in place of the hated police, the U.S. military had decided to rely instead on militia forces, or "constabulary" as they rather quaintly called them. Unhappily for the islanders, the constabulary (with or without the help of the American Military Government) turned out to be as terrifying as the police they had replaced.

During the year of fighting that followed 3 April 1948, Jeju islanders were killed by the security forces because they were identified as insurgents, or because they were simply suspected of left-wing sympathies. They were killed by the insurgents because they were suspected of being police spies, and they were killed by the authorities because they were suspected of providing food and water to the rebels in the mountains. Young people were abducted by the rebels to swell their thinning ranks, and their parents were then killed by the police or constabulary because their children had joined the "Reds." To create a *cordon sanitaire* between the coast (which was largely under the control of government forces) and the slopes of Mount Halla, where they hoped to contain and eliminate the insurgents, government forces ordered some 130 villages to be evacuated and razed to the ground.

People who refused orders to leave their villages were killed, too.

As the day draws toward a close, Mr. Oh takes us to see the place where one of Jeju's lost villages stood. We make our way up a narrow lane lined with thickets of stunted bamboo. In the hazy, thickening light, everything is still—nothing but the sound of the wind and the distant call of a cuckoo. Ahead, the rutted lane curves out of sight. To the left stretches a grassy meadow surrounded by low stone walls. But for the bamboo, I might be back in the English countryside of my childhood.

Bamboo, Oh Seung-Kook explains, was always planted next to Jeju village houses to provide poles and fishing rods, and wild bamboo are a sign—the only sign—of the houses that once stood there. Speaking rapidly, almost as though the words were tumbling out unbidden, he begins to tell the story:

"In 1948, eighty-nine families—about four hundred people—lived here. On 16 November 1948, an order was issued that all the villages on the lower slopes of Mount Halla should be burnt down—this was one of them. When the village was burnt to the ground, some of the people who lived here were killed, but others managed to escape. About a hundred villagers fled and hid in a cave. But their hiding place was discovered, so they fled again to Mount Halla. There they were captured and herded into a temporary camp which had been built near the top of the the Jeongbang Falls [the beautiful waterfall we had visited the previous day].

"They were never seen again.

**Figure 5.1. The Jeongbang Falls, Jeju Island
(Author's photograph)**

"Relatives who went looking for them later heard how the captives had all been ordered out of the camp and to the head of the falls. There they were shot and their bodies were thrown onto the rocks below, where the power of the water washed them out to sea. The surviving villagers eventually returned and built new houses not far away from here. A few have come back here to make 'empty graves'—places where they can remember their dead—but none can bear to live on this spot again."

As suddenly as they began, Oh Seung-Kook's words stop. He gives a small sigh, and bends down to rummage around among the weeds on the embankment. When he straightens up he holds two things: in his right hand, a fragment of roof tile, and in his left, the base of a broken rice-bowl.

Sea currents know no frontiers. For centuries, they have carried fruits and seeds, flotsam and jetsam, and small boats with their human cargoes north from the Korean island of Jeju to the Japanese island of Tsushima. In 1948, the current carried bodies. Nameless and faceless, their identities dissolved by the sea, they washed up one by one on the southern shores of Tsushima, and the Tsushima islanders gave them a dignified Buddhist burial.

We walk in silence back down the lane. In the gathering dusk, I imagine the ridges of thatched rooves half-hidden behind clumps of bamboo in the fields. Quite vividly, I hear in my head the sound of feet running along the lane and the cries of children calling to one another as they make their way home from the fields.

At the place where the lane rejoins the main road we pause, and I feel a touch of coldness on the back of my neck as Han Heung-Cheol translates the words engraved on the small stone monument that has recently been placed there. The village that once stood in this place was called Mudong-i-wat. The name means "the Field of Dancing Children." The village, it seems, was given that name some two hundred years ago by a visiting official, who was struck by the energy and joy of the children he saw playing in its meadows.

The monument invites visitors to these fields to recreate in their minds the voices of the dancing children, and to pray for peace.

The precise number who died in the aftermath of the Jeju rebellion of 3 April 1948 will probably never be known. Until recently, when 4/3 was still a dark, suppressed memory to be spoken of in whispers, there were rumors of fifty thousand or even eighty thousand dead. Now that research can be conducted openly, the figures have been revised downward, but they are still chilling. The local government, which is engaged in a process of truth and reconciliation for the victims of 4/3, has collected the names of almost fifteen thousand victims and believes the total number to be between fifteen thousand and twenty thousand. Mr. Oh thinks that it is around thirty thousand.

Somewhere in the gap between the earlier rumored figures and today's count of the dead are the thousands—tens of thousands perhaps—who boarded any fishing boat willing to carry them, and fled across the sea to Japan, swelling the tide of stowaways who washed up on the shores of Tsushima and the seaboard of southwestern Japan.

Not all the refugees from Jeju headed for Japan, others went to Busan, seeking an escape from the fighting on the Korean mainland. But Busan proved a harsh and dangerous place of refuge, for in 1950 the Korean

War—the "Forgotten War," as it is so often called in other parts of the world—broke out.

In the streets of Busan's Yeongdo it begins to be possible to imagine—however dimly—the experience of an event that has been described as "one of the most devastating of modern conflicts." The origins of the conflict are complex and contentious—border disputes between North and South had flared intermittently since 1949. But in June 1950 North Korean troops, with the support of the Soviet Union, swept across the thirty-eighth parallel and down the peninsula with surprising speed, leaving a trail of death and destruction in their wake. Within two months, they were just forty-five kilometers away from Busan.

For a period in August 1950, before the counteroffensive from the South began, only a tiny part of the southernmost tip of Korea remained under the control of the South Korean government and the United Nations (in practice, mostly U.S.) forces who supported it. Into this little arc of land between the battlefront and the sea poured hundreds of thousands of frightened and exhausted refugees—many wounded, many separated from their families, most hungry and homeless. Then the tide of war turned, and the South Korean and United Nations forces swept north, inflicting equal destruction on the northern half of the peninsula.

By the time a ceasefire was signed in 1953, the two sides were almost exactly where they had started, and the border (now with a few more curves and meanders than before) still ran along the thirty-eighth parallel. The cost of the war included the lives of over three million Koreans, about half a million Chinese, and around forty thousand United Nations troops.

Among the other lasting scars of war was the disappearance of many thousands of people. In the late 1950s, the South Korean government claimed that hundreds of thousands of its citizens were still being held prisoner in North Korea. In fact, the real fates of many of the disappeared have remained unknown ever since. Some indeed were probably executed by the North Korean government or held in prison camps for years. Others were among the dead of war whose remains were never found. Others again had chosen to flee north across the border, just as tens of thousands had chosen to flee south. Whatever their fates, the fear, uncertainty, and silence surrounding the disappeared of the Korean War still casts its shadow over the lives of many Korean families today.

For much of the war period, Busan was crammed with desperate refugees who were looking for food and shelter and hunting for parents or children from whom they had become separated in the confusion of flight. Even as

late as 1956, when two Red Cross officials from Geneva visited Korea as part
of a confidential mission to investigate the repatriation issue, Busan left them
with a "very powerful impression of desolation and poverty. This comes from
the fact that the city and its surroundings are still full with refugees, living in
conditions which seem miserable from our European point of view."

In the narrow streets of Yeongdo, many hundreds of refugees sought
boats to take them across the water to the relative safety of Tsushima or
other parts of Japan. At the height of the fighting, there were appeals to the
highest authorities to allow refugees from Korea to enter Japan, but they
met with firm refusals. A top secret telegram was sent from Washington to
Tokyo, dated 6 January 1951. It reads: "General MacArthur has pointed out
that refugee problem out of Korea is increasingly pressing for decision, but
that he does not repeat not believe it feasible to bring refugees to Japan."
Douglas MacArthur, supreme commander of the Allied powers in Japan
and of U.N. forces in Korea, was (according to the telegram) concerned
that accepting refugees "might well enrage the Japanese people because of
past relationship between them and Korean race," and might aggravate
"Japan's own pressing problems with Korean minority already in Japan."

The dead who drifted across the border to Tsushima could find a rest-
ing place on Japanese soil, but no such privileges were to be accorded to the
living.

So the crossings remained furtive and illegal. Money was exchanged
quietly in the backs of shops or on street corners of Yeongdo, sometimes
with the captains of fishing boats, but often too with diving women, whose
knowledge of the sea and business acumen enabled them to act as a link between sea captains and their desperate passengers.

No one knows how many Jeju islanders—women like Ms. Yang the diving
woman, whose story is told in Haramura Masaki's documentary film—
managed to slip past the watching eyes and find their way to the shelter of
friends' or relatives' homes in Japanese cities. But those who succeeded in
crossing the border found themselves living an uneasy life. Without proper
papers or entry permission, they were liable to deportation from Japan at
any moment, and anyone who had fled Jeju in the wake of 4/3 was inevitably regarded by the authorities in South Korea as a dangerous "Red."

Ms Yang, after leaving her little girl behind because the captain of the
boat she boarded would not let her take a baby with her, did not see her
daughter again for fifteen years; and having become a Red, a North Korean, she was forbidden to return to her birthplace of Jeju until the democratization of South Korea took firm hold in the late 1990s.

Now I am beginning to understand the origins and meaning of the political fissure that opened up in the midst of Japan's Korean community. Some of the forces that went into the creation of "North Koreans in Japan" begin to be visible. It no longer seems quite so strange that many people from Korea's southernmost province of Jeju were among the tens of thousands who, from December 1959 onward, boarded the ships in Niigata to go "home" to North Korea.

Yet flying back from Korea to Japan, I have a feeling that, despite the dark history we have encountered, Jeju Island today is a place of hope.

Though life in the villages is still hard, and bent-backed old women still hoe basalt stones from the red soil of the fields, the work of generations and the shifting currents of East Asian society have brought a new prosperity to Jeju. Thousands of tourists flock to smart resorts on the southern fringes of the island; the underground malls of Jeju City are full of young people, shopping for the latest fashions and chatting to one another on their cell phones. Jeju can even afford to send crate loads of its delicious oranges to North Korea as aid.

The islanders speak enthusiastically of Jeju as "the peace island." They have grand dreams of creating a place where people from all over the deeply divided East Asian region can come together to talk, to share histories and visions for the future. The political forces at work, both on Jeju and in the region as a whole, are complex and volatile, and twenty-first-century prosperity brings shadows as well as light.

But there is nothing that weighs more heavily on the human heart than silence; and on Jeju, the silence has finally begun to lift.

6

THE BORDERS WITHIN

The divisions that tore the society of Jeju Island apart in the late 1940s and that devastated the whole peninsula in 1950–1953, also carved deep fault lines through the Korean community in Japan. But for *Zainichi* Koreans their effects were compounded by the peculiarities of the national borders separating Japan from North and South Korea.

The man sitting opposite me in the lobby of a small hotel in central Tokyo is one of those who has experienced the full force of those effects first hand.

He is precisely the same age as I am, born in 1951—a middle-aged man with a face that seems rather sad in repose, but that is every now and again transformed by a broad smile. A musician by training, he was once a horn player in a provincial symphony orchestra but now works mainly as an interpreter.

I first met him at a conference shortly before my visit to Busan and Jeju. At that time, we merely exchanged brief greetings, and I was rather surprised to receive an email from him soon after, with an attached article he had written about the repatriations to North Korea. "I have a close personal connection to the repatriation story," he wrote, "and if you would like, I'd be happy to talk to you about it."

Intrigued, I called him up to make an appointment. "How much time can you spare for a meeting?" I asked.

"How much time have you got?" came the answer. "I can talk for many, many hours."

In Japan, as in Korea itself, liberation brought joy and hope to former colonial subjects. All over the country, new political, social, and cultural groups sprang up almost overnight. Korean students established newspapers and journals in their long-suppressed native tongue, and community groups somehow found spaces amid the burnt-out landscapes of Japanese cities to set up Korean schools for their children. For the first few months, the heady sensation of freedom brought people together. National pride overwhelmed political differences. But very quickly, the insidious line drawn across the Korean Peninsula began to make its presence felt.

The largest community organization—the League of Koreans—was launched as a broad social movement, advocating the rights and welfare of *Zainichi* Koreans across the political spectrum. But fissures soon appeared within its ranks. Its leaders were left wing and increasingly aligned themselves with the Communist groups then establishing their ascendancy in the Soviet-occupied North of the peninsula. Conservative and liberal nationalists became disillusioned by this drift toward Communism, and many left the organization, eventually forming their own group, *Mindan*, which became closely linked to the South Korean regime.

Meanwhile, the Allied occupiers observed the activities of the League of Koreans with growing suspicion. In 1948, just as the events of 3 April were unfolding on Jeju Island, the Japanese government moved to close down Korean ethnic schools in Japan, arguing that they did not meet the educational standards established by the Japanese Ministry of Education. A mass protest movement erupted, with the League of Koreans playing the central role. In the eyes of General Douglas MacArthur's occupation headquarters, this seemed like an alarming extension of the revolutionary activities on Jeju. A state of emergency was declared, the Allied forces stepped in to put down the demonstrations, and the League of Koreans was outlawed and disbanded.

The Japanese government reacted even more strongly. In 1949, Japanese Prime Minister Yoshida wrote to MacArthur asking for authority to allow the Japanese government to forcibly deport the Korean minority en masse to South Korea. MacArthur was unwilling to allow such a drastic "solution," though he agreed that Koreans should not be encouraged to remain in Japan.

After the outbreak of the Korean War, Japan's political leaders returned to the theme of deportation, this time putting forward a somewhat more modest proposal. In December 1950, Chief Cabinet Secretary Okazaki Katsuo, an influential politician with close links both to the occupation authorities and to Prime Minister Yoshida Shigeru, announced that an agreement had been reached with the South Korean government on "the compulsory returning of subversive Korean residents in this country to their homeland."

There were, however, a few technical hitches to this scheme. Until the end of the Pacific War, Japan's Korean and Taiwanese colonial subjects had been Japanese under international law. If they traveled outside the empire, they did so on Japanese passports; if they competed in the Olympic Games, they competed for Japan. So the breakup of Japan's colonial empire—like the end of empires elsewhere—raised important problems of nationality. Throughout the occupation of Japan, the Allied authorities repeatedly emphasized that Koreans living in Japan legally retained Japanese nationality until some clear agreement about their citizenship could be reached between Japan and the newly independent Korea.

So the "subversives" whom the Japanese government was proposing to deport were formally Japanese, and many of them had been born and spent all their lives in Japan. As the occupation authority's advisors pointed out, this raised awkward questions about the legality of deporting one's own nationals. Besides, nobody had the slightest illusion about the fate that awaited so-called Reds deported to South Korea in the middle of the Korean War. In the words of one General Headquarters, Supreme Commander for the Allied Powers (GHQ-SCAP) memo: "The General Headquarters thinks that it is not desirable to deport them to Korea knowing that Koreans to be deported from Japan will be executed in Korea." Instead, (less reassuringly) the memo suggested that it would be better for them to be "given [the] death sentence in Japan according to law." ?

Rumors of impending mass deportations sparked large protest demonstrations in Korean communities across Japan. In fact, the issue proved (as the Japanese police noted) to be one of the few things capable of evoking a united response from Korean residents of every political persuasion. Some likened the proposed deportations to "the Jewish expulsion conducted by Hitler."

In the end, the Japanese government was persuaded to drop its mass deportation plan for the time being at least. Instead, a former U.S. immigration official, who had previously been in change of America's wartime internment camps, was brought to Japan to help draw up an Immigration Control Ordinance, giving the Japanese minister of justice wide discretionary powers to deport "subversive aliens."

But to transform Koreans in Japan into aliens, one further step was necessary. The story that I am about to hear is the story of that further step and its effect on individual lives.

In the Tokyo hotel lobby, my visitor and I settle into our leather armchairs. Chopin preludes tinkle over the music system, and our coffee grows cold on the table as we talk. I am feeling tentative, uncertain what to ask, and the man sitting opposite me prefaces his answers to my first questions with long silences, moments where he seems to be turning inward in search of words to encompass his experiences. But the more time passes, the more fluent and passionate his flow of words becomes.

This is the start of his story.

Rika Hiroshi (as he was then called) was born and grew up in the town of Toyohashi in Aichi Prefecture, roughly halfway between Tokyo and Osaka. His father ran Acacia Books, a little secondhand bookstore in the center of town, and the family lived on the second floor of the building above the shop. Books and writing were an important part of family life. Hiroshi's parents had met at a local poetry circle, where both indulged their passion for *tanka*, the short evocative poems often seen as the epitome of Japanese literary taste.

Like many people of their generation in Japan—people who had come of age during the Pacific War—Rika Hiroshi's parents were left-wing. Socialism appealed to postwar intellectuals and literati, both for its promise of a better future and because it offered a way of drawing a firm line between themselves and the elders whom they blamed for allowing Japan to slide into the disasters of war.

Hiroshi was a bright child who did well at the local school. By the third year of primary school, he was receiving top marks in most subjects and had been elected class representative. There was, however, one thing that his classmates liked to tease him about: his very unusual surname. Although the characters used to write it were different, the pronunciation of his name was identical with the Japanese word for "science." Not only to be top of the class, but also to be blessed with a name that sounded like science, seemed an unfair advantage.

But it was a different sort of teasing that precipitated the shattering of all Rika Hiroshi's assumptions about himself and his place in the world.

"In those days," he recalls, "Japanese school kids had an expression which they sometimes used to tease one another. When one kid said something silly or incomprehensible, the others would sometimes say 'Hey, don't speak Korean!' It was one of those thoughtless phrases that children use. We didn't really understand what we were saying."

One day, when Rika Hiroshi was eight years old, his mother caught him using that expression.

"My mother said 'Sit down. I want to talk to you.' Then she explained to me, 'You're not Japanese. You're registered as a foreigner; you are a Korean.'"

He pauses for a long time, and then continues, "I felt . . . I felt that I had been totally negated. I knew nowhere but Japan. I spoke only Japanese. I couldn't grasp the reality of what it meant to be Korean. I didn't know a single Korean song, didn't speak a word of Korean. Nothing. It wasn't so much the fact that I was not Japanese that was shocking—well, that was a shock too of course—but what was worse was the sense of having nothing to put in its place. If I'm not Japanese, I thought, then what on earth am I? My parents had no answer to that question—just the bare facts. My mother had been Japanese until she got married and lost her nationality. Dad was Korean by birth, but had come to Japan as a small child and was a Japanese public servant when he got married. He had no close relatives in Korea and didn't speak the language."

Certain things, though, did suddenly start to make sense For instance, the strange food served at his grandparents' ancestral ceremonies, which was quite unlike anything he had eaten at his friends' houses. And then there was that unusual surname "Rika." In 1940, Korea's colonial rulers had decreed that all Koreans were to adopt "Japanese-sounding" names. To avoid discrimination, many Koreans in Japan went on using those Japanese names, in public a least, in the postwar period—indeed, many still use them today. Rika is a Japanized version of his family's Korean name. His real surname was Yi— also often pronounced *Ri*—and the name that he uses today is Yi Yang-Soo.

His family's branch of the extensive Yi clan had been farmers in a small village near Jinju, an old town in Korea's South Gyeongsang Province. His ancestors had been landlords, but his grandfather had lost much of the family's wealth and, like so many others, they had joined the swelling ranks of migrants to Japan.

"Dad was only five years old when he came to Japan, so he didn't speak Korean," Yi recalls. "Grandma and Grandpa spoke Korean to one another, but—you know how it is—little kids don't really listen to adult conversations properly. My grandparents spoke with a local southern Korean accent. In their dialect, the word for 'Grandpa' was *Halbae* and the word for 'Grandma' was *Hanmae*, so I used to say *Halbae, Hanmae*. But, well, I just thought that was what my Grandma and Grandpa were called. After all, if you ask most little children, they wouldn't be able to tell you what their grandparents' real names are. I didn't think anything of it."

Yi Yang-Soo's father, Yi Sun-Weon, had married twice. His first wife was also a Korean migrant; the marriage had been arranged by their parents, but soon after the birth of their first son, his wife fell ill and died. When Sun-Weon decided to remarry, this time to Yamaguchi Miyo, a young Japanese woman he had befriended at the poetry writing circle, their relationship was strongly opposed both by both families. But this, after all, was postwar Japan—a time of democratization and individual freedom. The young couple went ahead with their wedding, and Miyo's name was removed from her birth family's register.

In modern Japan, the family register is the all-important fount of identity and belonging. Family registers are birth, marriage, and death certificates rolled into one; they are not only the official record of individual identity, but also a record that places each individual firmly into the patrimonial lineage of family and of local and national community. No child can be enrolled in school and no passport can be issued without an officially certified copy of an entry in the family register.

In colonial times, the family register was also the marker that divided ruler from ruled. Although prewar and wartime Korean and Taiwanese colonial subjects possessed Japanese nationality in terms of international law, within the empire, they were eternally differentiated from "ethnic Japanese" by the fact that their families were registered not in "Japan proper" (*naichi*) but in the "external territories" (*gaichi*). In colonial times, when Japanese women married Korean men, their Japanese registration would generally be expunged, and they would acquire their husband's external territory registration. But since the end of the war and the independence of Korea, this transfer of family registers had become impossible. Miyo, on her marriage, was left with no family registration at all. Her son, too, was left without a registration, his uncertain legal identity an embodiment of all the unresolved problems of Japan's postcolonial history.

By the time Yi Yang-Soo was born in 1951, the postwar Allied occupation of Japan was drawing to a close. The United States and other occupiers were able to look back with a degree of justifiable pride at their achievements. Many areas of Japanese politics and society had been transformed since the Day of Defeat. Farmland had been redistributed, a more democratic education system had been introduced, women had gained the vote, and Japan had acquired a new constitution that committed it to a peaceful future. Boosted, ironically enough, by the effects of the Korean War, the Japanese economy was well on the road to recovery. A defeated empire, in short, had been successfully transformed into a bastion of capitalism and democracy in a troubled and divided Asia.

There were, however, a few awkward odds and ends that needed to be tidied up as the occupiers prepared to hand their powers back to the Japanese government, and one of these was the position of Koreans in Japan. What was to become of the nationality of *Zainichi* Koreans when the postwar Peace Treaty came into force and Japan was formally and irrevocably severed from its former empire?

The Allied occupation's legal experts had a firm view as to what *should* happen. Similar problems had arisen before in many other parts of the world when colonial empires fell apart. In such cases, special arrangements had generally been made, giving dual citizenship or special residence rights to emigrant communities created by colonialism. Legal precedent suggested that, at the very least, individuals should be offered a choice between old and new nationalities—in this case, the right either to retain their existing Japanese nationality or to adopt the nationality of the newly independent Korea.

There was, however, an obvious complication—there was not one newly independent Korea, but two. Syngman Rhee's Republic of Korea in the south insisted that all Koreans in Japan were its citizens, but it was clear in 1952 that a majority of Koreans in Japan did not want to be defined as South Korean nationals. Some—including a substantial number of people who originated from the south but had left-wing sympathies—wanted to define themselves as nationals of the northern Democratic People's Republic of Korea. A larger number still saw themselves just as "Koreans"— citizens of a single homeland who refused to have their identity split by the thirty-eighth parallel.

Meanwhile, the Japanese government's view of the matter was simple. Now that the empire was gone, they no longer wanted Korean or Taiwanese former colonials to be Japanese citizens. As the end of the occupation approached with no resolution in sight, the occupation authorities quietly washed their hands of the whole problem, leaving it for Japan and South Korea to work out by themselves.

In April 1952, the Japanese government unilaterally announced that, with the implementation of the San Francisco Peace Treaty, Korean and Taiwanese residents in Japan would lose their Japanese nationality. They were given no say in the matter. The change of nationality would take effect on 28 April 1952, the day when the San Francisco Peace Treaty came into force and Japan regained its independence.

Japan's approach to the issue evoked heated protests from South Korea. The South Korean government did not object to the redefinition of Koreans in Japan as Korean citizens—in fact, it too defined all *Zainichi* Koreans as citizens of the Republic of Korea. However, it demanded that, instead of being treated like other foreigners in Japan, Koreans should be given special rights reflecting the peculiar circumstances in which they had become foreigners. On the other hand the Syngman Rhee regime in South Korea, which was burdened with its own problems of poverty and unemployment, showed no serious interest in supporting any large-scale return of *Zainichi* Koreans to its territory. Instead, it tended to use the issue of Koreans in Japan as one of the many bargaining counters deployed in the painfully prolonged series of normalization talks with Japan.

Policy on nationality in Japan is normally handled by the Ministry of Justice, but the issue of the nationality of *Zainichi* Koreans involved the delicate matter of relations with the two Koreas, so a central role was played by Foreign Minister Okazaki Katsuo, the man who had announced the earlier abortive mass deportation scheme. When the minister of health and welfare was questioned in the Diet (parliament) about the effect that the loss of nationality would have on Korean's rights to welfare, he referred questioners to the minister responsible, Mr. Okazaki. When Okazaki was asked about this, he agreed that it left many Koreans in Japan in an ambiguous position. It was not clear whether those who failed to take up South Korean citizenship really had any nationality at all.

However, Okazaki comfortingly assured questioners that the government was engaged in negotiations with South Korea about the status of Koreans in Japan.

"As far as the change of nationality is concerned, in relation to property rights and so forth," he said, "Koreans who have been living in Japan up until now have been running all kinds of businesses and received various rights as Japanese people. We have therefore more or less reached an understanding that the government will take special care that the change of nationality will not cause them any particular inconvenience."

By the time Yi Yang-Soo learned that he was Korean, he was also becoming increasingly conscious of another force that threatened to shake his world apart.

His parents' marriage was not a happy one. Yi Sun-Weon was an autocratic husband and father, given to violent bouts of temper in which he would strike out at his wife and children over the most trivial of incidents. In the late 1950s, Miyo decided that she could endure it no longer, and was going to leave home, taking her son with her. Yang-Soo, who was old enough to understand what was going on, was deeply anxious about the future.

"Although I was only a kid," says Yi Yang-Soo, "I kind of understood that it would be difficult for a woman to manage on her own. Mum suggested that we might go to live with relatives in Tokyo. But I thought, If we go and move into a new household, what happens if we face the same problems all over again? What happens if we are really unhappy there? I was just so uneasy about the whole idea."

The only alternative was for mother and son to find some way of supporting themselves. But in postwar Japan, the prospects for a single mother with a young son were not good—and the prospects for a *foreign* single mother were grim indeed. For despite the bland assurance by Foreign Minister Okazaki that Koreans and Taiwanese would not be "caused any particular inconvenience," the loss of nationality in fact meant that Koreans in Japan—including women like Miyo—faced a drastic deprivation of social rights.

It was unclear how far Japan's existing migration control law applied to Koreans, because they had not been foreigners when they migrated to Japan. A hastily introduced ordinance permitted them to go on living in Japan until such time as the Japanese government devised a long-term policy on the subject, but said absolutely nothing about social, political, or human rights.

As foreigners, from 28 April 1952 on, Koreans in Japan lost the right to public housing and a range of other welfare benefits. This exclusion was reinforced and became all the more painful as Japan's welfare system developed in the postwar decades. For example, when major new national health insurance and national pension insurance schemes were introduced in 1959, just before the departure of the first repatriation ship from Niigata to North Korea, they explicitly excluded foreign residents.

Because of their foreign status, Koreans in Japan were also now excluded from professions such as medicine and debarred from public employment—everything from elite bureaucratic jobs to driving trains for the national railways or sweeping streets for local councils.

For over two decades, Koreans in Japan would also have no automatic right of reentry to Japan if they traveled overseas, and spouses or children of *Zainichi* Koreans who had been left behind in Korea at the end of the Pacific War or during the chaos that followed would have no right to enter Japan for family reunions

The loss of welfare rights was particularly devastating. In colonial times, many large Japanese companies had employed Korean workers, paying them wages lower than those given to Japanese employees. After the war, this wage discrimination ceased. However, when Korean workers were no longer a source of cheap labor, large firms lost interest in employing them—particularly as many managers viewed Koreans in Japan as potential troublemakers. At the beginning of the 1950s, more than three-quarters of *Zainichi* Koreans of working age were either unemployed or engaged in casual work with very unreliable earnings.

To prevent complete social chaos in impoverished Korean communities, the Ministry of Health and Welfare, as a special act of "benevolence," did agree in 1952 that Koreans and Taiwanese in Japan, having been stripped of all other social entitlements, could continue to claim the most minimal form of assistance given to the very poor—livelihood protection benefits.

But a discretionary act of benevolence by the powerful is a two-edged sword. What is given may also, discretionarily, be taken away. Above all, the power to take away can become a tool to discipline, to control behavior, to manipulate the actions of whole communities.

When Miyo and Yang-Soo decided to leave home at the end of the decade, the future was terrifyingly uncertain. But then, quite suddenly, what seemed like a ray of light had appeared on the horizon. Both of Yi Yang-Soo's parents had begun avidly reading information that was appearing almost daily in the Japanese media and in left-wing *Zainichi* Korean circles in the middle of 1958. These newspaper articles were about the opportunity for Koreans to be repatriated free of charge to North Korea. There were glossy, illustrated magazine stories about the wonderful free housing, welfare, guaranteed income, and careers for women offered by the Democratic People's Republic of Korea's burgeoning socialist system; the articles featured alluring pictures of the brand new apartment blocks already being built to house those who wished to return.

And so it was that in the rainy season of 1961, Yi Yang-Soo and his mother Miyo—a woman who had been born into a Japanese farm family and never traveled outside the country in her life—boarded a train for the journey to Niigata, for the first leg of a journey "home" to the Democratic People's Republic of Korea. For that reason, too, they appear fleetingly in the gray box files full of documents in the basement archives in Geneva, unnamed but unmistakable: "A Korean woman (ex-Japanese) of 35 years old who came from Aichi Prefecture with her second son [actually, her husband's second son] of ten years old."

But I am running ahead of the story. For to understand how Yi Yang-Soo and his mother came to be recorded in the files in Geneva, we need first to understand how the repatriation scheme came into being. And to make sense of that, it is necessary to go back to a time when Yi Yang-Soo was just four or five years old and still secure in the unthinking certainty that he was Japanese.

III

STRATAGEMS

.

7

THE SHADOW MINISTRY

A single page from a newspaper lies on the desk of my Tokyo hotel room. It has been printed from microfilm. The words are dark and difficult to read; the small photograph in the top left-hand corner is indistinct. I have left it lying there as I go to open the windows, in the hope that fresh air will help to clear my head and help me to see through the opaque phrases on the page.

But the air outside is tepid and still. Large drops of rain splatter against the windowpane and onto the umbrellas of the small figures who scurry up and down the hill below the hotel. At the bottom of the hill, just out of sight, is the YWCA, where I stayed when I first came to Japan over thirty years ago. Back then, the narrow side streets of Tokyo were lined with gray tiled wooden houses, built in the aftermath of the bombing raids that flattened the city during the Pacific War. During my first winter in Japan, I remember noticing how, as dusk fell, the air would fill with the smell of charcoal and paraffin stoves. Here and there, you could still encounter tiny, bow-legged old women bent double under the load of vegetables that they had brought to the city to sell.

A great deal has changed in three decades. The wooden houses are almost all gone, replaced by the steel and glass of office buildings or by the rectangular creations that in Japan are imposingly termed "mansions": small apartment blocks clad with tile, concrete, or pseudo-marble. The trains on which the old women once traveled to market are now crowded with orange-haired teenagers exchanging photographs on their i-mode cell phones.

The transformations since July 1955, when the page of newsprint on my desk was published, have been even more profound. I try to imagine the city in the 1950s, as wartime recovery was just beginning to give way

73

to rapid economic growth. The year 1955 was only three years after Japan had regained its independence from postwar occupation. Lingering scars of bombing would have been visible amid the noise and dust of construction. Limbless ex-soldiers would have haunted the street corners, playing the forlorn melodies of military songs on their harmonicas. In the middle of that year, the Soviet Union was seething with intrigue as Georgy Malenkov, Vyacheslav Molotov, Nikolai Bulganin, and Nikita Khrushchev battled to succeed the late and little-lamented Joseph Stalin; in Washington, D.C., Dwight D. Eisenhower was just starting to plan his reelection campaign.

But some things, after all, do not change. In November 1955, a coalition of Japanese conservative groups joined forces to form the Liberal Democratic Party (LDP) and established a government under the leadership of Prime Minister Hatoyama Ichirô. The same party has been in power almost continuously ever since. It is still in power today.

I inhale a deep breath of damp city air and go back to the page on my desk. Alerted by a reference in Chang Myeong-Su's book, I have tracked down this newspaper in Japan's National Library. The small article in the corner of the page would have been easy to miss. It reports the appointment of retired diplomat Inoue Masutarô to the position of director of the Foreign Affairs Department of the Japan Red Cross Society. I peer again more closely at the grainy oval photograph—a middle-aged man with a slightly elfin face, prominent ears, and an uncertain smile. It is one of those rather unfortunate photographs that seems to have caught the subject unawares. His forehead is furrowed; his eyes, beneath their drooping eyelids, glance sideways, giving him a faintly furtive air.

Mr. Inoue's new posting was a significant one. In recent years, says the article, the Japan Red Cross Society's Foreign Affairs Department has become famous for handling those ticklish diplomatic tasks that the government itself dare not touch, particularly issues concerning Japan's contentious relationship with Communist countries. The department's triumphs in these sensitive areas, indeed, have given it a special aura—the reputation of being a "second Ministry of Foreign Affairs." But now the government itself is embarking on fresh foreign policy initiatives, including plans to establish diplomatic relations with the Soviet Union. How will the Red Cross's shadow foreign ministry fare in the new era? The answer lies in the hands of its newly appointed chief, Inoue Masutarô.

The three columns of print that follow, together with a few fragments of extra information that I have picked up along the way, compose everything I know about Inoue. For despite the latent power of his position, Inoue himself remains oddly obscure. I wish that I knew more about him. If I did, I might be able to make better sense of the words on the page in front of me. And if I could do that, I might be able to see more clearly how the repatriation story begins.

For historians, beginnings are all important, but always equivocal. Nothing in history has a real beginning or a real end. Each event is always a product of what came before. The art is to find a starting point that omits nothing essential but that does not confuse with a miasma of irrelevant background detail. The task is delicate, though, for the choice of starting points shapes the whole story that follows. At the moment, my quest for a beginning of this story is like a search for the start of a tangled skein of wool; everything seems to be inextricably tied to something else, and many of the threads lead back to the life and character of Inoue Masutarô.

The little information I possess suggests that Inoue's background closely mirrored Japan's own twentieth-century rise as a world power. His ancestors came from a small silk-farming village in the mountains of central Japan, but in the 1880s one young member of the family embarked on the path to wealth and success. The young man, Horikoshi Zenjirô (a cousin of the Inoues), established the Horikoshi Trading Company, specializing in the export of Japanese silk brocades to the American and European markets. The silk trade was the foundation of Japan's early industrialization, and by the end of the decade Horikoshi Trading had grown into a flourishing family concern. Among those who benefited from its rise was Inoue Masutarô's father, Inoue Kinjirô, who was offered a job as head of the firm's Paris office.

Inoue Masutarô was born in Paris in 1899 and learned French in infancy. In fact, as Inoue told the author of the 1955 newspaper article, when his family came back to Japan in the first decade of the twentieth century, he spoke hardly any Japanese at all, so his parents enrolled him in an exclusive private school, known in Japanese as Gyôsei Gakuen and in French as l'Ecole de l'Etoile du Matin. The school had been set up by French missionaries to teach Japanese children alongside the children of expatriate families and offered a bilingual curriculum in Japanese and French.

From l'Ecole de l'Etoile du Matin, Inoue's education progressed along the well-defined path that led to a place in Japan's administrative and political elite. He studied at the fiercely selective Number One High School (*Ichikô*) and then at Tokyo Imperial University, where he majored in politics in the law faculty. Given his cosmopolitan background, it was not surprising that he should have chosen a diplomatic career. In the mid-1920s he joined the Ministry of Foreign Affairs, where his immediate seniors included a fellow *Ichikô* and Tokyo Imperial University graduate, the tall, athletic, and talented Okazaki Katsuo, who was two years older than Inoue (and who was to become chief cabinet secretary at the time of Japan's abortive 1950s deportation plan and the foreign minister who oversaw the revocation of the Japanese nationality of Koreans in Japan). Inoue was soon joined at the Ministry of Foreign Affairs by his brother Takajirô, who was three years his junior. Indeed, the brothers Inoue were to pursue strangely parallel careers.

During the early part of his career with the ministry, Inoue Masutarô spent several years going back and forth between Tokyo and the newly established Japanese puppet state of Manchukuo, where his task was to investigate the subversive influence of Chinese Communism. But he also traveled more widely to France, Belgium, the United States (serving as commercial attaché in the New York Consulate-General in the late 1930s), Poland, Hungary, Yugoslavia, and Portugal (where he held the post of counselor in the Japanese Embassy in Lisbon at the end of the war).

Inoue's diplomatic career, moreover, also included one significant moment that is recorded, not in the *Asahi* newspaper article, but in the archives of the U.S. Central Intelligence Agency.

After the surrender of Nazi Germany in May 1945, some members of the Japanese political elite recognized that Japan was facing imminent defeat. Until that time, the Soviet Union, desperately defending its western flank from German assault, had maintained a pact of neutrality with Japan. But now, with the German threat gone, Stalin's government was preparing to turn its attentions eastward.

It was at that point that a trickle of tentatively worded messages began to reach the U.S. and British governments by roundabout routes: via the Vatican, Sweden, Portugal, and other neutral countries. Elements high up in the Japanese government were trying to open up a channel for a negotiated surrender. The key figures behind these peace feelers included Japan's wartime foreign minister, Shigemitsu Mamoru, and his favorite protégé, Okazaki Katsuo, who was at that time head of the Foreign Ministry's Information Bureau—Japan's main civilian intelligence agency.

In Portugal, a message stressing American and Japanese "common interests" against the USSR, and expressing Japanese willingness to seek a negotiated surrender, was conveyed to the local agent of the U.S. Office of Strategic Services (OSS—the forerunner of the CIA) on 7 May 1945 and duly passed on to President Truman. The person who had been chosen to

Figure 7.1. The surrender ceremony on the USS *Missouri*, 2 September 1945. Shigemitsu Mamoru (with top hat and walking stick) stands in the front row, with Okazaki Katsuo (also in top hat) just behind him. (Courtesy of the Naval Historical Center, Washington, D.C. Photo no. USA C-2719)

make this extremely sensitive and secret contact was none other than the Japanese Embassy in Lisbon's counselor, Inoue Masutarô.

In the end, his message (and others like it) proved futile. The Allies were only interested in an unconditional surrender, and the conflict was to be played out until the bitter end. Shigemitsu and Okazaki went on to play central roles in the transfer of power to the incoming Allied occupation authorities—roles publicly symbolized during the official surrender ceremony onboard the U.S. battleship *Missouri* on 2 September 1945, where Okazaki presented the credentials of the Japanese delegation, and Shigemitsu signed the surrender document on behalf of the Japanese imperial government.

Foreign Minister Shigemitsu Mamoru, Information Bureau Chief Okazaki Katsuo, mid-ranking diplomat Inoue Masutarô. . . . It is difficult to tell how close the relationship between these three men was, for Inoue was very much more junior than the powerful and well-connected Shigemitsu and Okazaki. But their roles in the middle of 1945—as the Pacific War came to an end and the Cold War order began to take shape—are of interest because they foreshadow another coming together in the mid-1950s, when the repatriation plan was formed. At that time, Shigemitsu

Mamoru would again be foreign minister, Okazaki Katsuo became the political power broker to whom the LDP entrusted the handing of the repatriation issue, and Inoue Masutarô was the Red Cross official most actively responsible for putting the repatriation plan into effect.

In the immediate postsurrender period, the destinies of the three men diverged. The Soviet Union insisted that Shigemitsu should be prosecuted for his part in overseeing Japan's wartime military expansion. He was accused of Class A war crimes and imprisoned in Tokyo's Sugamo Prison. It was only after the end of the Allied occupation that he was released from prison and returned to political life.

Meanwhile, his protégé Okazaki, who spoke fluent English, served as a personal go-between, carrying communications between the Allied occupation authorities and the new star of Japanese politics, Yoshida Shigeru, who was to become Japan's most influential postwar prime minister. In 1949, Okazaki was elected to the Lower House of the Japanese Parliament and was quickly appointed first to the key political post of chief cabinet secretary and then to the position of foreign minister.

As for Inoue Masutarô, during the Allied occupation of Japan he took up a series of temporary jobs, including a place on the defense team for a military strategist accused (and eventually convicted) of war crimes at the Tokyo Trials. But in 1952, when his former colleague Okazaki Katsuo became foreign minister, Inoue was summoned back to the Ministry of Foreign Affairs to work as a senior analyst. In this capacity, he was able to make use of some the skills and know-how he had developed during his work on Manchuria in the early 1930s, for his main mission was once again to gather information on East Asian—particularly Chinese—Communism.

During the immediate postwar years, Japan's information-gathering activities were hampered by the closure of Japan's overseas embassies and the dissolution of the country's prewar intelligence agencies. Against this difficult background, one important strategy for intelligence analysts was to develop contacts with immigrant communities in Japan, and particularly with Chinese, Korean, and other immigrant groups closely linked to Communist regimes abroad. Inoue's time as a foreign affairs analyst undoubtedly provided knowledge, skills, and relationships that stood him in good stead after his appointment to the Japan Red Cross Society in the middle of 1955.

The 1955 Japanese newspaper article reporting Inoue's appointment to the Red Cross concludes on a slightly curious personal note. An unnamed "friend" of Inoue's describes him as "a scholarly type who attacks specialist

topics with great energy," but adds, "He's no good at things like forming social relationships, and that's why his abilities haven't been fully appreciated."

Was the foreign-born Inoue an eternal outsider, never quite able to
feel at home among the Japanese social elite? Did he, for that very reason,
struggle all the harder (too hard?) to be accepted? Certainly, the double-
edged compliment from his unnamed friend makes some sense of the
mountain of correspondence from Inoue that I found in the Red Cross
archives in Geneva. Most of it is in English, though he occasionally wrote
in French. In either language, Inoue expressed himself fluently but with
idiosyncratic grammar. Many of his letters ran to four or five pages of
densely typed text; many of them enclosed essays or reports setting out his
views on various subjects at even greater length. Reading these documents,
I feel that I can almost hear the sighs of the officials in Geneva, as yet another fat airmail envelope from Tokyo landed in their in-trays.

To read this correspondence is also a disconcerting experience. The
unguarded candor of Inoue's language, and of the language used by some
other officials involved in this story, suggests an overweening bureaucratic
faith in the power of the inscriptions "secret" or "highly confidential,"
stamped across the top of their letterhead. No one (these letters seem to as-
sume) will ever know.

Or maybe it is something more disturbing still: a quiet confidence that
all the people who matter in the world will share their views of the issue.
The returnees to North Korea, after all, were leaving forever. If they had
complaints to make, their voices would never be heard.

Even if people *knew*, no one would ever *care*.

What puzzles me most about the page of newsprint on my desk, though,
is not the account of Inoue's career, but the article that fills most of the rest
of page. This is a long and extraordinarily detailed analysis by "the Japanese security establishment" about recent developments within Japan's Korean community. The origins of the article are enigmatic. It is unclear
whether it is written by a journalist or by a member of the Japanese security establishment itself. The information, however, clearly comes from an
official, or several officials, engaged in intelligence activities.

The analysis offered by the article is intriguing. The Korean community in Japan, we are reminded, is deeply divided. Some Koreans in Japan
belong to the pro–South Korean organization *Mindan,* but a larger number
are left wing, and many express a degree of support for the North Korean
government. Up to this point, left-wing Koreans have tended to associate

themselves with the Japanese Communist Party, conspiring with Japanese Communists to launch revolution and overthrow capitalism in Japan. But in May 1955, after a bitter factional struggle, pro–North Korean members of the community formed a new organization, the General Association of Korean Residents in Japan (abbreviated to *Sôren* in Japanese or *Chongryun* in Korean), which, the article's security sources believe, marks a dramatic turning point in the politics of the minority community. The General Association defines Koreans in Japan as citizens of the Democratic People's Republic of Korea and insists that they should hold themselves aloof from Japanese politics, working instead to build closer diplomatic ties between Japan and North Korea and to bring about the reunification of their fatherland. Instead of plotting revolution, the association was concentrating on things such as rebuilding the network of Korean community schools in Japan.

The members of the Japanese security establishment whose views are represented in the article present these trends in an optimistic tone. The recent moves seem to offer the prospect of a new stage in the relationship between the Japanese state and the Korean minority, a stage that coincides rather nicely with the government's plans for fresh diplomatic initiatives in the Cold War world. The article ends, though, with a stern warning that, whatever its current strategy, the General Association is still a "Marxist-Leninist" body whose members may yet be persuaded once again to return to their old revolutionary ways.

Can it be a pure coincidence that this analysis appears side by side with the announcement of Inoue's appointment as head of the Red Cross Foreign Affairs Department? Does the article give a glimpse of the thinking behind the repatriation plan? Is it even possible that Inoue himself—the ministry's expert on Asian communism—is a source for at least part of the security establishment's analysis?

Not for the first time in pursuing this strange tale, I wonder whether my imagination is beginning to run away with me. It is time to get out of my hotel room, away from the desk and the perplexing page of newsprint. I need to move, to walk around. It is time for a visit to the headquarters of the Japan Red Cross Society.

By early afternoon, when I reach Shiba Park, the rain has lifted. The park is an oasis of sparkling leaves in the midst of the city. Pigeons peck around the puddles and amid flowerbeds thick with lavender; homeless people sleep on the benches. From somewhere beyond the park's perimeter comes the rhythmic chant of schoolgirls, performing their calisthenics in a neighboring sports field.

As I walk through the park, I think how often Inoue Masutarô, Shimazu Tadatsugu, and their colleagues of the 1950s must have come here from their offices just around the corner.

The tall aristocratic Shimazu, groomed from early adulthood for his role as president of the Japanese Red Cross, drove past here every morning on his way to work from his home in the nearby Shibuya district. His presidential office with its long boardroom table looked out across the lawns and tennis court of the Japan Red Cross Society compound. Above, on the second floor, were the imperial quarters and special meeting hall set aside for occasional visitation by the Society's honorary president, Empress Nagako, for the Society had connections to the most eminent in the land.

Two of Shimazu's predecessors as Red Cross presidents had been Tokugawas, descendants of the Shoguns who ruled Japan until the mid-nineteenth century. His own ancestors had for centuries controlled the vast domain of Satsuma in southern Kyushu and had helped to plan the imperial restoration that prepared the way for the emergence of a modern, centralized Japanese state.

Sadly, the magnificent mock-Renaissance brick Red Cross headquarters where Shimazu and Inoue worked no longer stands. Built in 1912, the last year of the Meiji Era that had witnessed the emergence of the modern Japanese state, it was torn down in the 1970s, shortly before the centenary of the Japanese Red Cross to make way for an (if anything) even more imposing monument to modernity designed by renowned architect Kurokawa Kisho. All that remains is a perfect replica of the baroque, cream and gold Imperial Meeting Hall, incongruously transplanted into the matrix of Kurokawa's angular geometry.

The great forecourt and the breathtaking expanse of the new building's façade of mirror-glass and pink marble dwarf the human figures that venture though the front gate. The scale and grandeur are almost enough to deter an uninvited intruder like myself. But one corner of the building is set aside for public information, complete with a souvenir stand selling Red Cross pens, T-shirts, and telephone cards. I slip rather nervously inside and into the Information Room, with its permanent exhibition on the history of the Japanese Red Cross movement.

On the wall immediately opposite the entrance is a panel outlining the history of repatriation to North Korea. The display is dominated by a big and familiar photograph of a repatriation ship, festooned in bunting, leaving the port of Niigata. But there is also a smaller picture that I have never seen before: a photograph of the scene inside one of the "Special Rooms" in the Niigata Red Cross Center. A young woman returnee sits with her back to the camera, facing a middle-aged western woman and a Japanese man with a Red Cross armband. An ashtray and a basket of sweets have been placed on the table between them. The sun streams through a window, illuminating the big Red Cross flag on the wall of the room.

I find myself thinking of Mr. Yoon, sitting in that room in total silence, while the bewildered officials on the other side of the table struggle in vain to persuade him to speak . . .

"Excuse me! Excuse me! For you." My thoughts are interrupted by the young woman attendant, who touches my arm and thrusts an English pamphlet about the exhibition into my hand. She is bright eyed, charming, and eager to help. When I explain my interest in the postwar history of the Japan Red Cross Society, she shows me the Information Room's small library, points me to the imposing multivolume official history of the Red Cross, and offers to help photocopy the sections I need.

Volume Seven deals with the 1950s and devotes more than eighty pages to the repatriation of Koreans to North Korea. The account of the repatriation is clear and straightforward and includes Japanese versions of a few of the letters and memoranda that I have read in the archives in Geneva, as well as some that I have never seen before. The documents included are mostly correspondence sent to the Japan Red Cross Society from Geneva, Pyongyang, and elsewhere. Rather few of the society's own letters are given space in the volume.

According to this version of the story, Japanese Red Cross involvement in the whole affair was a strictly humanitarian response to demands from within the Korean community in Japan, the first stirrings of which appeared in April 1956. In that month, a small group of Koreans began a prolonged sit-down demonstration in the forecourt outside the Japanese Red Cross Society's headquarters, demanding repatriation to North Korea. Meanwhile some Koreans interned in Ômura Detention Center and awaiting deportation to South Korea had started to plead to be sent to North Korea instead. Following a meeting between Japanese and North Korean Red Cross representatives in Pyongyang in February 1956, the North Korean side urged the Japan Red Cross Society to help these detainees fulfill their wish.

Two representatives of the International Committee of the Red Cross (ICRC) happened to be visiting East Asia in the spring of that year. They inspected Ômura Detention Center and also witnessed the demonstration outside the Japan Red Cross headquarters. The envoys collected information on the problem that they took back to Geneva with them. It was at this point that the ICRC recognized the importance of the plight of Koreans in Japan and presented a series of proposals to the national Red Cross Societies of the region on ways to address the problem. All this explains why the Red Cross movement, both nationally and internationally, was able to respond so swiftly when a much larger movement demanding repatriation to the DPRK suddenly erupted from within the *Zainichi* Korean community in the middle of 1958.

I thank the assistant and walk out of the Information Room and into the forecourt of the Red Cross building carrying my photocopies from the official history. The thanks are heartfelt. I am touched by her kindness and sincerity, and I hope that she would not be hurt if she could read the negative thoughts about this episode in Red Cross history that fill my head as I stand looking around into the forecourt where, nearly half a century ago in April 1956, the first demonstrators gathered to demand repatriation.

There is just one problem with the official Japan Red Cross version of this history. It is, to borrow the phrase coined by former British cabinet secretary Sir Robert Armstrong, remarkably economical with the truth.

To put it another way, it is a perfect illustration of the fact that where you choose to start a story fashions the meaning of the tale you tell. By starting in April 1956, the official account conveniently omits to mention the fact that, in the six months before the arrival of the first protestors at the gates of the Red Cross compound, a great many interesting and highly secret messages had been flying back and forth between the headquarters of the Liberal Democratic Party, various ministry buildings nearby, the Red Cross compound in Shiba, and the headquarters of the International Committee of the Red Cross on the shores of Lake Leman.

These messages cast an entirely different light on the origins and meaning of the repatriation scheme.

8

THE TIP OF THE ICEBERG

My hotel in Tokyo is next to a large private university, and in the evenings the narrow lane outside is filled with the cheerful voices of students heading home. A little way down the hill is a rehearsal room where they gather after class for orchestra practice. When I open the window, the faint sounds of tuning instruments drift in from outside. This evening, a saxophonist is practicing "Stranger on the Shore," the theme tune from a long-forgotten television drama of my childhood, and it is against this incongruous background of plaintive echoes from 1960s Britain that I set out the evidence on my desk.

In one corner is the page of newsprint that I was studying this morning. In front of that is my stack of photocopied pages from the headquarters of the Japan Red Cross Society. To the side is a laptop that—thanks to twenty-first-century technology—contains more than a thousand digital images from the archives in Geneva. Spread out on the floor (since I have run out of space on the desk) are an array of additional bits and pieces collected from other published sources.

I am ready to try to piece together a different beginning to the story. It is not, of course, a perfect beginning. The records on which I draw are fragmentary and full of silences. The story itself is complex, and telling it involves strategic choices of inclusion and omission.

But this version at least casts some new light on one part of the narrative that has very successfully been concealed from sight for half a century.

This is, indeed, a story all about concealment. The tale begins with a group of people within the Japanese establishment who were determined to promote a mass exodus of members of the Korean minority from Japan to North Korea, but to do so in such a way that their own role in the process would be invisible. They were by no means the only architects of the repatriation scheme, but they were its most influential initiators. The silence that has surrounded their role for the past fifty years is a measure of their success.

Inoue Masutarô made his mark on the Japanese Red Cross very quickly. When he took up his position with the society on 1 July 1955, it was in the midst of a repatriation in the opposite direction: an attempt to rescue a small number of Japanese nationals who had remained in North Korea since colonial times, and who desperately wanted to come home. Negotiations on the issue had been dragging on for more than a year, but within a few weeks of Inoue's arrival, events began to move at high speed.

The whole issue also suddenly became far more secretive and politically charged than ever before and quickly became inextricably linked to the problem of the repatriation of Koreans from Japan.

Two months after his appointment, Inoue Masutarô was already planning a trip to Geneva to test the waters on these sensitive issues. On 22 September he flew out of Tokyo's Haneda Airport on for what was be the first of many visits to the International Red Cross headquarters in Geneva. On his way he stopped in Rome to visit his brother Takajirô, who was then Japan's diplomatic representative to the Vatican.

It was probably on this visit that Inoue Masutarô began his tradition of staying at the Hotel des Bergues, which became his favorite base camp in Geneva. From this grand stucco building on the Quai du Mont-Blanc in the heart of Geneva he could look down at Rousseau's island, where a statue of the political visionary sits on its plinth with quill pen in hand; and beyond, he could look across the fast-flowing narrows where lake turns into river, to the old town with its cathedral tower silhouetted on the skyline.

As it happened, Inoue arrived in Geneva just as an important transition was taking place in the leadership of the International Committee of the Red Cross. Long-serving ICRC president Paul Ruegger had retired, and his place had been taken by Leopold Boissier, who was to hold the position of ICRC president throughout the crucial phases of the repatriation project.

Suave, gentle, and tactful, Boissier was some six years older than Inoue Masutarô and had long family connections to the Red Cross movement. His father had been vice president of the ICRC in the early twentieth century, and Leopold himself had as a young man served as assistant to the ICRC president during the negotiations surrounding the 1919 Versailles Peace Treaty.

The day after his arrival in Geneva, Inoue was invited to a private lunch with Boissier. There is no official record of the two men's conversation over this meal, but their subsequent correspondence suggests that it may have led Inoue to see Boissier as a man of the world with a grasp of the political considerations that inevitably cast their shadow over any humanitarian action. This would explain why he soon developed the habit of sending Boissier long, confidential, and startlingly frank letters elaborating the political complexities surrounding the activities of the Japanese Red Cross, often in excruciatingly minute detail.

After his lunch with Boissier, which went on well into the afternoon, Inoue spent an hour and a half in the ICRC's headquarters on the hill above the lake, deep in talks with officials. The discussions focused on practical matters. Inoue's main counterpart during this meeting, and his principal host throughout his visit, was Eugène de Weck, a stout, balding, middle-aged man with a ready smile. De Weck was a career Red Cross bureaucrat who was at that time a section chief in the ICRC's Executive Division and was to play a central role in the repatriation story.

It was in the course of this meeting on the afternoon of 27 September that the outlines of Inoue's mission began to emerge.

The conversation began predictably enough. Inoue briefed de Weck and his colleague on the protracted negotiations with North Korea about the return of Japanese nationals. The North Korean government, he explained, seemed willing to invite a delegation from the Red Cross to Pyongyang to discuss the problem.

But Inoue soon went on to raise a new issue that, as he himself pointed out, was potentially much more politically explosive than anything discussed so far: "The presence in Japan of a significant Korean community." In de Weck's record of the meeting, this statement is followed by a parenthetical description of Japan's Korean community as "quite well organized, when one considers the attacks [*attentats*] made by certain members of the community against United Nations forces."

This is an extraordinary statement. It is not clear which "attacks" are referred to, but the description was probably provided by Inoue, since the ICRC had virtually no information at all about the Korean community in Japan at that time. So during Inoue's very first mention of Koreans in Japan, during his very first meeting with the staff of the International Red

Cross, Japan's Korean minority was already being viewed as violent and subversive.

The conversation then took a somewhat vague and speculative line. Comparisons were made between negotiations with North Korea and a recent agreement under which the Red Cross had secured the return of Japanese nationals in China. In the Chinese case, Inoue stressed, the agreement had resulted in a simultaneous repatriation of some Chinese residents in Japan who wished to go home. Perhaps the return of Japanese from North Korea might similarly be reciprocated with a repatriation of Koreans in Japan who wished to return to the DPRK? But this, said Inoue, would undoubtedly be more contentious than the Chinese case, for it was sure to evoke the anger of the South Korean government. As a hypothetical question—a possibility "to be kept in reserve for the moment"—Inoue asked whether the International Red Cross might be willing to play an intermediary role, neutralizing political problems in dealings with North Korea "to avoid the various inconveniences mentioned above." The response was diplomatic and equally vague— the ICRC was willing to do whatever it could to assist in resolving international humanitarian problems between Japan and its neighbors.

Inoue's visit to Geneva was not quite the first time that the Japanese Red Cross had raised the possibility of "exchanging" Japanese in North Korea for Koreans in Japan. In January 1954, president Shimazu Tadatsugu had sent a message to Pyongyang, asking the North Korean Red Cross for its cooperation in securing the repatriation of Japanese, and volunteering, in return, to help repatriate Koreans in Japan who wished to return to the DPRK. When the North Koreans replied, however, they made no mention at all of this suggested reciprocal arrangement.

Despite the lack of encouraging response, on his return from Europe in the autumn of 1955, Inoue began to pursue the link between the two topics with great vigor.

Several weeks after leaving Geneva, on 14 November 1955, Inoue sent Boissier the first of the long "personal and confidential" letters that were soon to be adding to the bulk of the ICRC's files on East Asia. As in his meetings with ICRC officials, he began by raising the problems of rescuing Japanese stranded in North Korea. But, also as he had done during his meeting with de Weck in Geneva, Inoue soon moved on to a more sensitive topic: "As far as North Korea is concerned, there is another much more serious question in relation to the question of repatriation, unlike the case of repatriations [of Japanese] from Russia and China. This is the fact that there are six hundred thousand Koreans in Japan."

Both North and South Korea claimed Koreans in Japan as their own citizens, and both tried to influence them politically. This question of the political and national allegiance of the Koreans was, Inoue noted, "a great issue not just for North and South Korea, but also for Japan itself."

Inoue hastened to assure Boissier that the problem of Koreans in Japan was not a "minority question": Koreans were not a national minority, since "all these Koreans are foreigners under international law." Perhaps advisedly, he refrained from going into the historical reasons for their alien status. "Most of these people," he continued, "clearly wish to stay in Japan. There are, however, a certain number who wish to return either to North Korea or South Korea. But since the total number is very great, the number of those repatriated will come to a huge figure: for example, if one person in a hundred wished to return, the figure would be six thousand."

The "real difficulty" was going arise in relation to the repatriation of these people to their homeland. The time was approaching when the Japanese Red Cross might have to "act in the name of humanity to resolve the problem of the two [categories of] Koreans present here.

"The question of the North Korean repatriation," Inoue warned Boissier, "is just the beginning. It is only the tip of the iceberg."

Was Inoue acting on his own initiative, or did he have more powerful political backing? In his first contacts with Geneva, it is difficult to be sure. But by December, the answer was becoming evident; for at that point the Japanese Red Cross decided to activate the possibility that it had so far been "keeping in reserve," and explicitly asked the International Committee of the Red Cross to mediate in a mass repatriation of Koreans from Japan to North Korea.

What also becomes clear in this request is a strategy by which repatriation might be achieved, as it were, through "remote control," with its most active proponents pursuing their aims from backstage, concealed from public gaze.

The request came in the form of a letter sent to Boissier by Japan Red Cross president Shimazu on 13 December 1955, and written (as Shimazu himself noted) with "the full approval of the competent authorities in the Japanese Foreign Office and in the Ministry of Justice."

Shimazu's letter enclosed an English translation of an appeal for repatriation by a group of Koreans calling themselves "The Tokyo Rally of Koreans Wishing to Go Home." This, he said, had been handed to the Red Cross by an official of the North Korean–affiliated community association *Chongryun*. Strangely, the translation, though dated 8 December, includes no indication of the names or number of people who signed the appeal. Shimazu, however, insisted that this was a demand for a "mass repatriation." Although "the Japanese side has no objection to and rather hopes that the repatriation of North Koreans in Japan will be carried out," the Japanese government was afraid that it might create havoc in the delicate diplomatic relationship between Japan and South Korea; so the Japanese authorities and the Japan Red Cross Society were, in effect, asking the ICRC to carry out the repatriation on their behalf.

That December, the Red Cross building in Shiba was not the only place where things were starting to stir. Three days after Shimazu wrote his letter, Shigemitsu Mamoru—by then released from prison and back in his old wartime post of foreign minister—told a parliamentary committee that he personally would like to see the introduction of a policy to help North Koreans return to their homeland.

At this point, Inoue's initial cautious feelers turned into a gathering stream of correspondence on repatriation, written in tones that rapidly moved from the diplomatic to the importuning, and then to something verging on hysteria.

Boissier's cautious and tactful response to Inoue's letter of 14 November said nothing at all about the issue of Koreans in Japan, so in December Inoue tried again. He suggested to Boissier that the Japanese Red Cross delegation, on its forthcoming visit to Pyongyang, might ask the North Koreans to join Japan in requesting ICRC to supervise a mass repatriation of Koreans to North Korea. Conscious of the likely response to this from South Korea, Inoue went on to propose a wider regional three-way exchange of people: a repatriation of Japanese from North Korea to Japan, and of Koreans from Japan to North Korea, combined with a Red Cross mission to return South Korean missing people from the Korean War days.

This time, Boissier promptly responded with a counterproposal. In view of the great political sensitivity of the whole issue, he suggested, the best strategy would be to let the International Committee of the Red Cross send its own fact-finding mission to East Asia. On the basis of their report, the ICRC would decide how to respond to the problem. The International Committee, Boissier stressed, wished to keep this first exploratory mission strictly confidential. He asked the Japan Red Cross to await its outcome and, in the meanwhile, to avoid discussing either the proposed ICRC visit or the question of Koreans in Japan during their negotiations in Pyongyang.

Inoue and his colleagues were clearly delighted that the international organization was becoming interested in the repatriation issue. They were also very eager to keep the ball rolling, and to ensure that the ICRC mission visited Japan and the two Koreas as soon as possible. So Inoue quickly replied with a message to the ICRC's executive director Roger Gallopin warning that "North Koreans" in Japan were becoming restive and were "preparing to hold nationwide rallies to enhance their repatriation." This was alarming (in Inoue's words) "in view of the large number of Koreans, their very violent character, and the fact that they are divided into several parties, which may turn into unfortunate accidents at any moment." The result, Inoue grimly predicted, was likely to be "affairs of bloodshed."

This was the first, but by no means the last, of such messages. In the year that followed, Inoue and Shimazu would repeatedly use warnings of impending outbursts or riots by Koreans in Japan to pressure the ICRC for a quick decision on the repatriation issue. On this occasion, Inoue urgently requested the International Committee to forestall imminent mayhem by openly announcing their willingness to help conduct a mass repatriation to North Korea. He also wanted Geneva's blessing for a campaign by the Japanese Red Cross "to promote a public opinion in Japan that 'the only way to solve the problem of North Koreans in Japan is to leave the whole matter in the hands of the ICRC.'"

This letter is interesting for many reasons, not the least because Japanese media reports show no signs of mass rallies in favor of repatriation by the Korean community at that time. There are, it is true, a few small reports of a meeting of some would-be returnees in Tokyo in July 1955—perhaps this was the source of the petition that Shimazu sent to Geneva in December. But the first significant public demonstration on the repatriation issue seems to have been the one that took place outside the Japan Red Cross Society's headquarters in April 1956, three months after Inoue wrote his letter and at a time when the Red Cross was already heavily involved in developing its repatriation plan. And even then, this rather small gathering, many of whose participants were uniformed high school students and parents with children, seems far removed from Inoue's dark forebodings of blood in the streets.

Almost before Gallopin and his colleagues could catch their breath, let alone reply, however, Inoue was writing to them again in equally excited but now more positive tones to share with them some important news. First he reported that the Japanese Red Cross had identified the recently established North Korean–affiliated community association *Chongryun*—Inoue refers to it in English as the "General League of Koreans in Japan"—as having the most direct contact to the North Korean government. To avoid unnecessary political complications, the Red Cross was planning to pursue the repatriation issue by seeking "mutual understanding" with the Korean community through its contacts with *Chongryun*.

Second, and with an even greater air of drama, Inoue informed Geneva of "an indication that the Japanese Governmental party, the Conservative Party [i.e., the Liberal Democratic Party (LDP)], would start a movement to support the repatriation of the Koreans. Such influential members of the Conservative Party as Mr. Hitoshi Ashida (former prime minister) and Mr. Katsuo Okazaki (former foreign minister) have informed us unofficially that if the Koreans really wish to go back to North Korea, they will materialize a policy to help those Koreans in Japan."

The new policy, Inoue added with a hint of pride, could be attributed to the hard work of the Japan Red Cross Society, which had "approached higher levels of our political circles, in view of the importance of the question." It is difficult to be sure whether Red Cross lobbying had really turned the government's attention to the problem, or whether it was the government that had passed yet another prickly diplomatic problem to the Red Cross.

The key facts of Inoue's account, however, can be confirmed.

Three days before his letter was written, on 16 January 1956, former Japanese prime minister Ashida Hitoshi noted in his diary that the ruling LDP's Foreign Affairs Committee had discussed "the rapid repatriation of North Koreans who wish to return to their homeland." Immediately after the meeting, Ashida telephoned Japan Red Cross vice president Kasai Yoshisuke, who was about to lead the Red Cross mission to North Korea.

"We think," Ashida told Kasai, "that North Koreans in Japan who want to go home should be sent back, so we'd like you to discuss this with the Kim [Il-Sung] regime."

Kasai's response was cautious: "The Ministry of Foreign Affairs won't go along with this, because they're worried about opposition from South Korea," he warned Ashida.

As it turned out, whatever the Foreign Ministry's concerns, Kasai's mission would indeed soon convey to the North Koreans a strong (if somewhat confusing) message about Japan's interest in a mass repatriation.

Meanwhile, within the Japanese ruling party, the issue was placed in the hands of former foreign minister Okazaki Katsuo—Inoue's erstwhile senior colleague in the Ministry of Foreign Affairs; the man who in 1950 had announced the agreement to deport subversive Koreans to South Korea; the man who (unbeknownst, it seems, to Boissier and his colleagues in Geneva) had overseen the transformation of Koreans into aliens, and who had cheerfully assured the Japanese parliament that the transformation would not cause Koreans in Japan "any particular inconvenience."

In humanitarian dilemmas, underlying issues often matter more than the numbers of people involved. But in this story, numbers, as well as principles, are all-important.

In the middle of the 1950s there were certainly Koreans in Japan who wished to be repatriated to North Korea. Some were left-wing detainees awaiting deportation in Ômura Detention Center, who feared persecution at the hands of the Syngman Rhee regime if they were sent to South Korea and pleaded in terms of real desperation to be deported to the North instead. Others originated from the North, and wished to rejoin the families they had left behind there. There were also students at the Korean schools run by *Chongryun*, who were disqualified from entering most Japanese universities and hoped to complete their education in North Korea instead. And then there were the politically committed—the true believers who longed to share in the realization of Kim Il-Sung's vision of a glorious future for the Socialist Fatherland.

Helping these people achieve their wish was a perfectly respectable humanitarian project. If the Japan Red Cross Society had simply tried to arrange transport and travel documents for them, the repatriation movement would have been everything that the official history makes it out to be—a piece of humanitarianism fully in accord with the best principles of the Red Cross.

In fact, the society had clearly embarked on a much more ambitions venture.

As the messages from Tokyo became more insistent and more alarming, and as the ICRC prepared to send its confidential mission to East Asia, officials in Geneva began to press the Japanese Red Cross for some basic information about the *Zainichi* Korean community. For example, could the Japanese side provide a figure, "however approximate," of the number of Koreans in Japan who might wish to return to the DPRK? And were there also people who wished to be repatriated to South Korea?

The response they received from Tokyo is intriguing. There were, the ICRC was informed, about 646,000 Koreans in Japan, of whom 575,000 were officially registered as foreign residents. Of these, twenty-one percent belonged to the "South Korean" side, fifty percent to the "North Korean" side, six percent were "neutral" and twenty-three percent were "diverse."

Since the South Korean government showed no interest in receiving returnees from Japan, the ICRC was informed, there was little prospect of the repatriation of those on the South Korean side.

As far as individuals seeking repatriation to the DPRK were concerned, if the "number of Koreans wishing to return to [the] North is 60,000 as said by the North Korean League, it will mean that about 9% of total Koreans or about 18% of North Koreans in Japan are to be repatriated."

The North Korean League mentioned in this message is clearly the North Korean–affiliated association *Chongryun*, which was indeed the main proponent within the Korean community of a program of repatriation to North Korea. But sixty thousand people wishing to return to the North? From December 1955 onward, this figure was cited again and again by the Japanese Red Cross as the likely number of returnees. In fact, by March 1956 Inoue was writing that sixty thousand was the minimum number of returnees, and soon after, in a letter approved both by president Shimazu and by officials of the Ministry of Foreign Affairs, he reported that the Japan Red Cross Society's advisory board had unanimously assented to his proposition that it was "indispensable to repatriate at least 60,000 Koreans within this year."

Yet the origin of this figure is a mystery. There is only one contemporary estimate from *Chongryun* that comes anywhere near this order of magnitude. In May 1956, when the ICRC mission finally arrived in Japan, Inoue Masutarô arranged for its members to have a highly confidential briefing by three senior *Chongryun* officials, including the organization's secretary general, Han Deok-Su (who was then in the process of establishing his powerful personal role in the association's affairs). At this meeting, the *Chongryun* officials informed the envoys from Geneva that they estimated the number of Koreans in Japan wishing to return to North Korea at thirty thousand. They claimed to have arrived at this estimate through a process of registration. For good measure, Han Deok-Su and his colleagues added the information that three-quarters of the Korean community were North Koreans, and that, if a repatriation scheme could be started, most would choose to go to North Korea.

The difficulty here is not simply that Han Deok-Su's figure is only half the number that the Japanese Red Cross was hoping to repatriate by the end of 1956; equally important, the statement by *Chongryun* is itself simply not credible.

The association produced no evidence of the alleged registration of would-be returnees. More strikingly still, the estimated number of people seeking repatriation that the *Chongryun* presented to its own members and to the Japanese public was dramatically different from the information that Han Deok-Su and his colleagues gave in secret to the ICRC. So too, it would emerge, were the estimates of would-be returnees made by the North Korean government itself.

Japan's parliament is housed in a somewhat forbidding gray building in central Tokyo that was completed in the 1936, just as the nation's democracy withered before the blasts of ascendant militarism. Following the Germanic tradition, it is known as "the Diet."

The streets around the Diet are a barometer of the security climate. News of terrorist attacks in Europe or heightened political tensions in East Asia brings out convoys of blue and white police buses, which park along the streets emitting staccato crackles of radio communication. Today, though, everything is quiet. I am heading not for the Diet itself, but for Japan's National Diet Library, which stands just across the road from the nation's political heart. I do not really need to come here to pursue the question that has been bothering me. Japan has a wonderful electronic database of the records of its parliamentary proceedings that can be searched anywhere online. But I have to collect some photocopies that I have ordered from the library, and it seems a good opportunity to browse the Diet debates of the mid-1950s. Besides, I can combine this with an early lunch in the library's basement café, looking out at the quiet inner courtyard with its trees and bronze statuary and watching the motherly waitresses make a fuss of their customers: the wizened old professors with armfuls of books and the earnest groups of postgraduates discussing neonationalism or global warming.

Sometime in early 1956, I recall, the Foreign Affairs Committee of the Lower House of Parliament devoted a whole session to the subject of the "return" of Koreans from Japan to North Korea. I have glanced at the records of the meeting before. Now I want to look at them again more carefully.

The committee meeting, as it turns out, took place on 14 February 1956, less than a month after the ruling party officially decided to take up the issue of repatriation. Six people were called to give testimony, including two senior officials of the Japan Red Cross Society and three representatives of *Chongryun*.

No one was there to speak for the Koreans who were "on the South Korean side," "neutral," or "diverse."

Japanese politics in the 1950s were deeply divided. As the Cold War intensified, democratizing energies that had surged to the surface of Japanese society after the shock of defeat in war were on the retreat. The education and labor reforms of the occupation era were being rolled back, and fierce debates were underway over rearmament and Japan's security relationship with the United States. The largest opposition group, the Socialist Party, favored pacifism and neutrality but, greatly outnumbered by the ruling Liberal Democrats, could do little but resort to delaying tactics, backroom deals, and occasional bouts of fisticuffs on the floor of the Diet.

There was, however, one thing on which all sides of politics could agree: the desirability of repatriating ethnic Koreans to North Korea. The Left, of course, was not immune from ethnic prejudices. Besides, many Socialists supported repatriation because they really believed Kim Il-Sung's promises of a new and better world. South Korea at that time was an impoverished right-wing dictatorship where opponents of the regime were regularly tortured and executed. North Korea—more industrialized and in the midst of a highly publicized development plan—was more effectively controlled and rather better at concealing its tortures and executions. Even among those who knew that the Democratic People's Republic of Korea was no utopia, there were still some hopes that its tough brand of revolutionary socialism might carve a path to a bright future.

The Liberal Democrats harbored no such illusions, but many of them were only too happy to lend their political muscle to any feasible proposal for a mass exodus of Koreans from Japan.

Foreign Minister Shigemitsu Mamoru did not attend the Foreign Affairs Committee Meeting on 14 February 1956, but his deputy Morishita Kunio did, expressing general support for the proposition that it was "necessary to return the Koreans who are living in our country." The main problems were to find boats to take them and raise sufficient funds to pay for transport and resettlement costs.

The Japan Red Cross's social affairs director was questioned about this issue and made it clear that the society was committed to repatriation. The Red Cross, he reported, was indeed already exploring possibilities of using foreign ships, perhaps those belonging to the Hong Kong–based British firm Butterfield and Swire, although there were concerns that this company's vessels might not be large enough for the task at hand. Alas, however, his organization lacked the large sums of money needed to assist and encourage the Koreans to go home.

The three *Chongryun* representatives who were called to give evidence to the committee had many issues that they wished to raise. They wanted, for example, to discuss the unreasonable way in which the Ministry of Health and Welfare had recently begun cutting Koreans' already very limited access to assistance. They wanted to talk about the harsh conditions in

Ômura Detention Center and about the large number of Korean forced laborers who died in Japan during the war, and whose remains still lay in mass graves on alien soil.

But their parliamentary questioners kept steering them firmly back to the topic at hand: repatriation. On this, the Korean representatives were cooperative. They too strongly believed that the government should make it possible for those who wished to do so to return to the Socialist Fatherland.

The *Chongryun* representatives were also quite specific about the number of people seeking repatriation. Because of increasingly punitive welfare policies, they noted, the number was rising, but

> As of December 1955 there were 1,100 members of the general [Korean] community wishing to go home [i.e., to North Korea]. Most of them are in Tokyo. There are also people detained in Ômura detention center who wish to return to the Republic. These currently number seventy-one. Then there are 120 people who have been separated from their families. Furthermore, there are 133 students who have left high school and cannot go on to further education, so wish to go and study in the Republic.

Neither sixty thousand nor thirty thousand, but a total of 1,424. Oddly enough, communication between *Chongryun* and Pyongyang seems to have been less than perfect, for at the very same time the North Korean government was estimating the number at about half this level.

I do not know who was responsible for producing the estimates of volunteers for repatriation given to the ICRC, which multiplied the number given to the Japanese Diet twenty-five- to fifty-fold. But it is not difficult to surmise some reasons why the figure may have been so drastically approximated upward.

At the time when the debate on repatriation was taking place in the Diet's Foreign Affairs Committee in February 1956, the long-awaited, important, and somewhat mysterious meeting between representatives of the Japan Red Cross Society and its North Korean counterpart was underway in Pyongyang. In fact, a large part of the Diet debate was taken up with speculation as to what was going on at the meeting. Were the delegates only negotiating the return of Japanese stragglers from North Korea? Or were they also taking up questions of the status and future of Koreans in Japan? No clear answers to these questions were forthcoming during the debate on

14 February, nor in the media reports published after the completion of the meeting on the last day of the month. In fact, the real story of the Pyongyang negotiations has remained unknown until today.

But as it turns out, the discussions taking place in Pyongyang in February 1956 are crucial to understanding the factors behind the repatriation to North Korea. They also raise uncanny echoes that resound across the political landscape of twenty-first-century Northeast Asia.

9

THE PYONGYANG CONFERENCE

The border between China and North Korea is marked by two rivers that flow in slowly broadening streams from the mountainous central watershed toward the coast: to the northeast, the Tumen; to the southwest, the Yalu (known in Korean as the Amnok). On the Chinese side of the Yalu estuary stands Dandong, now a booming city whose commercial center is adorned with advertisements for MP3 players and mobile phones. New hotels and offices line the Yalu's shores, their reflections glittering on the surface of its gray-brown waters.

The overnight train from Beijing to Pyongyang grinds to a prolonged halt in Dandong station, while Chinese border guards clamber into the carriages and wander up and down the corridors distributing exit documents and checking our passports. Then the train draws out of the station and rumbles slowly over the long river bridge spanning the frontier.

Sinuiju, on the Korean side of the border, offers a startling contrast to Dandong: a forlorn and run-down industrial town, with gray-streaked concrete apartment buildings and crumbling factory chimneys standing stark and smokeless against the clear autumn sky.

To understand the repatriation story, I have realized, it is necessary to see North Korea. Here, of course, I have no hope of reading archives. I also have no plans to attempt interviews with returnees; even if I could obtain official permission to meet them, returnees would be unable to speak freely and might even be put at risk by my questions. But I need to see with my own eyes the landscape to which they returned and, if possible, to gain some sense of the way in which the repatriation is remembered in North Korea itself. So it is that I have arrived in Sinuiju on the overnight train from Beijing in the last week of October 2005, and now sit waiting for the North Korean border guards to examine my passport and luggage.

As I wait, I chat to "Mr. Choi," one of the other passengers in my carriage during this long train journey. He is returning, laden with baggage, from an overseas business trip. The gregarious and multilingual Mr. Choi explains that he works for a North Korean state-owned corporation, and has been negotiating with potential foreign investors. It is, he adds wistfully, quite difficult to persuade foreign companies to invest in North Korean projects.

When the customs officer opens my bag and searches it for suspect foreign books, Mr. Choi's eyes light up as he notices the English translation of Balzac's *Eugénie Grandet* that I have brought with me to read on the journey. He picks it up and turns the pages with a deep, nostalgic sigh.

"I studied French at university," he says. "Balzac, Hugo, Maupassant . . . Ah, I used to read them all. How I loved those books. No time for that now, though. It's all English in international business these days. I hardly use my French at all."

Once my bags have been cleared, I step down onto the platform, dominated by its two giant portraits of Kim Il-Sung and Kim Jong-Il. The morning air is crisp and the platform almost deserted. I wander along to the little souvenir shop to buy a guidebook. From some invisible clock tower, the slow electronic chimes of "The Song of General Kim Il-Sung" mark the hour. It is, I think, the saddest sound I have ever heard, an aching echo of all the sorrows of the Korean past and present.

When I get back to my carriage, I find my fellow traveler engaged in a seemingly friendly conversation with the customs officer who, as they talk, is meticulously thumbing though Mr Choi's magazines, pausing now and again to rip out an offending page, scrunch it up and drop it into the garbage bag he carries with him for the purpose.

As we head south from Sinuiju toward Pyongyang, still some ten hours away, I gaze out of the compartment window, trying to absorb as much as I can of this country about which I have heard so much and know so little.

After years of dearth, the 2005 harvest is said to have been good, and to my inexpert eye this seems to be true. Everywhere, the dry brown fields are lined with stooks of harvested rice. Here and there, villages of small white houses, each surrounded with its tiny walled courtyard, lie bathed in autumn sunshine. Wildflowers flourish along the railway banks, and kestrels circle in the still air.

Yet nothing can conceal the extreme poverty of the country. Women squat, washing their clothes on the banks of the shallow rivers. The main road that runs alongside the railway track is unpaved, and but for the occasional truck that roars past in a cloud of dust, the only traffic is the endless stream of pedestrians and cyclists, trudging across the landscape with the measured stride of people who have a long journey ahead of them. There are children on their way to school or to work in the fields; young women chatting to one another as they balance bundles of goods on their heads; farmers walking alongside wooden carts drawn by spindly oxen; people bent double under massive bundles of firewood. Once, we pass a middle-aged man carrying on his back a whole tree, more than two meters long and neatly chopped off at the roots.

The harvest may have been good, but there are still small figures out in many of the fields, stooping with meticulous care to pick up every grain of rice that the harvesters have left behind.

I find myself thinking of the stories of life in North Korea that Yamada Kumiko told me when I met her a few months earlier in her suburban apartment in Japan—stories about the back-breaking labor that she endured for forty years, between the time of her repatriation and her final secret crossing of the border out of North Korea.

When she and her family first moved from a provincial Japanese town to North Korea in the early 1960s, they were allotted a home in a rural area in the far north of the country, an area much like the one I can see from the train window. Their two-bedroom apartment was on the top floor of a four-story apartment building. It was newly built and had an indoor flush toilet, but this was unusable, as there was no running water. All water for washing and drinking had to be fetched in buckets from the river, and the dirty water was then carried downstairs again to be thrown out.

"You had to get down to the river at first light, even in the depths of winter," said Yamada-san. "Once other people started to do their washing there, the water would get too dirty to use." To boil the water that she had carried in buckets up four flights of stairs, the heavily pregnant Yamada Kumiko had first to chop the rock-hard tree roots that were the only available form of fuel.

At this point I become aware that Mr. Choi, sitting opposite me in the carriage, is watching me with a rather wry expression on his face.

"Wasn't your family worried when they knew you were going to visit . . . what do they call it . . . 'the Axis of Evil'?" he asks.

His unexpected use of the phrase makes me smile. "Only a little," I say.

Curious to know his reaction, I add, "Some of my friends in Japan have visited this country. I have Korean friends in Japan whose relatives moved to North Korea in the 1960s and 1970s. Some of them have been over to visit family members here."

Mr. Choi's brow furrows into a puzzled frown as he considers this.

"I don't understand. You mean, their families originally came from this part of Korea, and then some of them returned here after Liberation?" he says.

"No," I reply, "these are people who originally migrated to Japan from the South. From places like Busan and Jeju."

I will later learn from a tour guide that the mass repatriation of Koreans from Japan is officially known in North Korea as "the Great Return to the Fatherland." But the Great Return does not seem to be commemorated with much enthusiasm or pride, for the curiosity on Mr. Choi's face is unmistakably genuine as he asks,

"Eh? So . . . why did they come here?"

Sinuiju and its surroundings do not seem to have changed much in the last half-century. Nor do its border control rituals. When Inoue Masutarô and his two Red Cross fellow delegates stopped here on their way to Pyongyang on the morning of 27 January 1956, their luggage, too, was opened by customs officers, who carefully checked each page of the documents they were carrying. In the process, Inoue was startled to notice that the bags belonging to one of the delegates, Miyakoshi Kisuke, contained a very large number of "documents and papers from Koreans, Korean organizations, and communist organizations in Japan to various organizations and associations in Korea." Among them was a petition from a group of Korean detainees in Japan's Ōmura Detention Center, addressed to the government of the Democratic People's Republic of Korea and pleading for rescue from the prospect of deportation to South Korea.

What attracted Inoue's attention to this document, though, was not so much the import of its words as their color. As a symbol of its signatories' desperation, the petition had been written in blood.

Thus began one of the most bizarre and misunderstood episodes in the troubled history of Japan's relations with its neighbor North Korea: the 1956 Japan Red Cross Society's mission to Pyongyang.

The mission was a significant event. A number of Japanese groups, including a delegation of parliamentarians, had visited North Korea before, but these had all been unofficial visits, made without the approval of the Japanese government. The Red Cross mission was the first Japanese delegation to travel to North Korea with government blessing and using official Japanese passports. Similar postwar Red Cross missions to the Soviet Union and the People's Republic of China had led to the opening of political dialogue with their governments and, in the Soviet case, were soon to lead to the normalization of diplomatic relations.

There can be no doubt that the North Korean officials preparing to meet the delegation in Pyongyang had high expectations. The meeting was also taking place at a particularly sensitive moment. The Red Cross Society of the Democratic People's Republic of Korea had not yet been recognized as a member of the international Red Cross movement, but just before the arrival of the Japanese delegation, the society had applied to Geneva for official recognition. Since North Korea was excluded from membership of almost all international organizations (including, of course, the United Nations), the application was invested with great symbolic significance, and the response was awaited with suspense. Good relations with the Japanese Red Cross Society, the oldest and by far the richest Red Cross Society in East Asia, would certainly help the cause.

If all went well, the Pyongyang Conference might mark the start of a new opening of North Korea to the outside world.

There were, however, some curious aspects to the Japanese mission to North Korea. Though few media reports seem to have commented on this point at the time, one enigma was its membership. The three-member negotiating team consisted of the Japan Red Cross Society's vice president Kasai Yoshisuke, Inoue Masutarô, and a man named Miyakoshi Kisuke, who was generally referred to in the media simply as a member of the Japan Red Cross delegation. Just occasionally, a newspaper report would add parenthetically that he was the former deputy director of the Japan-Korea Association, on secondment to the Japan Red Cross Society.

In fact, Miyakoshi was a politician who had previously had little connection to the Red Cross. He did, however, have a close connection to the Democratic People's Republic of Korea. A member of the small Progressive Party (*Kaishintô*), Miyakoshi was best known for his enthusiastic efforts to promote closer ties between Japan and Communist countries. The Japan-Korea Association (*Nicchô Kyôkai*), of which he was deputy director, had succeeded in developing good relations with a number of North Korean political leaders. Miyakoshi had been included in the delegation because of these connections and to satisfy demands from North Korea, but a secret agreement had been signed between the Japan-Korea Association and the Japanese Red Cross, enabling him temporarily to be "rebadged" as a Red Cross official in order to maintain the image of the mission as a purely humanitarian venture. Predictably enough, however, he in fact pursued his own association's agenda, and even (to Inoue Masutarô's great annoyance) used the opportunity to sign an unofficial trade agreement between Japan and North Korea.

In the circumstances, the atmosphere in the train compartment must have been rather tense, as the Japan Red Cross delegates made the final stage of their journey down the western side of North Korea from Sinuiju to Pyongyang, through a landscape of snow-capped hills and dry, frozen fields, still scattered here and there with the wreckage of the Korean War.

The delegation reached Pyongyang around 9:00 p.m. Snow was falling, and the station was largely in darkness, but for the brilliant lights that illuminated three statues of Kim Il-Sung, Mao Tse-Tung, and Nikolai Bulganin (the Soviet leader who was at that time expected to emerge as Stalin's successor, but in fact was soon to fall from grace). The travelers were greeted at the station by officials from the North Korean Red Cross and driven down the broad and tree-lined Stalin Street to the hotel where they would spend the next month.

The following morning dawned clear and icy, with a daytime temperature of minus seven degrees and a biting wind whipping across the Daedong River. On the drive from their hotel to the building on the willow-lined river

Figure 9.1   Pyongyang 1956—the new city rising from the ruins of the old (Source: Russian National Archives Photographic Collection no. 0-244248)

bank that housed the headquarters of the North Korean Red Cross, Inoue and Kasai caught their first glimpses of the North Korean capital.

Just a couple of years earlier, Pyongyang had lain in ruins, devastated by wave after wave of U.S. bombing raids. According to a Soviet estimate, twenty-eight million square meters of North Korean housing had been destroyed during the war, of which only two million had been rebuilt by 1954. Since then, though, the North Korean government had poured massive energy and resources into reconstruction—particularly into the reconstruction of Pyongyang. As the Japanese Red Cross visitors noted, in January 1956 there were cranes and construction sites all over central Pyongyang, making the city look just like "Tokyo four or five years ago."

During this first courtesy call on their North Korean counterparts, it seemed as though the Japanese delegation's mission to Pyongyang would be brief and straightforward. The North Korean government had identified a group of thirty-six Japanese people who wished to return home, and had brought them to Pyongyang in preparation for their repatriation.

The most important remaining task for the Japanese delegation was to obtain further information about the fates of the uncertain number of their compatriots still believed to be alive somewhere in North Korea.

The events of 1956, indeed, strangely foreshadowed the kidnap crisis of the early twenty-first century. Then as now, Japanese media and family support groups insisted that there were many more Japanese people still remaining somewhere in North Korea. Press reports put the total number at around two thousand and suggested that some were possibly being held in prisons or labor camps. Relatives of these missing people urgently appealed to the Japanese government and Red Cross to press the North Koreans for information on their whereabouts.

Meanwhile, Inoue Masutarô was astonished and somewhat suspicious at the hospitality that the North Korean side lavished on the Japan Red Cross delegation. All their accommodation and meal expenses were covered by their North Korean hosts. Three cars were placed at their disposal throughout their stay; special bookings were made for them at theatres, and they were treated to private movie screenings in their hotel. The North Korean Red Cross had even arranged for a nurse to visit their hotel rooms every morning and check their pulses.

Other aspects of North Korean life, though, left a less favorable impression. Inoue's comments in fact give an interesting glimpse of the country where he was hoping to resettle sixty thousand people for humanitarian reasons. Soon after his return to Japan, he offered some friendly advice to the ICRC officials who were finalizing plans for their fact-finding mission to East Asia. During their visit to North Korea, Inoue warned, they should exercise great caution with the food, which was "barely edible." Inadequate medical facilities meant that they should also be sure to bring medication and spare pairs of spectacles with them. Other essentials for the journey included toiletries, shoe polish, photographic film, and ball-pen refills, all of which were scarce or unobtainable.

In addition, Inoue advised the Swiss visitors to bring their own supplies of whisky "to pacify one's nerves after a hard day of discussion."

This last recommendation was eloquent testimony to Inoue's own experiences during his month in Pyongyang. Barely twenty-four hours after the Japanese delegation's arrival, negotiations with the North Koreans had degenerated into acrimonious wrangles that dogged the remainder of their stay. The problems began when the North Korean side proposed that the meeting should discuss two extra topics in addition to the repatriation of the Japanese nationals: first, relations between the Japanese and North Korean Red Cross Societies; and second, the situation of Korean residents in Japan.

The Japanese Red Cross delegates were themselves, of course, extremely eager to talk about Koreans in Japan: specifically about the possibility of "returning" them to the DPRK. They had, after all, been requested by former Prime Minister Ashida Hitoshi to do so. However, they faced a dilemma. They had also been very firmly instructed by Leopold Boissier and other officials in Geneva *not* to discuss the topic with the North Koreans at this stage, but to await the outcome of the forthcoming confidential ICRC mission to East Asia. There was a real risk that any public discussion of repatriation in Pyongyang would enrage the South Koreans and destroy the chances of success for the all-important ICRC mission.

It was Inoue who devised a way around the problem. Publicly, the Japanese delegation insisted that they sympathized with the plight of Koreans in Japan and hoped some day to do something to help them, but that this was complex political topic that the Japan Red Cross Society had no mandate to consider at present. The formal sessions of the conference were to be limited to the question of Japanese citizens still in North Korea.

But the formal conference was to be preceded by informal and highly confidential talks between Inoue and his North Korean counterpart, Shin Yeong-Geun. The media were aware that these talks were taking place, but did not, of course, know the details of their content. In fact, the Inoue-Shin talks focused almost entirely on the question of Koreans in Japan; and it was there that the Japanese side communicated to North Korea its desire for a large-scale repatriation.

Meanwhile, on 11 February, Miyakoshi Kisuke had upstaged his fellow delegates by securing a private audience with the man who was ultimately to become one of the chief architects of North Korea's repatriation policy, Nam Il.

North Korean Foreign Minister Nam Il had a special and personal interest in overseas Koreans, for he had been one himself. His parents had been among the Koreans who had fled rural poverty into Siberia and subsequently been relocated *en masse* to Central Asia by Stalin (who ironically suspected all Korean immigrants of being Japanese spies). Nam returned to Korea only after the arrival of Soviet troops in the North in 1945. He spoke perfect Russian and maintained close links to his old homeland, becoming one of the most influential of the returnees from the USSR within North Korea's deeply factionalized politics.

From 1954 on, Nam had made a number of statements about the problem of Koreans in Japan, and in February 1955 he had issued a pronouncement on the need for North Korea to develop closer relations with Japan. During a meeting with Soviet Ambassador Ivanov on 1 October, Foreign Minister Nam provided some intriguing insights into the strategy behind these initiatives.

After the Korean War, political contact between North and South Korea had been totally severed, making it impossible even to find a forum in which the future relationship between the country's two halves could be discussed. From the North Korean point of view, some form of contact with the southern half of the peninsula was essential to future dialogue between the two Koreas and was also important both for information gathering purposes and as a possible channel for exerting influence over South Korean public opinion. Since the end of the Korean War, the DPRK had in fact tried on several occasions to open informal dialogue with the South, but to no avail. In his discussions with Ivanov, Nam Il began by lamenting the ongoing failure of North Korea to find any channel of communication with the South.

Nam then went on to observe that an improving relationship with Japan might provide a solution to the problem. Perhaps Japan could become a kind of steppingstone across which information could flow to and fro between the two halves of the divided Korea. In particular, said Nam, it seemed possible

> To make use of Koreans living in Japan—traders, students, and other groups. Contacts, even by private individuals, might help us to establish links with representatives from the South, and might strengthen the movement towards a meeting between the governments of the North and South with the purpose of resolving the problem of the reunification of the country. With these aims in mind, the Korean government considers it essential to provide material support for Koreans living in Japan.

The details of this support became clearer three months later, at the end of December 1955, when Nam Il used the North Korean Red Cross as an intermediary to send a long telegram to Japan, criticizing the Japanese government for failing to protect the rights of Koreans in Japan and for preventing the free movement of people between the two countries. The treatment of detainees in Ômura attracted particularly hostile comment.

On a more positive note, Nam's message outlined the North Korean government's plans to assist the education of Koreans in Japan by providing textbooks for Korean schools and offering scholarships for university students. For the North Koreans, unlike the Japanese side, repatriation was clearly just one part of a larger set of policies toward Koreans in Japan. Besides, the numbers of returnees envisaged by the two sides were very different.

The contrast between the Japanese and North Korean positions became clear as soon as Inoue Masutarô and his North Korean opposite number Shin sat down for the confidential exchange of opinions that was to be the prelude to the plenary conference.

One of the trials that frayed Inoue's nerves during his stay in Pyongyang, requiring regular recourse to a soothing glass of whisky in the evenings, was the North Korean negotiating style. His hosts, he soon discovered, were inclined to launch into long monologues about abstract principles, heavily laced with phrases such as "non-intervention in domestic affairs," "the five principles of peaceful coexistence," and so forth. In order to help his opposite number come to the point, Inoue asked Shin Yeong-Geun to draw up a draft of the items that the North Koreans would like to see included in the conference's final communiqué. Inoue himself also drew up his own very brief draft, postponing concrete decisions on all issues except the return of Japanese citizens. These drafts were then used as a basis for a frank exchange of ideas between the two sides.

Shin's draft communiqué was long and detailed and elaborated the points made in Nam Il's telegram to Japan. It committed the Red Cross societies of both countries to the goals of promoting the free movement of people between Japan and North Korea and of "stabilizing the livelihoods" of expatriates in the two countries—Japanese in North Korea and Koreans in Japan. The North Korean Red Cross promised to assist in discovering the whereabouts of Japanese remaining in Korea. In return, the Japan Red Cross Society was requested to help prevent ethnic discrimination against Koreans in Japan in terms of work, education, and welfare.

The draft put forward by Shin also called for a delegation from the North Korean Red Cross to be allowed to visit Japan, and pledged both national Red Cross societies to "cooperate so that the 70 (assumptive figure) Koreans desiring for going home [*sic*] in the Omura Detention Camp and other Koreans in Japan who desire to return home can return to [their] homeland by the repatriation boat to be sent for the Japanese nationals in Korea."

In responding to these proposals, Inoue drew on his experience as a former ministerial expert on Communism, mobilizing a little ideological jargon of his own. By applying "the dialectical method of Marx," he assured Shin, the two sides should be able identify the "greatest common factor" shared by their contrasting positions, and so achieve consensus.

Inoue's dialectical reasoning had no difficulty identifying the point of synthesis between both sides. It was, he insisted, mass repatriation. Inoue argued that it was "meaningless, if not ridiculous" to discuss stabilizing the livelihood of Koreans in Japan. Of the six hundred thousand Koreans in Japan, he told his North Korean hosts, one hundred thousand were receiving welfare. "Therefore, it is obvious that if we could eliminate this one-sixth who cannot earn their living, we can stabilize the livelihood of Koreans in Japan." As Inoue later reported to the ICRC in Geneva, in his discussions with Shin, "the point [on which] I laid the emphasis was the necessity for mass repatriation. . . . In fact, once the way of mass repatriation of Koreans in Japan be opened, it is evident that all Koreans who cannot earn their living in Japan will request to be returned to Korea."

The North Korean side, Inoue noted, was unimpressed by this reasoning because, as far as they were aware, the probable number of Koreans actually seeking repatriation to the North was "less than 1,000," a number much too small to make an appreciable impact on the overall living standards of Koreans in Japan.

At that point, the Japan Red Cross Society's arguments for repatriation appear to have performed a somersault. For the few months before, their correspondence with the ICRC had been pressing the need for repatriation as an urgent response to the potentially violent demands of sixty thousand Koreans in Japan who were desperately longing to return to the North Korean homeland. In his private discussions with Shin, however, Inoue's explanation was clearly very different. His main argument for mass repatriation, as he further elaborated in his report on the Pyongyang Conference, was now simple and hardheaded:

> The economic situation in Japan is not yet adapted to the conditions following the end of the Pacific War and, accordingly, the livelihood of Japanese themselves is very hard. . . . In these circumstances, I presume, it is impossible for the Japanese Government to accomplish the stabilization of the livelihood of Koreans in Japan with success, when the Japanese Government has too many problems to solve for the relief of its own people. . . . Consequently, I am of the opinion that to realize the mass repatriation of Koreans is the most appropriate way to stabilize the livelihood of Koreans and, at the same time, this is necessary for the Japanese side, too. Without this repatriation, this problem will never be solved at present.

Here, indeed, we seem to be approaching the heart of the matter. Japan in the second half of the 1950s was moving from postwar reconstruction into rapid industrial growth. The scars of war and poverty were rapidly disappearing. But many of the former colonial subjects who still lived in Japan remained impoverished, unemployed, ghettoized—seen, in short, as an unwelcome reminder of the past and a possible source of future social and political disturbance. In a report that Inoue compiled later in the same year (in consultation with government officials and his superiors in the Japanese Red Cross), he was to emphasise that "certain Koreans" in Japan were employed in day laboring, "anti-social occupations" (like illegal alcohol distilling), and other occupations (such as scrap collecting, running pachinko parlors, etc.), which, in his words, do not give a "sound impression."

Inoue's explanation of the reasons why these forms of work are so prevalent in the minority community was unequivocal. Koreans were largely excluded from other, more respectable forms of employment. This exclusion, however, was not to be blamed on the Japanese government, nor on employers: "The reason why the capitalists do not wish to employ Koreans is because some Koreans were so unlawful during the period succeeding the end of the war," and employers were "afraid of the ideological string which may be attached to Korean laborers."

As the Japanese economy recovered, Inoue argued, the informal sector in which Koreans were employed would steadily shrink. However, because of their social "weakness," they would be unable to adapt to the new conditions of a more prosperous Japan. Their unemployment would therefore rise, and they would become a growing burden on the national welfare budget:

> Therefore I believe that . . . <u>whatever they may try, certain Koreans cannot live on under present circumstances in Japan and there seems to be no prospect of solution in the near future and the only way left is repatriation.</u>

The suggestion put to the North Korean side during the Pyongyang Conference, and spelled out in more detail in Inoue's report, was in effect that North Korea should relieve the former colonial power of part of its welfare burden; and the response from the North Koreans seems to have been a pained silence. Shin Yeong-Geun did, however, thank Inoue for taking part in an honest exchange of ideas: "The sole gratitude," Inoue tartly noted, "that I received from the Korean side during the whole session."

But when on 23 February the private talks between Inoue and Shin ended and the plenary conference opened, discussions again collapsed into mutual recriminations. The Japanese side believed they had received a commitment that the formal conference, at which the media would be in attendance, would only address the issue of Japanese returnees from North Korea.

The North Korean chief negotiator Ryu Gi-Chun, however, saw things differently, and insisted on reading out to the assembled delegates and media representatives a draft communiqué based on the one drawn up by Shin. Perhaps in response to the private discussions between Shin and Inoue, the reference to repatriation had then been reworded to read, "The Japanese Red Cross will give active cooperation to repatriate seventy odd Koreans desiring repatriation among Korean detainees in the Omura Camp and [the] *other seven hundred odd Koreans* [my emphasis]."

As Ryu read this communiqué, a horrified Inoue scribbled a note to Kasai Yoshisuke saying, "We will leave Pyongyang tomorrow." Kasai nodded and, as Ryu finished speaking, stood up to announce that the Japanese side had "neither preparation nor competence" to discuss the issues raised in the North Korea draft communiqué. The next day, he paid a formal visit to the North Korean Red Cross to inform them that the Japanese side was breaking off negotiations and returning home. After some discussion, the

Japanese were eventually persuaded to stay on for a further two days in Pyongyang, during which they managed to finalize arrangements for the return of the thirty-six Japanese nationals already awaiting repatriation. A face-saving joint communiqué was also hammered out and signed at 2:00 a.m. on the morning of the Japanese delegation's departure. On Japanese insistence, this included the statement that the question of Koreans in Japan had not been put on the formal agenda, since the Japanese delegation had no competence to discuss it, but that it was a "humanitarian question" on which both Red Cross Societies hoped to negotiate in the future.

The collapse of the negotiations meant that the fate of other Japanese remaining in North Korea could not be determined. The issue was left in the hands of the North Korean Red Cross, who promised to follow it up. Sure enough, within a few weeks of the Japanese delegation's departure, a further twenty-one Japanese would-be returnees had been identified. In the end, however, the thirty-six Japanese citizens whom the Red Cross delegation had met in Pyongyang were the only Japanese to be repatriated. The rest soon disappeared from the Red Cross agenda. By the time Inoue and Shin next met in great secrecy in June 1956, the repatriation of Koreans in Japan had become the sole focus of discussion, and the issue of Japanese in North Korea seems not to have been raised at all.

The Japanese delegation left Pyongyang by plane on 28 February. On the way to the airport, Inoue Masutarô, who was sharing a car with his North Korean counterpart Shin Yeong-Geun, expressed satisfaction with the results of the talks and asked Shin how he felt about their outcome. Shin, "having corrected his words many times through the translator, said he was pleased to hear that the Japanese side was satisfied with the outcome of the Conference."

Reading the expression on Shin's face, Inoue "sympathized" with him and expressed his own belief that "the solution of the problem of Koreans in Japan should be carried out resolutely," but that various other avenues should be explored before the Japanese and North Korean Red Cross societies attempted to resolve it themselves.

Inoue did not specify what these avenues were, but he was of course thinking of the ICRC mission, which (as he knew) was about to embark on its visit to Northeast Asia.

10

SPECIAL MISSION TO THE FAR EAST

In the forty-five-year history of the Cold War, the year 1956 stands out as a landmark. The death of Stalin had opened the way to a wave of reform within the Soviet Union, creating hopes for a new age of democratization throughout the Communist Bloc. Buoyed by these hopes, in October 1956 a spontaneous movement for political reform erupted in Hungary, as citizens took to the streets calling for a withdrawal of Soviet forces and for the right to free speech and free elections. The Hungarian Communist Party's Central Committee responded quickly, replacing its leadership with a reformer, Imre Nagy, who promptly started to dismantle the one-party state.

But these developments provoked great alarm in Moscow; it was one thing to allow a limited and localized critique of the excesses of Stalinism in the USSR itself, quite another to let satellite states transform their political systems in ways that might lead to the complete fragmentation of the Soviet camp. The United States, fearful of provoking a nuclear conflict, refused to intervene on behalf of the Hungarian reformers. On 4 November, Soviet tanks rumbled into the streets of Budapest, and the Hungarian uprising was crushed.

Meanwhile, just five days before the Soviet occupation of Budapest, British and French planes, supported by Israeli ground forces, launched an unexpected military strike on Egypt, bringing the Middle East to the point of all-out war. The attack was a response to Egyptian leader Gamal Abdul Nasser's nationalization of the Suez Canal, which both the UK and France saw as a lifeline to their still-extensive colonial possessions in Asia. But if the United States had been reluctant to give support to the Hungarian uprising, it was equally reluctant to back what it saw as a reckless military adventure by the European imperial powers. The United Nations condemned the attack on Egypt, and the United States and USSR worked behind the scenes to bring the parties to the negotiating table. The Suez Crisis ended in a humiliating backdown by Britain and France and marked a further shift of power from the old colonial centers of Europe to the new western superpower, the United States.

The International Committee of the Red Cross was deeply involved in these crises. In Hungary, it provided medical supplies and relief, and also offered assistance to the refugees who streamed out of the country, often with nothing but the clothes on their backs. In the Suez Crisis, the main task for the ICRC was to ensure that all sides in the conflict adhered to the Geneva Conventions, a task that, in the case of France, was handled by the Committee's Paris representative, William Michel.

For Michel, this marked the end of an eventful year. Six months earlier, he had been on the other side of the world. To be precise, six months before the Anglo-French attack on Egypt, he had been sitting on a flight from Hong Kong to Tokyo, in the midst of the ICRC's complex and highly confidential fact-finding mission to East Asia. Next to him on the plane, on that last day of April 1956, sat the portly figure of Eugène de Weck, the ICRC section chief who had looked after Inoue Masutarô during his trip to Geneva and who was Michel's companion on a long itinerary that had already taken the two men to India, China, and North Korea.

It was after 10:00 p.m. when Michel and de Weck's airplane came in to land at Tokyo's Haneda Airport. They were looking forward to the coming weeks with curiosity, for they were well aware that their meetings in Tokyo would hold the key to the success or failure of their mission.

So far, their visit to East Asia had been perplexing and physically taxing. Michel was still recovering from a bout of pneumonia that had struck him in Beijing, giving him an unwelcome opportunity to experience the services offered by the Chinese Red Cross firsthand. The mission's one-week stay in North Korea, from 5 to 12 April, had also failed to produce the results they were expecting.

Like Inoue and his colleagues before them, Michel and de Weck had stayed in Pyongyang's International Hotel, and like the Japan Red Cross Society's delegation in February, they had been showered with hospitality by their North Korean hosts, who covered all their expenses and lavished them with free boxes of chocolates and packs of cigarettes. The North Korean Red Cross had also prepared a comprehensive—indeed exhausting—itinerary for them, a whirlwind tour of the wonders of socialist reconstruction and development.

They had visited the building sites of Pyongyang, inspected a textile factory, traveled out of the city to a collective farm, and driven 100 kilometers each way along "terrible, dusty roads" to view a massive irrigation project. There had been tours of Red Cross hospitals, displays of singing and dancing, and an outing to the theater to watch a revolutionary ballet set during the Korean War. Evenings had been devoted to film showings on everything from Korean history to the soon-to-be-completed Three Year Plan and the heroic achievements of North Korean construction workers, the latter viewed by the Swiss visitors with a slightly sardonic eye. As Eugène de Weck observed, "Seeing the speed with which the bricks were laid, we finally understood why every section of our newly constructed hotel shakes so alarmingly."

All this left very little time for formal negotiations with the ICRC's newly accredited national affiliate, the Red Cross Society of the Democratic People's Republic of Korea. And when the ICRC delegates did manage to snatch a few hours for quiet discussion with North Korean Red Cross officials, they made little progress with the main topics on their agenda.

Michel, who did most of the talking during their meetings, conveyed to the North Koreans an offer from the International Committee of the Red Cross to assist with two problems: first, tracing the missing of the Korean War; and second, repatriating ethnic Koreans from Japan to North Korea. But the response from the North Korean side was politely negative. They were grateful for the ICRC's offer, but they were dealing with these issues quite satisfactorily by themselves.

North Korean Red Cross secretary-general Ri Chun-Sik expressed his country's concern about the Koreans interned in Ômura Detention Center. But as far as the general issue of Koreans in Japan was concerned, he pointed out that the North Korea Red Cross had only recently discussed this with their Japanese counterparts. His society, he said, had "confidence that the promises of the Japanese Red Cross would be fulfilled, and that they would be able to achieve a direct solution." Though Ri did not spell this out, in terms of North Korean policy, the whole point of an initiative toward Koreans in Japan was of course to strengthen direct contact with Japan and with the *Zainichi* Korean community, and outside intervention by an international organization was more likely to hinder than to help the process.

Influenced perhaps by the earlier discussions with Inoue, the North Koreans' estimate of the likely scale of repatriation from Japan had now risen somewhat; in answer to a question from the ICRC delegates about the number of potential returnees, Ri said that there were "700 according to the letters and lists which we have received, but there are certainly many more, a considerable number."

Michel and de Weck could hardly fail to notice, though, that this was very different from the information they were receiving from Tokyo. As they were to report at the end of their travels in East Asia, their mission received enormously varying estimates of the numbers of Koreans seeking repatriation: "North Korean circles themselves are much more modest in their estimates than the Japanese RC [Red Cross], which seems to amplify the problem."

By the time their plane touched down on the Haneda runway and taxied to a halt before the arrivals hall, Michel and de Weck had a long list of questions to which they were seeking answers in Tokyo.

As I pore over the meticulous account of their visit, which has lain unread in the ICRC archives for almost fifty years, there are just two questions that loom very large in my mind: How did seven hundred—or at most a few thousand—would-be repatriates of 1956 become the ninety thousand who ultimately "returned"? And why did the International Committee of the Red Cross—a body officially dedicated to apolitical humanitarianism—ever agree to involve itself in this scheme?

When they stepped out of the airplane into the mild spring Tokyo night and made their way down the metal stairway to the tarmac, the two ICRC delegates were startled to be greeted by the popping flashbulbs of press cameras. At the bottom of the steps, among a bevy of journalists, cameramen, and others, stood Miyakoshi Kisuke of the Japan-Korea Association and, next to him, the tall and elegant figure of Harry Angst, Tokyo representative of the International Committee of the Red Cross.

Beyond the customs hall the weary travelers were confronted by a further melee of journalists, well wishers, and petitioners. People crowded forward, asking questions or offering greetings in Japanese, to which Michel and de Weck nodded politely but uncomprehendingly. William Michel found a large bouquet of flowers wrapped in red ribbons thrust into his hands, while bowing men presented name cards introducing themselves as officials of the General Association of Korean Residents in Japan (*Chongryun*). The Swiss visitors had little means of knowing which of the people in the crowd were Japanese and which Korean, and of the Koreans, who was affiliated with the North and who with the South. They were grateful for the reassuring presence of the Japanese-speaking Harry Angst, who steered them through the crush to a waiting car, dismissing importuning newspapermen and others with a firm, "Not now. Contact us later."

They sped through winding city streets to the Imperial Hotel, the splendid if slightly down-at-heel Frank Lloyd Wright building in central Tokyo where Michel and de Weck were to stay. It was after 1:00 a.m. by the time the ICRC emissaries finally checked into their hotel, but Inoue Masutarô was there to greet them, eager to let them know that all of Japan had been awaiting their arrival with great impatience, and that Japanese public opinion expected their mission to produce a solution to problems of Japanese-Korean relations. In response, Michel and de Weck reminded the excited Inoue that their mission to East Asia was a strictly exploratory one, and that they wanted to keep it as discreet as possible.

Michel and de Weck's stay in Japan was to prove very different from their visit to North Korea. There were dinners and glittering receptions, to be sure; but here there would be no tours of showplace factories and irrigation projects. Instead, large amounts of time would be devoted to very serious discussions with Red Cross officials, senior Japanese bureaucrats, and prominent political figures from both government and opposition parties. In the course of their stay, Michel and de Weck managed to have an audience with Foreign Minister Shigemitsu Mamoru (an honor specially arranged for them by Inoue Masutarô), and even to exchange greetings with Prime Minister Hatoyama and with Emperor Hirohito himself—clear signs of the importance with which their visit was regarded in Japanese official circles.

As in North Korea, however, so too in Japan, they relied on the local Red Cross to arrange most of their itinerary. On their first morning in Japan, during discussions about the agenda for their stay, Inoue happily agreed to arrange a meeting with *Chongryun*, which the Japanese Red Cross had now chosen as its main counterpart in pursuing the repatriation project. Inoue insisted, though, that this meeting should include only Chairman Han Deok-Su and a couple of other senior officials, rather than *Chongryun*'s rank and file.

Depending as they did on the Japanese Red Cross for introductions during their stay, Michel and de Weck had only one real alternative source of information and contacts in Japan: Harry C. Angst, the Japan-based representative of the International Committee of the Red Cross. The handsome and charming Angst certainly knew Japan well, for he had lived there since 1931, when he had arrived in Yokohama as a recent college graduate to take up a position in the Japanese offices of the Swiss trading company

Siber Hegner. Being a citizen of neutral Switzerland, Angst had been able to stay on in Japan during the Pacific War; in 1943 he was appointed to the position of deputy ICRC delegate in Japan, responsible for visiting Japanese prisoner-of-war camps and detention camps for civilian detainees, and on the basis of this work he was later promoted to chief delegate.

As one prominent ICRC figure approvingly remarked, Angst's familiarity with Japan allowed him to "move with ease in all the social circles of the capital, whether amongst businessmen, government ministers or the Red Cross." But his very ability to blend into such circles seems to have made it difficult for him to take positions that contradicted government or Japan Red Cross policy. In the postwar years, indeed, he was fiercely criticized by many former allied prisoners of war, who (in the words of one long-time foreign resident in Japan) felt that Angst had been "spineless, disinterested in their fates and that he played up to the Japanese."

On the first day of their stay in Japan, however, Angst accompanied Michel and de Weck to meet one person who would give them an outsider's perspective on their mission: the Swiss minister to Japan, Max Troendle.

A politically shrewd and plainspoken man, Troendle had been briefed about the purpose of the ICRC mission, and he left Michel and de Weck in no doubt about his views on the subject. De Weck, in his notes of their meeting, recorded that Troendle "regards all these things as extremely explosive, and he is persuaded that their humanitarian aspect, at best quite dubious, is in any case greatly outweighed by political considerations." Japan, Troendle went on, "would like nothing better than to get rid of its entire Korean population. Failing this, partial departures are very welcome. But for that to happen, it is necessary make South Korean opposition disappear."

Japan's position, the Swiss minister explained, would be greatly strengthened if it were to become clear to the rest of the world that South Korea's opposition to the repatriation scheme was contrary to the policies of the International Red Cross.

Troendle then went on to brief Michel and de Weck about the likely U.S. position on a possible mass repatriation to North Korea. The United States, he noted, was in a state of "incompetence" because of its forthcoming presidential elections. Besides, U.S. diplomats in Japan and South Korea had been ordered not to take any initiative on this and "in any event, not to get mixed up in relations between Japan and South Korea."

In retrospect, the information Michel and de Weck received during the rest of their stay in Japan appears all too clearly to confirm Max Troendle's cynical analysis.

During a special briefing session with senior bureaucrats held the following day in the discreet surroundings of a private house in central Tokyo, the head of Japan's Immigration Control Bureau provided Michel and de Weck with figures illustrating the high crime rate of Koreans in Japan. "The Korean community," he informed the visitors, "was the source of great concern to the Japanese authorities." Next, it was the turn of the Ministry of Health and Welfare, whose representatives presented a detailed report claiming that ethnic Koreans constituted a disproportionately heavy burden on the Japanese budget.

This report, as it happens, also offers a disturbing clue to the forces that would soon increase the numbers volunteering for repatriation.

Meanwhile, the head of the Health and Welfare Ministry's Repatriation Bureau provided estimates of the cost of a one-way ticket from Japan to the Chinese city of Tianjin (Tientsin)—the most likely route for repatriates heading to North Korea—and assured the Swiss delegates that "if the number to be repatriated was significant (60,000, for example) the Japanese government could consider the question of covering the costs itself."

On the Monday of the following week, Michel and de Weck spent the entire day closeted with a group of officials who included representatives of the Police and National Security Agencies. Here they were given figures on the involvement of Koreans in criminal activities (particularly smuggling), and were told that the "excessive" claims on the welfare system by the Korean community had a deeper political purpose: they were part of a campaign by left-wing Koreans, who sought to prevent Japan from rearming by diverting government funds to other purposes—in short, not just a financial problem but a matter of national security.

Interestingly, though, the police representative cast doubt on the high estimates of potential returnees that the ICRC had received from the Japanese Red Cross and *Chongryun*. Although the police had no figures of their own, noted de Weck, "They think the estimates which have been made are too high."

On 9 May, the ICRC mission made a brief detour to South Korea, where they visited Busan and Seoul before returning to Japan the following week. Back in Japan, Michel and de Weck were able to report some of their findings in South Korea when they called on Japanese Foreign Minister Shigemitsu Mamoru. The minister greeted them warmly and told them that the problem of Koreans in Japan was a matter that "greatly preoccupied his government." It was necessary, Shigemitsu told them,

> To find a solution which would permit those who do not have the means to live in Japan to attain a better existence in their homeland. He

[Shigemitsu] is counting on the ICRC to help realize this 'wish'. He would particularly like to return the women and children, who were leading a miserable existence in Japan, to their homeland.

Inoue Masutarô expressed himself in rather less moving terms than his former Foreign Ministry departmental head Shigemitsu. During a long and "intimate" exchange of views with the ICRC envoys, he confirmed impressions that (as William Michel observed) had "until now been impossible to acknowledge, but [were] none the less true": According to a rather startled Michel, three of the points now spelled out in black and white by Inoue were as follows:

1. The total absence of humanitarian considerations in relation to the whole Korean problem in Japan.
2. The desire of the Japanese government to rid itself of several tens of thousands of Koreans who are destitute and vaguely communist, thus solving at a stroke a security problem and a budgetary problem (because of the sums currently spent on destitute Koreans).
3. According to Mr. Inoue, the Japanese government has decided to begin the repatriation, if necessary by instigating individual demands to go to the North.

This last point, Michel noted in parenthesis, "seems rather 'excessive and fraught with serious consequences.'"

On 18 May, a week before they left Japan, William Michel and Eugène de Weck flew from Tokyo to Fukuoka and traveled from there by train to Nagasaki and on to the small port of Ômura, where they inspected the Detention Center and spoke to Korean detainees awaiting deportation. While in Tokyo, they also received a lengthy briefing from Inoue, who used photographs to illustrate to them the dire living conditions of Koreans in Japan.

But the ICRC delegates did not actually visit any of the Korean communities themselves. If they had done so, they might have discovered that, in May 1956, there was one topic of conversation that was on everybody's lips.

In February 1956, the Japanese Ministry of Health and Welfare had suddenly launched a large-scale and concerted campaign to weed out "excessive welfare claims" by Koreans in Japan. The campaign was conducted in cooperation with the police, who descended in force on Korean communities, going from door to door to demand documentary evidence of welfare entitlements and checking living quarters and backyards for signs of hidden wealth or illegal money-making activities.

Livelihood protection payments to the very poor were, of course, almost the only form of welfare still granted—on a discretionary basis—to Koreans in Japan after the government unilaterally declared them foreigners. At the time of their loss of nationality rights in 1952, about sixty thousand Koreans in Japan had been receiving welfare, but by March 1955, the number had more than doubled. There were several reasons for this rise.

The temporary downturn that affected the Japanese economy after the Korean War boom had had a particularly severe effect on the precarious informal sectors of the economy where many Koreans were employed. Meanwhile, between 1953 and 1955, Communist-affiliated Koreans had been involved in a joint campaign with Japanese left-wingers to improve the lot of the poor. In the course of this campaign, they encouraged their compatriots to apply for welfare and (according to the Health and Welfare Ministry's accusations) sometimes pressured officials to grant welfare to those who did not really deserve it. The radicals' campaign had subsided with the founding of *Chongryun* in 1955 (since this new association discouraged Koreans in Japan from engaging in Japanese domestic politics), but the effects of the campaign had lingered on, and in early 1956 the number of Korean welfare claimants remained at over 130,000.

It is doubtless true that there were some questionable welfare claims by Koreans in Japan—as there also were by some Japanese claimants. But in a situation where Koreans in fact had no legal *entitlement* to welfare at all, and where there was only a thin line between absolute unemployment and intermittent money earning from casual work, it was very difficult to distinguish the deserving welfare claimant from the undeserving. The process of documenting claims was all the more difficult because many Koreans in Japan (particularly of the older generation) did not speak perfect Japanese, and many were unable to read and write.

One small example of the consequences of the welfare crackdown is recorded in a study of the Korean community in Japan, written by *Zainichi* Korean social researcher and activist Pak Jae-Il and published in 1957. Pak had been conducting a social survey of a Korean community in a country town in northeastern Japan—a group of forty-one households, of which fifteen were receiving welfare. After the Ministry of Health and Welfare sent the police in to investigate the community in March 1956, six of the fifteen families had their livelihood protection payments canceled, and a further three had their payments drastically cut. Pak noted that the crackdown focused not on the poorest of the poor, but on those who had until then just been managing, with the help of livelihood assistance, to make ends meet. In the months that followed, these people were reduced to desperate poverty, in one case even forced to go out on the streets begging.

There was nothing secret about the Ministry of Welfare's campaign; on the contrary, it was broadcast all over the Japanese media. Just one of many examples was a large illustrated article published in the *Asahi* newspaper on 26 April 1956. Entitled "Koreans' Livelihood Protection: Ten Times the Level of Japanese People's," the article began by revealing the existence of Korean welfare recipients who, "when compared to their Japanese counterparts," were "said to be living quite luxurious lives." Readers were then regaled with a whole series of stories, provided to the press by police sources, of Korean recipients who had been found in possession of such telltale evidence of opulent living as a decorated tea chest, an "expensive" pet dog, or a western style dressing table.

Four weeks later, the newspaper was able to report with satisfaction that the Welfare Ministry's crackdown had led to 117,073 Korean welfare recipients being investigated. As a result, it had been possible to cut the amount of livelihood protection paid to the Korean community by 27.7 percent. Between the end of 1955 and the middle of 1957, the number of Koreans receiving Livelihood Protection payments was reduced by around eighty-one thousand.

What the Japanese media and public did not know (though Michel and de Weck did) was that the Welfare Ministry's crackdown had been launched immediately after the secret decision by the ruling Liberal Democratic Party to "start a movement to support the repatriation of the Koreans to North Korea." There can be no doubt that the Health and Welfare Ministry was perfectly well aware of a connection between its campaign and the simultaneous efforts by the government and Japan Red Cross Society to promote the repatriation plan. After all, the ministry's representatives gave Michel and de Weck details of their efforts to reduce welfare demands by Koreans at the very same time they expressed their willingness to consider covering the costs of a mass repatriation.

Japan Red Cross officials also recognized the capacity of the ministry's campaign to instigate demands for repatriation to North Korea. As Shimazu Tadatsugu noted in a letter sent to Geneva soon after Michel and de Weck's visit, Koreans in Japan were struggling to exist in an environment where

The total amount of livelihood relief fund for them has been cut down, thus driving them into more difficult situation, in contradiction to the elevation of the Japanese standard of living. Their only way of living is therefore to repatriate to North Korea where the construction is demanding more labour.

The uncertainty and inadequacy of welfare in Japan is a recurrent refrain in the repatriation story; and of course, the consequences of the welfare policies determined in the 1950s went on affecting Koreans in Japan—both those who chose to leave for North Korea and those who chose to stay—for decades to come.

Taniguchi Hiroko, a *Zainichi* Korean returnee who is now back in Japan after around a quarter of a century of harrowing experiences in North Korea, was not yet born at the time when Michel and de Weck visited Japan. Her family joined the repatriation in the 1970s, when she was high school student.

Her family's motive was simple. Her father, who had held a steady job as a janitor for years, had become chronically ill. There was no pension, no health insurance, no public housing, and only the extremely uncertain prospect of "discretionary" livelihood protection payments from the Ministry of Health and Welfare to fall back on. With children still at school, and no reason to have confidence in the ministry's benevolence, Hiroko's father took the advice of a friend and registered his family for repatriation to North Korea where, they had heard, housing, health care, and education would be provided free. Hiroko, a teenager who was hoping to go on to college to study foreign languages, passionately opposed the decision. She wanted to stay in Japan with her friends and the life she knew. But she was just too young to make her own independent decision.

On the evening of Thursday, 24 May, William Michel and Eugène de Weck had dinner with Harry Angst and were then driven to Haneda Airport, where Inoue, Kasai and other Japan Red Cross Officials were waiting with bouquets of flowers to bid them a fond farewell. Around midnight, they boarded their flight for Hong Kong, promptly unloading the bouquets onto their radiantly smiling flight attendants.

In Hong Kong, the two men would part company, Michel traveling on to Indonesia and Malaya, while de Weck visited the Philippines, Vietnam, and Thailand. It was not until early July that they returned to Geneva and submitted the findings of their mission to the ICRC.

With the information they had gathered in Japan, they might have been expected to read the warning signs and conclude, as Max Troendle had done, that the issue of Korean repatriation was a diplomatic time bomb primed by the most dubious of political motives—a perilous object indeed for an apolitical and charitable organization to handle. Had they reached that conclusion, the mass repatriation might never have happened.

But in the world of international humanitarianism, nothing was as simple as it seemed.

11

THE FIRST "RETURN"

When William Michel and Eugène de Weck delivered their eagerly awaited report in Geneva in July 1956, there were two issues that made their task particularly difficult. One was the information they had gathered during their visit to Ômura Detention Center; the other was the scene that had greeted them in the courtyard of the Japan Red Cross Headquarters during their visit to Tokyo.

A casual present-day visitor, driving along the main road that runs beside the calm expanse of Ômura Bay, might be forgiven for assuming that the large glass and steel building not far from the sea is the local branch of some high-tech multinational corporation. The impression is reinforced inside the building's reception area, where the curved chrome sweep of the central staircase is tastefully coordinated with the abstract metallic shapes in silver and gold that adorn the walls.

The smiling staff are eager to show visitors their excellent facilities: the banks of computer monitors, the well-equipped clinics, the children's nursery stocked with toys (even though the building nowadays is empty of children). Only the massive steel side door through which the building's long-term occupants are admitted, the bare functional room where they are body-searched and checked with metal detectors, and the dormitories where they sleep, ten to a room, remind the outside observer of the harsher realities of this place.

Now known as Ômura Immigration Reception Center, this is Japan's oldest migrant detention institution, and its occupants today are a mixture of nationalities: Chinese, Southeast Asian, Middle Eastern, and others. But when ICRC delegates William Michel and Eugène de Weck (accompanied

Figure 11.1. Eugène de Weck (center), William Michel (carrying white sheet of paper), and Harry C. Angst (the tall figure at the back) visit the women's and children's section of Ômura Detention Center, 19 May 1956. (© ICRC)

by Harry Angst) went there in 1956, it was commonly known to the public as Ômura Koreans' Detention Center and was specifically intended to hold people awaiting deportation to South Korea.

The old detention center that Michel and de Weck visited was on the other side of the road from the present building, an area now overgrown with weeds and marked only by a small white signboard.

In 1956, the camp was surrounded by a high wall with a watchtower at each corner. Inside stood a row of five recently built blocks occupied by male detainees, and a single older two-story building (described by de Weck as being "in rather bad condition") occupied by the women and children. Roll call took place at 9:00 a.m. and 6:00 p.m., and meals were served on trolleys from a central kitchen three times a day.

On 19 May, the day when the delegation made its tour of inspection, there were 1,467 Koreans interned in Ômura, including 140 children under the age of fifteen, of whom 31 had no parents with them in the camp. Detainees were divided into two main categories. The largest number were people arrested for illegal entry to Japan, many of them having crossed the border to escape from the 4/3 Incident in Jeju and the Korean War or to join parents, husbands, wives, or other relatives already living in Japan.

A smaller category of detainees was made up of people who had completed sentences for criminal offenses. Under Japan's Migration Control Law, foreigners found guilty of crimes in Japan were to be deported after serving their sentences. When Koreans in Japan were turned into foreigners in 1952, it was decided that this rule should also be applied to them—even to Koreans who had been born in Japan and had been arrested for crimes committed before their loss of nationality.

The South Korean government, however, had other ideas. It insisted that these people were Japan's responsibility, and refused to take them back. As a result, Ômura contained a growing number of people who had served their time in prison but now found themselves incarcerated indefinitely, with no clear future in sight. Not surprisingly, this was a recipe for unrest in the increasingly overcrowded detention center.

Another problem was posed by the detainees who identified themselves with North rather than South Korea. By the time Michel and de Weck visited Ômura on 19 May 1956, their number had grown to ninety-seven, and their representatives complained of discrimination from camp authorities and clashes with other inmates. A miniature version of the Cold War, it seemed, was being played out within the walls of Ômura.

The North Korean–affiliated detainees gave the Swiss visitors a petition pleading to be sent to North Korea rather than deported to the South. These were the people who had earlier sent a petition written in blood to Pyongyang. There could be no doubting the sincerity of their pleas for help, and Michel and de Weck felt that this problem was one that the ICRC could not ignore.

And then there were the people whom the ICRC delegates found encamped outside the Japan Red Cross headquarters in Tokyo when they were invited there for a lunch by Shimazu Tadatsugu.

The first demonstrators had appeared outside the Red Cross building almost a month earlier, around 5:00 p.m. on 6 April 1956. Among them were representatives of forty-seven people who were demanding repatriation to North Korea. They had heard that a Japan Red Cross ship, the *Kojima*, was soon to depart to pick up the thirty-six Japanese nationals returning from North Korea, and asked the Red Cross to let them to board the ship and leave Japan to start new lives in the Democratic People's Republic.

According to the official history of the Japanese Red Cross, the demonstrators were told that this was impossible. The Red Cross was unsure what reaction such a voyage would evoke from the South Koreans and could not take the risk. Discussions dragged on late into the evening, and eventually around twenty protestors, who had traveled long distances to Tokyo, were allowed into the Red Cross headquarters. They spread their bedding on the floor of the grand main meeting hall, and in those elegant (though perhaps not very comfortable) surroundings, they spent the night.

The following day, they still refused to leave, and by the end of the week around thirty of them had set up permanent camp within the Red Cross compound, their numbers intermittently swelled by *Chongryun*-affiliated students and others who came to cheer them on. By 21 April, when the *Kojima* had already sailed for North Korea without them, the Red Cross offered them train fares back to whatever part of Japan they came from, and when this offer was refused, the Red Cross called in the police to eject them. However, the Koreans simply transferred their tents to the area outside the main gates of the compound, where they continued to camp, hanging their protest banners and their washing on the Red Cross headquarters' wrought iron fencing.

They were there when Michel and Weck visited the headquarters for lunch on 2 May; and they were still there when the Swiss delegates returned to the building on 21 May for a glittering cocktail party, whose guests ranged from the Emperor's three sisters-in-law, Princesses Chichibu, Takamatsu, and Mikasa, to the heads of rival Korean community associations *Chongryun* and *Mindan* and the newly appointed Soviet Chargé-d'Affaires.

Who were these forty-seven people whose longing to return to North Korea drove them to such lengths? Although their protest was reported in the Japanese media and generated a fat file of documents in ICRC headquarters in Geneva, the written records contain little trace of their lives, personalities, and circumstances or their feelings about the increasing hardships and frustrations of their protest.

Michel and de Weck saw the demonstration, but do not actually appear to have spoken to its participants.

The archives in Geneva include just one translated letter from a member of the protest group, Therng [*sic*] Ik-Sam, who explained to the ICRC that their "only motive to go to North Korea is to find means of livelihood and to join families or friends, because it is very hard, even practically impossible, to live in this country." The list of names that Therng attached to his letter shows that the group was made up of eight families and five single men. More than half of the forty-seven were children, and the birth of a new baby was about to increase their number to forty-eight.

One interesting extra detail, though, is provided by a highly confidential letter written by Japan Red Cross president Shimazu to the president of the North Korean Red Cross early in June. Shimazu pointed out that the forty-seven would-be returnees included three types of people: some were officially registered as foreign residents in Japan; others had been detained in Ômura awaiting repatriation, but had temporarily been released; and others again had never been registered in Japan at all, but were "100% illegal entrants." According to information obtained by the South Korean government (who were following events with mounting concern and anger), five of the forty-seven were in fact Ômura detainees released on parole.

The fear of arrest and deportation that hung over the heads of a number of the protestors makes their enthusiasm for repatriation to North Korea much easier to imagine.

As Shimazu eagerly explained to his North Korean counterpart, the distinctive composition of the group also meant that they constituted the perfect test case for the start of a mass repatriation.

Two days after William Michel and Eugène de Weck left Tokyo for Hong Kong, the demonstrations outside the Red Cross headquarters took a new turn.

Realizing that they had no hope of transport to North Korea in a Red Cross vessel, the forty-seven protestors decided that they would try to reach Korea via China, paying the costs of the journey by themselves, and they asked the Japan Red Cross Society to book berths for them on a Hong Kong–bound ship belonging to the British shipping company Butterfield and Swire. The Red Cross complied with great speed and efficiency. On 18 June, the protestors were told that the way was clear for them to leave for North Korea at their own expense, and the sit-in demonstration that had lasted for more than two months was called off.

In fact, the Japan Red Cross Society was unusually well prepared to respond to this request. As the evidence they had presented to the Diet in February shows, Red Cross officials had already been considering Butterfield's ships as a possible method for repatriating Koreans more than three months earlier. The Red Cross had also been busy for the previous several months canvassing other possible solutions to the transport problem.

A week before the start of the demonstration by the forty-seven, Inoue had written to inform Leopold Boissier of the Japan Red Cross Governing Board's unanimous view that it was "indispensable to repatriate at least 60,000 Koreans within this year." He then went on to discuss the problem of transporting such a large number of people in such a short time. One option, he observed, was to "remodel Japanese cargo-boats." However, while technically possible ("we did it during the war"), this was not a wholly desirable way of carrying out a humanitarian venture, and his preferred option was to ask the ICRC to assist in borrowing "liberty-style ships."

The protestors' plea provided a legitimate opportunity to find a practical solution to the problem. The Red Cross had promptly contacted Butterfield and Swire and the Hong Kong colonial authorities to book tickets for the forty-seven returnees and arrange their transit via Hong Kong to North Korea.

By the middle of June indeed, Inoue was already "planning to organize the second and third repatriation groups." He intended, however, to wait until the first group had reached North Korea safely before moving ahead with plans for subsequent shipments. As Shimazu wrote to the manager of Butterfield and Swire and to the Governor General of Hong Kong, "If the repatriation in question is carried out successfully through Hongkong, it means that an example has been established that the repatriation to North Korea in mass of Koreans in Japan is possible, and the Japanese Red Cross is decided to send the next group of Koreans via Tientsin [Tianjin] by the SS. Hupeh of the same company."

Meanwhile, Shimazu also wrote to Pyongyang to let the North Korean Red Cross know that this small repatriation of forty-seven people was just "the first step." Once this had been "carried out successfully without hindrance from the other side, only then can we consider the next step, which is the repatriation of those Koreans who are unable to afford their traveling expenses." Would the North Korean side, he asked, be prepared to cover the costs for such future returnees, which he calculated at around US$35 per adult (half-price for children)? Helpfully, the Japanese Red Cross had already confirmed that Butterfield would be happy to receive payments directly from North Korea. Less helpfully, neither Shimazu nor anyone else seems to have explained to the North Korean Red Cross that the number of returnees being contemplated in that year was sixty thousand.

The North Koreans quickly telegraphed back, confirming arrangements to welcome the forty-seven returnees. They did not, however, make any commitments about Shimazu's "next step." The ICRC, meanwhile, accepted a request from Tokyo to issue travel documents to the forty-seven protestors (none of whom had a passport).

By the second half of June, then, the return of the forty-seven seemed to be near fulfillment, and it was time to press ahead with plans for the future.

On 18 June 1956 (the day when the forty-seven protestors ceased their demonstration) Inoue flew out of Japan bound for Tianjin, where he was due to take part in a meeting with the Chinese Red Cross. Shortly before leaving, he contacted his North Korean counterpart, Shin Yeong-Geun, asking him to come to Tianjin for a highly secret meeting on a resolution to the problem of Koreans in Japan.

The private talks between Inoue and Shin, held in the last week of June, were (according to Inoue's account) "long and difficult." The North Korean side, though, seems to have seen the events unfolding in Japan in a positive light, and was already preparing to greet the forty-seven returnees.

On the eve of the secret meeting between Inoue and Shin, North Korean leader Kim Il-Sung put his signature to DPRK Cabinet Order No. 53—On Stabilizing the Living of the Korean Citizens Returning from Japan. This ordered the North Korean Red Cross Society and Pyongyang local authorities to provide "houses, food and all other things needed" to returnees from Japan, some of whom (according to the order) were expected to arrive "early in July." The decree also provided loans to enable returnees to set themselves up in agriculture, craft production, or commerce and offered assistance with health care and children's education. In addition, returnees were each to receive, free of charge, "one suit of summer clothes, one pair of footwear, one set of summer underwear and one blanket." The order was to be "effective whether the Korean citizens in Japan return home individually or collectively in the future." As later statements would make clear, however, the North Koreans at this stage seem to have had no notion of accepting a mass inflow on the scale that eventually took place.

In Tianjin, Inoue and Shin's arduous discussions succeeded in establishing further basic principles for financing the repatriation. First, it was agreed as a general principle that the sending side should cover travel costs within its own border, while the receiving side covered all other travel costs. In addition, the Japanese side acknowledged that it should cover all the costs of transportation for repatriates who had been forced laborers or recruits to the Japanese armed forces in colonial times. However, Inoue made it clear that the Japanese government could not in practice contribute to the costs of repatriation while it was still engaged in sensitive political negotiations with South Korea, since any visible Japanese support for repatriation would lead to an instant collapse of these negotiations. For the time being, then, it was agreed that North Korea would pay all the travel expenses of returnees.

Passing on this information to Geneva, Inoue acknowledged that North Korea was unlikely to be willing to bear the full costs of the plan for long, and he anticipated that Japan might be in a position to start picking up its share of the bill by autumn of that year.

By this time, travel plans for the forty-seven returnees seemed at last to have been finalized. Berths had been booked for them on a Butterfield ship, the *Hunan*, which was due to sail from the port of Miike in Kyushu on 7 July. The protestors, most of whom had sold their homes and belongings before the start of the demonstration, and many of whom had been camping out on the streets for months, packed their bags and (surely with profound sighs of relief) left Tokyo by train on 5 July, bound for Miike.

But at 11:00 a.m. on the day when they were due to board their ship, an urgent international telephone call was put through to the Japan Red Cross Headquarters in Tokyo. Butterfield and Swire were calling to say that the *Hunan* would no longer be stopping at the port of Miike during its current voyage.

The shipping company was withdrawing from the repatriation scheme.

As it turned out, the Japanese Red Cross, Butterfield and Swire, and others involved in the story had reckoned without the fury of the South Korean government.

The Syngman Rhee regime's position on repatriation to North Korea had been made clear to Michel and de Weck during their visit in May and could be summed up in a single sentence:

There is no North Korea.

As far as the South Korean government was concerned, it was the only legitimate government of the entire Korean Peninsula. All Koreans were its citizens, and repatriating any of them to the section of the country temporarily under "enemy occupation" was simply out of the question.

The Japanese government, of course, had been aware from the start that heated opposition could be expected from South Korea. That was why Japanese politicians and bureaucrats had sought to involve the International Committee of the Red Cross in the first place. Even they, however, had not quite been prepared for the ferocity of the South Korean reaction.

The South Korean side knew little or nothing about the complex negotiations that had been going on between Tokyo, Geneva, and Pyongyang. During their visit to Seoul, though, Michel and de Weck had cautiously raised the repatriation issue. The South Korean government realized that something was afoot, and their concerns were soon heightened by press reports emanating from Japan.

By late June, the Rhee government was seriously alarmed, and on 27 June it lodged what was to be the first of a series of strenuous protests with the Japanese Foreign Ministry. The message conveyed (as Shimazu reported to the ICRC) was that, if Japan did not take steps to prevent the repatriation of Koreans to North Korea, this would be regarded as a violation of the terms of the Korean armistice and an indirect declaration of war.

South Korea of course was in no position to contemplate a real war with Japan. Both countries were deeply dependent on the United States, which would certainly not allow the rising tensions between them to threaten East Asian security. But the Rhee government was deadly serious about its adamant opposition to a mass repatriation to North Korea, and if it was not in fact about to use military means to prevent it, it was at least prepared to deploy some more unconventional weapons.

First, there were the Ômura detainees. If Japan insisted on pursuing plans for repatriations to North Korea, the Rhee government could and would refuse to accept any deportees from Ômura at all, leaving the already overcrowded detention center to fill to bursting.

Then there was South Korea's own counterpart to Ômura: a walled compound of buildings on the outskirts of Busan, which William Michel and Eugène de Weck inspected during their stay in South Korea. This was where the South Korean government held some seven hundred Japanese fishermen whom it had arrested for violating its territorial waters.

At the start of the U.S. occupation of Japan and Korea, a rough dividing line—originally known as the MacArthur Line—had been drawn in the East Sea separating Japan from its former colony and defining the limits of each country's fishing rights. The contours of this line were revised in 1946, and became the source of growing controversy between Japan and Korea from 1949 onward. In 1953, the Rhee government had unilaterally adopted, and in some places extended, this line as the limit of Korea's territorial waters. The new boundary, known as "the Rhee Line" in Japanese and "the Peace Line" in Korean, ran as far as two hundred miles from the Korean coast in some places, and Japanese fishermen who crossed this line were liable to arrest by the Korean authorities for illegal fishing.

Until the mid-1950s, fishermen caught crossing the Rhee line had generally been sent home to Japan after a brief period of imprisonment, though their boats were often impounded. But as conflicts emerged over the deportation of detainees from Ômura, the South Korean government had come to realize that the fishermen made very useful bargaining counters in negotiations with Japan and began to detain them for prolonged periods of time. Conditions in the Busan Detention Center were tough, and detainees repeatedly complained of poor food and inadequate medical care.

As the indirect war over repatriation intensified, the number of Japanese fishermen in Busan Detention Center was to soar, reaching over nine hundred by the last months of 1957.

Meanwhile, the South Korean government also picked up rumors of the arrangement with Butterfield and Swire and immediately contacted the British colonial authorities (and possibly also the company itself) to ensure that they withdrew from involvement in the repatriation scheme.

Hence the sudden change to the itinerary of the passenger ship *Hunan.*

By now, life for the forty-seven people seeking repatriation to North Korea was becoming increasingly miserable. They were stranded in the provincial port of Miike. They had no source of income, and any savings they may have had were rapidly disappearing. They had paid for berths on a ship that had just sailed past without stopping to pick them up, and they were trying to survive on a budget that barely allowed them each two meals of soup and rice a day.

Chongryun, which had supported their initial protests, seems to have lost interest in them and (according to Inoue Masutarô) began to condemn the protestors for putting their own personal interests ahead of those of the wider community. Meanwhile, as they must have been at least vaguely aware, the Japanese Red Cross saw them as a small part of a much larger strategy. Hopelessly entangled in Cold War politics, they were bewildered by the unexplained and seemingly interminable delays to their repatriation, and increasingly suspicious of the motives of the Japan Red Cross Society.

Their plight was particularly ironic because there had in fact never been any insuperable barrier preventing their moving from Japan to North Korea. As the Japanese government pointed out from time to time, Koreans in Japan did not need official permission to leave the country. Individuals who could pay for the costs of their own transport were free to travel to China and on to North Korea, and although it was difficult to arrange the itinerary and travel documents, it was not impossible; a very small number of Koreans from Japan had done so already.

It was the fact that the forty-seven had staged a group protest, and thus become identified as a "test case" for a mass repatriation, which had involved them in the political machinations that now left them high and dry, their future uncertain, their days—during the height of the Kyushu summer—spent huddled together in a single room temporarily borrowed from a local community center.

On 26 August, ten of the forty-seven began a hunger strike.

In Tokyo, meanwhile, something like a strange shadow puppet play was starting to unfold. The Japanese government's nerve was seriously shaken by the strength of the protest from Seoul. The Foreign Ministry had, of course, been kept fully informed of Inoue's secret repatriation negotiations in Tianjin, and had clearly hoped that, by using the Red Cross as a humanitarian intermediary, the repatriation could be carried out without foreign opposition. But the events of July 1956 made it clear that the Rhee regime would hold the Japanese government responsible for actions taken by the Japan Red Cross Society.

The reaction from the Japanese side was not to abandon the repatriation project altogether, but rather to intensify efforts to pursue it by remote control, helping to propel events forward while trying as hard a possible to appear uninvolved in the whole process. To avoid further unpleasantness with South Korea, it was decided that the planned future repatriations must be carried out under the name of the ICRC, with the international body's representative in Tokyo, Harry Angst, making all the necessary travel arrangements. However, as Shimazu Tadatsugu carefully explained, in a letter sent to Geneva with the approval of the Foreign Ministry and Ministry of Justice, "I don't think the above arrangement would be a great burden on Mr. Angst because all the business would be carried out by the Japanese Red Cross itself. What we need is only to use, so to say, the name of the ICRC instead of that of the Japanese Red Cross."

The byzantine results of this approach were further illustrated in mid-July, when Shimazu Tadatsugu wrote to the newly appointed Soviet chargé-d'affaires in Tokyo, Sergei Tikhvinsky, in an effort to find a Soviet ship as a replacement for Butterfield and Swire's ships to transport the repatriates.

Shimazu carefully outlined the humanitarian purposes of the repatriation, but then went on to explain that he himself was not actually requesting the use of a Russian ship. Rather, he wanted the Soviet Mission, in the greatest secrecy, to transmit a message from the Japanese Red Cross to the North Korean Red Cross. The purpose of this message was to ask the North Korean Red Cross to ask the USSR to make a ship available for repatriation.

Tikhvinsky was understandably mystified by this circuitous approach. When Inoue Masutarô called on him a couple of days later to follow up the matter, the chargé-d'affairs said that he was perfectly happy to discuss the use of Soviet ships for repatriation, but that his Mission was not prepared to act as a post office for messages between national Red Cross societies. Inoue, however, was reluctant to discuss the issue directly with Tikhvinsky. An indirect approach was of the utmost importance.

If Soviet ships were eventually used for a mass repatriation, the request to the USSR must appear to have come from North Korea and not from Japan.

In the end, the Japanese Red Cross sent the telegram to Pyongyang itself, and the Soviet Union decided not to provide a repatriation ship. In 1956 there were still no regular shipping lines between Japan and the USSR. Besides, according to Inoue, the Soviet government was afraid of a possible attack on the ship by South Korea and was reluctant at that stage to provide a naval escort. However, Inoue did subsequently receive a private assurance from Tikhvinsky that the Soviet Union would be willing to consider the issue again once regular shipping links with Japan had been established.

It was against this turbulent background that, in July 1956, senior officials of the International Committee of the Red Cross met in Geneva to consider their response to the information brought back by William Michel and Eugène de Weck from their special mission to East Asia.

The dilemma confronting them was obvious. Discussions in Tokyo with Troendle, Inoue, and others had made it clear that the Japanese authorities' motives for supporting a mass repatriation to North Korea were, to say the very least, dubious. Michel was inclined to dismiss some of Inoue's more extreme statements, which he described as "puerile," but he was deeply aware of the tangle of prejudice and politics that surrounded the whole issue.

On the other hand, there were the Ômura detainees, whose plight seemed a truly humanitarian one, and some of whom were genuinely seeking to be sent to North Korea. Then there were the forty-seven protestors, still waiting in growing desperation for transport out of Japan. Though confused by the wildly varying estimates of numbers, the ICRC accepted that there were also some other Koreans who would welcome assistance to resettle in North Korea. In addition, and on an even greater scale, there were the "disappeared" of the Korean War and the millions separated from their families by the division of the Korean Peninsula. These were issues that could not simply be ignored. After long and intense debate, the ICRC concluded that it should try to find a means of extracting the truly humanitarian problems from the web of political conflict and intrigue in which they had become entangled.

On 16 July 1956, Leopold Boissier sent a letter to the governments of Japan, North Korea, and South Korea, via their national Red Cross societies, formally offering the ICRC's services in helping "certain Koreans—living at present either in Japan or in Korea itself—who wished to find a home of their choice on Korean soil." A month later he followed this up with a letter proposing that representatives of the three national Red Cross societies should come to Geneva in mid-October for a meeting to discuss the problem.

The response was predictable. Japan and North Korea agreed, and immediately began preparing to send delegations to Geneva.

South Korea angrily refused to have anything to do with the matter.

The forty-eighth would-be returnee was born in the height of summer, around the time when the hunger strike started.

Inoue reported to Geneva that the hunger strike had "electrified" the whole Korean community in Japan, and he yet again evoked the specter of imminent riots that might spread throughout the country. The crisis, indeed, raised his prose style to new levels of hyperbole: the hunger strike, Inoue wrote to Boissier, conjured up images of impending violence that "thrilled me with horror. I felt as though I peeped into the hole of the furnace of Dante."

Pressure was intensifying for the ICRC to provide a quick resolution to the repatriation problem. Unsure whether to treat the forty-eight as a special case or to push ahead with a general repatriation plan in which they could be included, the International Committee vacillated. Eventually, on 12 December, Boissier again wrote to national societies of Japan and the two Koreas. The proposed three-party talks, he acknowledged, were clearly not going to take place, but "the freedom to change one's place of residence or return to one's native country must remain the inalienable right of all human beings," and the ICRC was willing at any time to offer its services to interested parties to protect this right.

For those in the Japanese establishment who sought to accomplish a mass "return" of Koreans to North Korea, the experiences of the past year had vividly illuminated three large barriers that still had to be overcome.

The first and most visible barrier was the vehement opposition of the South Korean government. Second, despite the welfare cuts and the publicity surrounding the demonstration by the forty-seven returnees, there had not yet been a dramatic upsurge of demands for repatriation from the Korean community itself. Clearly, something more would be needed to generate the anticipated tens of thousands of volunteers for repatriation. Third, North Korea itself, though happy to welcome some arrivals of returnees as part of its strategy of building bridges to the Korean community in Japan, had yet to show any marked enthusiasm for the idea of receiving a mass influx of people from Japan.

Over the next two years, imaginative schemes would be developed to overcome some of these barriers.

Meanwhile, the Japan Red Cross Society responded to a renewed offer of assistance from Geneva with some very concrete proposals of its own. Shimazu Tadatsugu sent a long letter to Boissier placing the repatriation issue in the context of the global upheavals of 1956. Although the repatriation problem appeared "quite different from the problems in Egypt and Hungary," it was, Shimazu suggested, "of the same nature in essence and, as seen in your letter, the solution cannot be postponed even a day."

Since it was now obvious that no compromise agreement acceptable to South Korea could be reached, Shimazu proposed that the ICRC should abandon efforts to reach a tripartite agreement and take the initiative in proposing its own detailed plan for the repatriation of *Zainichi* Koreans to North Korea; and he went on to spell out point by point what the key elements of this plan should be.

Despite Inoue Masutarô's Dantean visions, once the Red Cross and the government agreed to provide some emergency relief to the forty-eight Koreans, the hunger strike ended with little fanfare—and no sign of riots. But the events of August had provoked sharp criticism by the protestors of the Red Cross handing of the affair. Following a lunch with Inoue in September, Harry Angst noted that the forty-eight demonstrators were increasingly being regarded as a "nuisance" by the Japanese government and by the Japanese Red Cross, and that both "will be most happy to see the day arrive when this group will be able to leave Japan."

After a long search, berths were finally found on a Norwegian ship for twenty of the would-be returnees. They sailed from the port of Môji on 2 December and traveled via Shanghai to Pyongyang, arriving there to a warm public welcome on 14 December.

The remaining twenty-eight were left behind in Japan until spring of the following year. In the interim, the South Korean government repeatedly demanded promises from Japan that these people would not be given official permission to leave the country. Perhaps for this reason, when they finally did depart, on the last day of March 1957, it was on a Japanese fishing vessel, which smuggled them across the border to the North Korean port of Cheongjin without official clearance from the government. Curiously, having inundated the ICRC with letters about the forty-eight protestors in the middle of 1956, the Japan Red Cross Society seems to have said nothing at all to Geneva about the departure of the last twenty-eight. There is also no evidence in the files to suggest that they had made arrangements for the North Koreans to receive the returnees at the other end.

But then again, the documentary records are riddled with strange silences, and many mysteries still surround this first return.

Was the 1956 protest, whose timing fitted so well with Michel and de Weck's visit and with wider plans for mass repatriation, really a pure, spontaneous coincidence? Or did this group of would-be returnees, with its illegal migrants and its detainees on parole from Ômura, receive covert encouragement from on high to start their demonstration?

Whatever its origins and however troubled its course, the first return played its part in the making of the mass repatriation. By the time the second group of twenty-eight left Japan on their clandestine voyage to Cheongjin, the ICRC had issued the memorandum that was to become the basis for the repatriation of tens of thousands more.

I cannot help thinking about those twenty-eight adults and children, arriving at the coast near Cheongjin on a Japanese fishing boat on 4 April 1957, after a five-day voyage that must surely have been rough, uncomfortable, and anxious. What happened to them when they stepped on to dry land? Was the North Korean Red Cross there to greet them? Were family and friends waiting for them? Did they receive the promised houses and loans, the blankets and shoes, the summer suits and underwear?

It is only fifty years ago. Though the adults may now be dead, at least some of the children who traveled on that boat should still be alive today. Are they there somewhere, among the elderly farmers whom I see trudging along the road with the ox carts and their loads of firewood? Or among the grandparents in their best clothes, brought into Pyongyang from around the country for the Arirang Festival and strolling along the park accompanied by wide-eyed grandchildren?

A few days after my arrival in the city, I go to Mangyeongdae, on the shores of Pyongyang's Daedong River, to visit the supposed birthplace of North Korea's late but eternal president, Kim Il-Sung. Many of the stories about Kim's birth and childhood exploits in the carefully preserved group of thatched farmhouses are of dubious veracity. But the legends surrounding his origins have provided a reason to create a large wooded park, whose immaculately swept paths wind through glades of autumn trees to a plateau overlooking the river and city beyond.

Though the park is thronged with visitors, on this afternoon I seem to be the only foreign visitor. Seeing one fragile, wrinkled old woman in her *chima jeogori*, who tugs on her grandson's arm to distract his gaze from my strange foreign face, I realize that there is an absence in the North Korean landscape that has been nagging subconsciously at the back of my mind— I have not seen any graves. Traveling around South Korea, you often pass small graveyards on the hillsides, containing the miniature tumuli of Korean tombs. In Jeju, wealthier rural families at least have family tombs in the midst of their fields, each surrounded by a low stone wall—the work of the living going on all around the presence of the ancestral dead. Where do North Korean communities, I wonder, bury their dead?

My guides have taken me to see historical tombs including the beautiful mausoleum of King Kongmin and his wife, not far from the thirty-eighth parallel, with its guardian statues looking out across the misty valley and squirrels and chipmunks playing in the canopy of the silent forest around. They have pointed out the Towers of Eternity, surmounted with red glass torches, which stand in the middle of so many villages, commemorating the Great Leader and Eternal President, Kim Il-Sung.

But the North Korean hillsides—many of them denuded of trees by chronic fuel shortage, scored to their very summits with tiny terraces of dry maize—seem devoid of monuments to the ordinary, everyday dead.

Where are the dead of the first return from Japan buried? And what stories did they take to the grave with them?

12

RESOLUTION 20

Humanity—The Red Cross, born of a desire to bring assistance without discrimination to the wounded on the battlefield, endeavours—in its international and national capacity—to prevent and alleviate human suffering, wherever it may be found. Its purpose is to protect life and health and to ensure respect for the human being. It promotes mutual understanding, friendship, cooperation and lasting peace among all people.

Impartiality—It makes no discrimination as to nationality, race, religious beliefs, class or political opinions. It endeavours to relieve the suffering of individuals, being guided solely by their needs, and to give priority to the most urgent cases of distress.

Neutrality—In order to continue to enjoy the confidence of all, the Red Cross may not take sides in hostilities or engage at any time in controversies of a political, racial, religious or ideological nature.

Thus the first three of the seven Fundamental Principles of the Red Cross, as codified by international human rights lawyer Jean Pictet. These principles, which guide the work of the Red Cross today, were condensed in the 1960s from a longer and more philosophical treatise on the subject that Pictet published in 1956.

Inoue Masutarô was very familiar with Pictet's principles, for he spent the first part of 1957 translating the longer version of the principles into Japanese. A copy of his translation, with a foreword by Shimazu Tadatsugu, was ceremonially presented to the ICRC in October of that year. In the autographed copy that he sent to Pictet himself, Inoue inscribed the French translation of a poem written by the Empress Teimei, consort of the Emperor Taishô, and regarded by the Japanese Red Cross as an expression of its core beliefs:

That all the countries of the world
May become friends, aiding one another
To come to the help
Of the unfortunate,
And that we may bring them
A little happiness.

In an age when the slogans of humanity, peace, and freedom are so often abused by those who seek their opposites, it is easy to be cynical about the lofty sentiments of Pictet's principles. It is tempting to see them as pious platitudes, thin veils for the Machiavellian realities of international politics. But dreams of peace and the relief of human suffering that they embody have in fact saved countless lives and inspired countless acts of compassion in almost every country of the world.

In Japan, thousands of ordinary local Red Cross volunteers, with at least the sketchy outline of these principles in their minds, have over the years visited the sick and elderly and helped provide relief after the earthquakes, floods, and the other natural disasters that are an inescapable part of the rhythms of Japanese life. The Cold War stratagems of the repatriation scheme were not of their making; and when the principles were manipulated for political ends, it was their good faith (among other things) that was betrayed.

In Geneva, the International Red Cross officials—Leopold Boissier, Roger Gallopin, William Michel, Eugène de Weck, and the rest of them—certainly also had the fundamental principles of their organization somewhere in mind while they wrestled with the repatriation issue.

At the same time, they were constrained by the distinctive ICRC tradition of humanitarianism.

As a body created to help the wounded of both sides during battle, the ICRC has always tried to work in cooperation with national governments, using negotiation rather than confrontation as its chosen weapon, and winning the trust of state authorities by respecting their confidentiality. Most of its projects are pursued through quiet diplomacy, conducted away from the media spotlight in small, anonymous meeting rooms.

This approach can produce remarkable results. But it is an approach that also contains its own particular risks.

One risk is that the international organization may become dependent on information supplied by national officialdom. And when (as in the case of repatriation to North Korea), officials in Geneva have little direct contact with the people whose suffering they are trying to relieve, that dependence can be a dangerous thing. Schooled in the traditions of quiet diplomacy, ICRC officials also tend to be wary of offending governments, particularly when these are the governments of countries with large and well-funded national Red Cross societies.

The dangers of this approach were to become all too apparent in the events that unfolded from the start of 1957 to the departure of the first repatriation ship in December 1959.

On 26 February 1957, Leopold Boissier sent a confidential memorandum on repatriation to the Red Cross societies of Japan and the two Koreas for transmission to their national governments. This February Memorandum, which was the outcome of much soul searching within the corridors of the ICRC headquarters, set out proposed guidelines for the repatriation of ethnic Koreans from Japan to Korea (North or South) and was ultimately (with modifications) to provide the basis on which tens of thousands of people boarded the repatriation ships in Niigata for the journey to North Korea.

On paper, the memorandum seems cautious, reasonable, and eminently responsible.

As soon as the Red Cross societies and governments of "the countries of present residence and destination" agree to the repatriation (its provisions state), the ICRC is to send a special mission to Japan to examine requests for "return" from *Zainichi* Koreans and to verify that they are truly departing of their own free will to the destination of their choice. The costs of repatriation are to be shared by the Red Cross societies of the sending and receiving country.

The memorandum, in fact, echoed key elements of the scheme suggested to the ICRC by Japan Red Cross president Shimazu Tadatsugu two months earlier. One of its proposals, however, came as a deep disappointment to Shimazu and his colleagues in Tokyo. They had hoped that the ICRC would supply Red Cross ships to carry the returnees. This, of course, would heighten the international humanitarian gloss of the project and reduce the visibility of the Japanese government's participation. But the international body refused to make such a large commitment to so politically contentious a scheme. Boissier's memorandum insisted that Japan must find the ships itself.

The ICRC officials who drew up the memorandum were not naïve. They knew that free will is an elusive thing, too easily created, molded, or destroyed by outside forces. Discussing the memorandum with Inoue Masutarô, for example, ICRC Executive Director Roger Gallopin was at pains to insist that, to have real value, any confirmation of the free will of repatriates "must be conducted peacefully and entirely without political propaganda."

What Gallopin and other ICRC members failed to recognize was their own utter powerlessness to turn these good intentions into reality.

The response to the February Memorandum from North and South Korea followed the then familiar pattern. North Korea sent a polite but guarded reply, expressing its continued preference for a face-to-face meeting between representatives from Japan and the two Koreas. South Korea refused to have anything at all to do with the scheme.

But the reaction from Japan, the most eager proponent of the project, was more complex.

By coincidence, the day before Leopold Boissier dispatched the February Memorandum, Japan had acquired a new prime minister, Kishi Nobusuke.

One of the most influential and controversial figures in postwar Japanese politics, Kishi was an enthusiastic nationalist who had been intimately involved in wartime economic planning. Like Shigemitsu Mamoru, he had subsequently been detained as a suspected Class A war criminal and spent a while in prison before returning to political life in the early 1950s. Kishi was also part of a political dynasty whose history has been inseparable from that of the Liberal Democratic Party. His brother, Satô Eisaku,★ was to become prime minister in the 1960s and early 1970s; his son-in-law, Abe Shintarô, was to serve as foreign minister; and his grandson, Abe Shinzô, became prime minister in September 2006.

While his immediate predecessors had been eager to strengthen Japan's economic and diplomatic links with the Communist world, Kishi Nobusuke had different priorities. A passionate supporter of the alliance with the United States, Kishi focused his foreign policy on the task of renewing the Japan–United States Security Treaty—a highly controversial issue at a time when many Japanese people would have preferred their country to take a less partisan position in global Cold War rivalries. Kishi also hoped to restore a resurgent Japan's economic influence in the non-Communist parts of Asia, including South Korea, and his administration

---

★Kishi was born Satô Nobusuke but (following a practice that is not unusual in Japan) was adopted into a wealthier family and took their surname.

promptly embarked on negotiations to try to resolve the crisis in relations with the Syngman Rhee regime.

Throughout 1957 and 1958, a slow and intricate dance of backdoor diplomacy between the Kishi government in Japan and Syngman Rhee government in South Korea unfolded, as both countries sought a path toward the establishment of diplomatic relations. The two partners would approach one another, almost reaching the point of contact, only for some sudden disturbance to send them swirling away in opposite directions; acrimony and estrangement would persist for a while, and then the gradual convergence would begin all over again.

With these delicate negotiations going on, some officials and LDP politicians felt that the scheme to send large numbers of *Zainichi* Koreans to North Korea was a dangerous distraction from more important issues and should be abandoned. But Kishi himself seems to have seen things a little differently.

The Republic of Korea's Syngman Rhee regime insisted that all Koreans in Japan were South Korean citizens, but—struggling with its own problems of rural poverty and high unemployment—it showed no enthusiasm for encouraging their return to the South. There was, therefore, a risk that, once diplomatic relations were established with South Korea, repatriation of *Zainichi* Koreans, whether to North or South Korea, would become impossible. Official hopes of radically decreasing the size of Japan's ethnic minority population would then be dashed. From this point of view, one appealing option was to attempt a large-scale repatriation to North Korea as soon as the immediate problem of the Busan and Ômura detainees had been resolved, but before the formal normalization of relations with the South.

Meanwhile, it had not escaped the notice of the Japanese government that the threat of a repatriation of Koreans to the North could, if handled with care, provide a powerful lever for putting pressure on South Korea should normalization talks stall.

Above all, repatriation to North Korea was popular with the Left as well as the Right. At a time when Japanese politics was becoming dangerously divided, this was the one issue that could win support from many Liberal Democratic Party members, while also building bridges to the Communist camp, thus tempering the Kishi administration's pro-American, hawkish public image.

For some figures in the Japanese government, then, it was not a matter of choosing between repatriation to the North or diplomatic relations with the South. Rather, deft juggling might make both aims achievable; it was all a matter of careful timing and skillful diplomatic gamesmanship.

In Japan, therefore, there was much debate about an appropriate response to the February Memorandum. Eventually, on 13 May 1957, Shimazu Tadatsugu officially informed the International Red Cross that the Japanese government agreed "in principle" with the plan set out in the memorandum. However, because of the "delicate situation" caused by the current round of negotiations about Ômura and Busan, the Kishi government wished to "deliberate cautiously on the time for the execution of the plan." The Japanese side would let the ICRC know when it felt the opportune moment for implementing the memorandum had arrived.

Kishi's perspective on repatriation became clearer in August 1957, when Shimazu Tadatsugu wrote to the prime minister and to several other Cabinet members, reminding them that the February Memorandum was still on the table, waiting to be put into action. The solution to the repatriation problem, Shimazu pointed out, had been "very much delayed."

Prime Minister Kishi, who concurrently held the foreign affairs portfolio, chose to reply in his capacity as foreign minister. He stressed that, in order to carry out a mass repatriation to North Korea with Japan providing the transport and logistical support, it would first be necessary to obtain the consent "or at least the tolerance" of the Rhee government. Otherwise, there was a risk of a South Korean attack on the repatriation ships themselves and a virtual certainty that South Korea would wreak revenge by increasing the number of Japanese fishermen held in Busan. What was needed, Kishi suggested, was for the ICRC to put moral pressure on South Korea to acquiesce in the scheme "by explaining its humanitarian intent." He urged the Japan Red Cross Society to take this suggestion up with the ICRC.

The timing was fortunate, for a great global celebration of humanitarianism, the International Conference of the Red Cross, was about to take place in New Delhi. The climax of the conference would be the passing of a series of resolutions to guide and strengthen Red Cross action in the coming years.

The outcome of Kishi's suggestion was the complex politics surrounding the New Delhi Conference's Resolution 20: a perfect and intriguing case of the multiple uses to which humanitarianism may be put.

The Red Cross movement's International Conferences (like the Olympics) are held once in four years and bring together participants from every corner of the globe. The nineteenth conference, which opened on 28 October

1957, met in the Vigyan Bhavan, a newly built convention center in the political heart of New Delhi, surrounded by the breathtaking monuments to imperial hubris that an independent India had inherited from the British Raj.

The conference's plenary sessions were held in the air-conditioned splendor of the Vigyan Bhavan's main meeting hall, which seated over a thousand people and was equipped with the latest simultaneous translation equipment. But away from the grand ceremony of the plenary sessions, there were plenty of opportunities for quiet diplomacy, as national societies and ICRC officials took advantage of the occasion to conduct private discussions in backrooms and hotel lobbies.

At the conference's opening session, with delegations from Japan and the two Koreas watching from the auditorium, Leopold Boissier took his place at the main dais, while other leading ICRC officials, including Roger Gallopin and William Michel, sat in a row beneath a giant Red Cross flag at the back of the podium, listening as Indian Prime Minister Jawaharlal Nehru addressed the assembled delegates.

A key task of the New Delhi conference was to strengthen international conventions for the protection of civilians in wartime. Another important issue (in the year when the desegregation of Little Rock High School marked the first upsurge of the U.S civil rights movement) was the worldwide campaign against racial discrimination. Responding to growing international awareness of the problem of racism, the conference's Resolution 34 appealed to national societies to make "special efforts to plan well conceived campaigns in the field of individual and social mental health against prejudice, discrimination and racialism and to extend aid to the victims of these evils in accord with the humanitarian traditions of the Red Cross."

While Resolution 34 was topical and a little contentious, Resolution 20, the main focus of interest for the Japanese delegation, was entirely unobjectionable and was passed unanimously. Indeed, it is hard to imagine anyone seriously opposing it. The resolution draws attention to the separation of families as a result of war and other disasters, and commits national governments and Red Cross societies to "facilitate by every means the reunion of persons, both adults and children, with their families in accordance with the wishes of such persons."

In fact, however, Resolution 20 was more than a mere set of benign platitudes. In response to Prime Minister Kishi's suggestions, the Japanese Red Cross had engaged in intensive lobbying in the weeks leading up to the

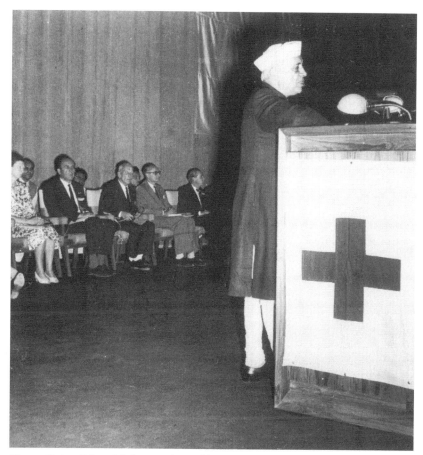

Figure 12.1.   Prime Minister Nehru addresses the opening session of the International Conference of the Red Cross, New Delhi, October 1957. (© ICRC)

conference. For one thing, the Japanese delegation to New Delhi energetically insisted that the ICRC use the conference as an opportunity to intervene in Japan's disputes with South Korea. This, it was hoped, would put pressure on South Korea to accept deportees from Ômura and release Japanese fishermen held in Busan. Once these problems were resolved, the way would be clear for Japan to move ahead with the repatriation to North Korea.

Meanwhile, the Japan Red Cross Society also proposed a conference resolution explicitly supporting the rights of displaced people to repatriation. The ICRC's reaction to this proposal, however, was cautious. Committee officials pointed out to Tokyo that such a resolution was unlikely to be accepted without thorough prior discussion, and there was no time for that at this late stage. Instead, the Japanese delegation was persuaded to throw its support behind the more vaguely worded Resolution 20 on the "reunion of families" which, with skilful interpretation, could serve its purposes equally well.

Despite the all-embracing language of the resolution, and despite the fact that a mass repatriation of *Zainichi* Koreans to North Korea would certainly divide more families than it reunited, Resolution 20 had (from the Japanese delegation's point of view) a very clear practical aim: to secure the return the fishermen detained in Busan and the departure of the detainees in Ōmura, and (above all) to pressure South Korea to acquiesce in a mass repatriation of *Zainichi* Koreans to North Korea. For, as Inoue Masutarô carefully explained in a leaflet sent to the world's national Red Cross societies at the beginning of 1959, "The whole Korean Peninsula is the 'home' of the Koreans residing in Japan in the meaning of Resolution No. 20 of the New Delhi Conference."

The aim of Resolution 20 was made particularly plain in an exchange about the conference that took place between Tokyo and Pyongyang.

No detailed records of the discussions between Japanese and North Korean delegates in New Delhi appear to have survived. But soon after his return to Tokyo, Japan Red Cross vice president Kasai wrote to Pyongyang, expressing his delight at having had another chance to meet the North Korean Red Cross' two vice presidents "and other old friends of mine" at the New Delhi conference. In particular, Kasai wanted to share with his North Korean friends his pleasure at the fact the conference had unanimously adopted Resolution 20, for this created "a positive foundation" for the issue of common interest to both their societies: the repatriation of *Zainichi* Koreans.

Based on Resolution 20, the Japan Red Cross Society was "now carefully studying how to materialize the long waited wish" of Koreans in Japan to return to their homeland.

As in 1956, the Japan Red Cross Society offered details of a "test case"—this time, a man who had been brought to Japan as a forced laborer and who had relatives in North Korea. "If we succeed in that case," wrote Kasai, "the way will be open for future repatriation."

Resolution 20 also helped the Japanese delegation to gain ICRC intervention in negotiations with South Korea. Immediately after the Conference, on 3 December 1957, ICRC executive director Roger Gallopin responded to Japan Red Cross requests by writing to the foreign ministers of Japan and South Korea. Citing the newly passed resolution, Gallopin volunteered the ICRC's services to help return the Busan and Ômura detainees to their homelands, and proposed a practical plan for the mutual release of detainees.

This intervention produced dramatic results. While the Red Cross delegates were meeting in the Vigyan Bhavan, the Kishi and Rhee governments had been locked in negotiations on the intractable problems of the Ômura and Busan detainees. As Shimazu Tadatsugu reported to Geneva in 1958, Japan had been trying the resolve the Ômura issue for more than six years, but "it was only last year, after the New Delhi Conference that any serious progress could be noticed."

Resolution 20, in short, had given the Japanese government the very thing that—as Swiss Minister Max Troendle had told Michel and de Weck more than a year earlier—they needed to pursue their aims: a way of isolating South Korea on the repatriation and related issues, by showing the South Korean position to be at odds with the globally recognized humanitarian policies of the international Red Cross.

On the very last day of 1957, an agreement on Ômura and Busan was signed by the Japanese and South Korean governments; Japan was to drop certain claims that it had attempted to assert over property left behind by Japanese colonists in Korea and would release on parole the Ômura detainees who had lived in Japan since colonial times. In return, South Korea was to agree to accept all postwar "illegal migrants" deported from Ômura and return the Japanese fishermen detained in Busan.

Full-scale negotiations on the normalization of relations between Japan and South Korea, in abeyance since 1953, were reopened, and both sides seemed ready to make concessions. But it very quickly became clear that the December 1957 agreement had a fundamental flaw: it had said nothing about the Ômura illegal migrants—over ninety people in all—who identified themselves with North Korea. The South Korean government assumed that Japan would deport them to South Korea; the Japanese government refused to do so. By January 1958, the North Korean government and Red Cross and left-wing groups in Japan were desperately lobbying the Japanese government to ensure that these people were not deported to the South.

As disputes over the interpretation of the agreement raged, some of the North Korean–affiliated detainees in Ômura, fearing that they were about to be deported to the South, began a hunger strike, and relations between Japan and South Korea once again deteriorated.

There was one particularly interesting feature of the Japanese delegation that had been formed to negotiate the normalization of relations with South Korea. A key member of the delegation was Japan's former ambassador to Argentina, who had been summoned home from Buenos Aires specifically for this task, somewhat to his own surprise since he had been out of Japan for the past five years and was (in his own words) "not really acquainted with Japan-Korea problems." The ambassador's name was Inoue Takajirô: He was none other than Inoue Masutarô's younger brother. The Japanese Ministry of Foreign Affairs had considered appointing the younger Inoue as chief negotiator, but eventually gave him the powerful but less visible position of deputy chief. They were aware that his family connections might alarm the South Koreans because of Inoue Masutarô known advocacy of repatriation to North Korea.

Meanwhile elder brother Masutarô was busy using Resolution 20 for some quiet but powerful lobbying activities of his own.

At the end of June 1958 the hunger strikers in Ômura received a visit from Angst and Inoue. The two men told them that the passing of the resolution in New Delhi had smoothed the way for their repatriation to North Korea. The Japanese government was willing to let them leave; the North Korean government was ready to receive them. It was only a matter of finding ships to carry them, and, since a regular shipping route had just been opened between Japan and the Soviet port of Nakhodka, this problem could now readily be solved.

The message from Inoue and Angst was not simply intended to cheer the detainees or encourage them to abandon their hunger strike. It was also designed as a loud and clear message to the Kim Il-Sung regime in Pyongyang. As Angst explained, since "the North Korean internees are in communication with their authorities in North Korea and considering that North Korea has an ambassador in Moscow," he and Inoue had urged leaders of the North Korean–affiliated detainee group to request that the Kim Il-Sung regime "approach the Soviets with a view to ascertaining whether or not Soviet vessels expected to call at Japanese ports in the near future could be used for repatriation of North Koreans in Japan."

To ensure that this request really reached its intended destination, on their return to Tokyo Angst and Inoue also held secret meetings with two officials of the General Association of Korean Residents in Japan (*Chongryun*) to discuss repatriation, On the afternoon of the same day, Inoue met Hatanaka Masaharu (chairman of the Japan-Korea Association, who had

**Figure 12.2.   Inside Ômura Detention Center during the Hunger Strike, June 1958.
The sign on the door reads "Life or Death!" (© ICRC)**

good personal access to the North Korean leadership) for talks which included a suggestion on the use of Soviet ships for repatriation.

A few days later, on 5 July 1958, Shimazu Tadatsugu sent a highly confidential telegram to the North Korean Red Cross, following up the contacts by Inoue and Angst, and urgently requesting North Korean cooperation with "our plan." Information sent by Inoue to the ICRC indicates that the plan in question involved a gradual release of detainees from Ômura on parole. Those released would then quietly be repatriated to North Korea on Soviet vessels as soon as these became available. There can be little doubt that the Japanese Red Cross leaders saw this (as they had seen the 1956 return) as the potential prelude to a mass repatriation.

Shimazu told the North Korean Red Cross that Inoue was about to make a formal request to the Japanese government to start the release of these detainees. The Japan Red Cross Society president also assured Pyongyang that he and his colleagues were confident of the "ultimate success of [the] plan," although it was "delicate, requiring time for repatriation." The Japanese Red Cross sought Pyongyang's "substantial help and approval" for the repatriation. Remembering the troubled course of the 1956 repatriation, however, Shimazu insisted that propaganda and publicity must at all costs be avoided. "Please recall our previous experiences," he wrote, "and give us quiet cooperation taking account [of] our very difficult position."

Meanwhile, during a parliamentary foreign affairs committee meeting on 3 July at which Inoue was called to give evidence, Foreign Minister Fujiyama discreetly implied that the Japanese government was considering calling in the ICRC to supervise a repatriation to North Korea, and soon after, with very little public fanfare, the government began to release the first North Korean affiliated detainees from Ômura on parole.

The negotiations with South Korea being conducted by Inoue Takajirô and his colleagues now grew increasingly acrimonious. Japanese negotiators were waiting to see whether the growing threat of a mass repatriation to North Korea would produce dramatic concessions from South Korea on other aspects of the normalization process. But the concessions failed to materialize, and by early 1959, discussions were once more gridlocked.

Opinion within the Japanese ruling party was still divided. Fujiyama favored the repatriation, but some members of the pro–South Korean lobby continued to oppose it. Prime Minister Kishi himself was cautious of making public statements on the issue, but by the start of 1959 was reported to be ready to move ahead with a repatriation scheme as soon as opposition from within the party was overcome. In January of that year, Kishi was re-elected party leader, and immediately after, the party's foreign affairs and public security committees decided to back the scheme.

Foreign Minister Fujiyama explained to the U.S. ambassador to Tokyo that the repatriation to North Korea was supported not only by the left-wing but also by conservatives in Japan because the "prospect of ridding [the] country of Korean minority is highly popular in view of their high crime rate, their political agitation and their pressure on [the] labour market." Another good reason for proceeding with the scheme, the foreign minister added, was the fact that "the burden of destitute Koreans on Japanese government institutions at all levels totals around 2.5 billion yen."

So now, finally, the Kishi government decided that the time had come; the implementation of the February Memorandum could be postponed no longer. On 13 February, the Japanese cabinet endorsed the policy, agreeing to "deal with the problem of the repatriation of *Zainichi* Koreans on the basis of the internationally accepted notion that the free choice of place of residence is a fundamental human right."

As demonstrations against the repatriation erupted throughout South Korea and the South Korean Defense Ministry threatened military action to stop the plan, the Japanese government moved quickly to set up a liaison committee that would put the mass repatriation into effect. The process would be supervised by the Japan Red Cross Society and ICRC, with backup from Japanese ministries as needed.

But by then, the circumstances surrounding the repatriation had been totally transformed.

For in mid-July 1958—a couple of weeks after the secret contacts by Inoue, Angst and Shimazu—the North Korean government had abruptly launched a new policy toward Koreans in Japan. As Shimazu had requested, this policy indeed offered "substantial help and approval" for a mass return to the socialist Fatherland. It also involved the use of Soviet ships. But far from providing the "quiet cooperation" which Shimazu had begged for, the Kim Il-Sung regime had chosen instead to trumpet its new policy to the world.

With the full support of the North Korean regime a massive propaganda campaign to encourage the return of Koreans from Japan was now in full swing.

IV

ACCORD

13

DREAM HOMES
ON THE DAEDONG

Han Deok-Su, chairman of the General Association of Korean Residents in Japan (*Chongryun*) was a sturdy, avuncular-looking man who seemed (at least to one of those who knew him) like a rather self-important, middle-aged farmer. His background was similar to that of many first-generation *Zainichi* Koreans. He had been born in a rural part of the Gyeongsang region of Korea in 1907 and had migrated to Japan in the 1920s, working on construction sites before becoming involved in labor organization.

Although left-wing in his politics, Han was above all a nationalist. In the early 1950s, he vehemently opposed the hot-headed young Korean Communists who joined their Japanese comrades in schemes to foment revolution within Japan. *Zainichi* Koreans, Han believed, should avoid entanglement in Japanese politics, behave as loyal citizens of the Democratic People's Republic of Korea, and follow the guidance of the Great Leader Kim Il-Sung—on whose personal style Han modeled his own leadership of *Chongryun*.

The creation of *Chongryun* in May 1955 marked the victory of Han Deok-Su's line over the revolutionary strategies of his rivals. But dissent surrounding the newly created organization did not disappear overnight. The first couple of years of *Chongryun*'s existence were a critical test of leadership for Han—a test from which he emerged triumphant.

He was to remain the organization's chairman for the next forty-seven years, until his death in 2001 at the age of ninety-four.

One of the sources of Han Deok-Su's power was undoubtedly the repatriation movement. From the start, he was a passionate advocate of a mass "return." Several members of his own family, indeed, would ultimately join the exodus to North Korea, though Han himself remained in Japan, living out the last years of his life in a large and well-guarded mansion in an affluent district of Tokyo.

Today in Japan, particularly since the revelations about the kidnapping of Japanese citizens by North Korea, *Chongryun* is reviled by the Japanese media and regarded with fear and suspicion by the public. It is seen as the sinister agency of a hostile rogue state. There are repeated rumors that some of its officials were involved in the kidnapping of Japanese citizens during the 1970s and 1980s.

Chongryun is also widely condemned for its central role in the repatriation. In 2003–2004, indeed, one Korean who had returned to North Korea and subsequently made his way via China to Seoul unsuccessfully sued the organization for damages, claiming that its deceptive propaganda had lured himself and other "returnees" to a terrible fate.

Condemnation of *Chongryun*'s role in the repatriation is well founded. Low-ranking members of the organization, to be sure, often acted in good faith. The dream of a socialist utopia seemed much more credible in the 1950s than it does today, and many of those who urged and helped their compatriots to return to the Socialist Homeland did so with a real belief that they were helping impoverished and oppressed people achieve a better life. Some now bitterly regret their actions.

But even among low-ranking members, there were those who knew enough about North Korea to harbor suspicions of *Chongryun*'s glowing propaganda images of the homeland. Senior cadres, who had far better access to information, had all the more reason to be aware of the gap between propaganda and reality.

Yet from the middle of 1958 onward, *Chongryun*'s leaders developed a massive and well-coordinated campaign to induce their fellow Koreans to leave Japan for North Korea. And as the repatriation project unfolded, the association assumed increasing control over its day-to-day management: drawing up lists of returnees; developing targets to be fulfilled; pressuring some Koreans to repatriate so as to meet those targets, while denying the requests of other would-be returnees whose desire for repatriation did not suit *Chongryun*'s or the North Korean government's political needs.

I am not sure how well Han Deok-Su was acquainted with Inoue Masutarô, but the two men certainly knew each other. As Inoue made very clear in his correspondence with Geneva, he preferred to deal with the repatriation issue via *Chongryun* rather than through the intermediary of other organizations like the Japan-Korea Association. Inoue's experience in dealing with Communist countries, particularly China, had shown him that the involvement of a variety of different interest groups only created confusion. Better by far to use a single intermediary with good links to the Communist government concerned—in this case, obviously *Chongryun*.

So two people whose social backgrounds were vastly different and whose political ideologies stood at opposite extremes of the Cold War divide found themselves engaged in a strange and steadily deepening collaboration. It was a very uneasy collaboration, often riven by bitter arguments over points of detail, but all the while cemented by their common commitment to a project that, for quite different reasons, served their own political aims.

This dangerous liaison went far beyond the personal level. In their pursuit of the goal of repatriation, key elements of the Japanese establishment promoted actions that greatly strengthened the power of *Chongryun*.

Repatriation enormously increased the influence of *Chongryun* over *Zainichi* Koreans and enhanced its profile in Japanese society at large. It ultimately enabled the organization to extend its control deep into the Korean community, operating as migration agency and de facto network of consulates combined. Since many of those who departed for North Korea entrusted the property they left behind in Japan to *Chongryun*, the scheme also generated huge inflows of wealth into the organization's coffers.

The results were not only a tragedy for many thousands of returnees. They also had lasting effects that haunt Japan's Korean community, and Japanese society as a whole, to the present day.

Han Deok-Su's enthusiasm for mass repatriation to North Korea was made very clear in the meeting that Inoue arranged for him with William Michel and Eugène de Weck in May 1956. There was, in fact, an interesting difference between the mood of this encounter and that of the meetings that Michel and de Weck held with officials in Pyongyang. While the North Korean Red Cross officials were reserved and cautious, quoting modest numbers of potential returnees and refusing the ICRC's offer to mediate in the repatriation, Han and his *Chongryun* colleagues were expansive and predicted the departure of tens of thousands of *Zainichi* Koreans to the Fatherland.

Over the two years that followed, *Chongryun* continued to promote the cause of repatriation with vigor, focusing its efforts most strongly on the return of detainees from Ōmura and students wishing to enter North Korean universities. But it was not until 1958 that the organization quite suddenly and dramatically embarked on a full-fledged, public campaign for a mass exodus to North Korea.

On 11 August 1958, a group of *Zainichi* Koreans living in Kawasaki, near Tokyo, held a meeting at which they spoke of their longing to return to the Socialist Fatherland. At the conclusion of the meeting, they decided to write a letter to Kim Il-Sung, asking for his support in realizing this dream.

As though this were a spark igniting a pile of kindling, within a couple of weeks, a mass movement for repatriation swept like wildfire across Japan. And this time it quickly became clear that the movement (unlike the small demonstration of 1956) had the wholehearted backing of the North Korean regime. On 8 September, at a public gathering celebrating the tenth anniversary of the founding of the People's Democratic Republic, Kim Il-Sung announced that his country would open its doors and its heart to the return of the Korean compatriots from Japan. A week later Foreign Minister Nam Il followed this up with an assurance that Koreans in Japan who returned to the Socialist Fatherland would find houses, jobs, education, and welfare waiting for them.

The response from *Chongryun* was ecstatic. The organization's newspaper *Chôsen Sôren* and sympathetic journals began to publish a flood of articles reporting the growing wave of people demanding return to North Korea. The miseries of life in Japan, particularly since the welfare cuts of 1956, were vividly contrasted with the hope of a new life in the Republic. In North Korea, readers were assured, the state provided all the basic necessities of life—housing, education, health care, even monthly food rations—free of charge. There would be no fear of unemployment or discrimination. Returning Koreans would be citizens in their own land.

The topic quickly became a sensation in the Japanese media, too. By October 1958, the Japanese press was reporting mass attendances at *Chongryun* rallies and quoting the association's claims that fifty to sixty thousand people might be repatriated "within this year." Socialist and Communist parliamentarians energetically lobbied the Japanese government to implement a repatriation plan at once and to abandon attempts at negotiation with South Korea.

The Japanese government, in media reports, tended to be depicted as an honest and innocent intermediary caught in the cross fire between the two Koreas. The Kishi administration was presented as being aware of the humanitarian issues at stake but fearful of offending the obdurately hostile Syngman Rhee regime. This image of the government's position was most vividly captured in a cartoon published by the *Yomiuri* newspaper in February 1959. Japanese Foreign Minister Fujiyama Aiichirô, wrapped in the Red Cross flag, is shown standing between a large and menacing thug in traditional Korean dress, labeled "South Korea," and a tiny, defenseless and weeping child, labeled "North Korea." The caption reads: "It's a humanitarian issue."

Like most media booms, the upsurge of Japanese press enthusiasm seems to have had many causes. It was very energetically encouraged by some of Japan's most influential people. On 17 November 1958, for example, a group of prominent Japanese politicians from across the political spectrum formed the *Zainichi* Korean Repatriation Cooperation Society (*Zainichi Chôsenjin Kikoku Kyôroku Kai*) to help fulfill ethnic Koreans' longing to return "home." The society, among other things, published pamphlets and newsletters, collected funds and signatures, and sent groups of prominent intellectuals and cultural figures on tours around the country to promote repatriation. Leading participants included former Prime Minister Hatoyama Ichirô, Japanese Communist Party Chairman Miyamoto Kenji, and Socialist parliamentarian Hoashi Kei, who was also a central figure in the Japan-Korea Association. One member of the Cooperation Society's three-person Representative Council was influential LDP politician Koizumi Junya, whose son, Koizumi Junichirô, was to become one of the most popular Japanese prime ministers of modern times.

Ever since 1955, when Inoue Masutarô had offered to "promote a public opinion in Japan" in support of ICRC intervention, the Japan Red Cross Society's director of Foreign Affairs had also shown great flair for the use of press releases and strategic leaks of information to the media, and he continued to do so in 1958 and 1959.

But press releases and public lectures do not by themselves create a media boom. Some other more inchoate element—a certain public mood, a communal emotion—is needed. In this case, that element was perhaps the fractured political landscape of 1950s Japan.

Though the country had been dominated since the Pacific War by conservative governments, Japan's postwar intellectual life had a strongly left-of-center flavor. There was widespread disquiet among Japanese intellectuals at the government's pro-American stance and particularly at the prospect of an impending renewal of the Security Treaty, signed between Japan and the United States at the end of the Allied occupation. In this polarized environment, repatriation was the one issue that brought people from both sides of politics together. It was also an issue with powerful human interest. No wonder so many newspapers and magazines across the political spectrum pushed the cause of the Koreans' return to their homeland,

Figure 13.1.   Copy of a prorepatriation poster produced by the
***Zainichi* Korean Repatriation Cooperation Society, 1959 (Source:**
Typescript by Hallam C. Shorrock Jr. held in ICRC Archives, B AG
232 105-011.02)

a cause that appealed to a public desire for Cold War neutrality without offending the political establishment.

You can find them still today, tucked away in the stacks of the larger libraries or on the shelves of obscure, secondhand bookshops—the multilingual, multicolored magazines with which North Korea advertised to
the outside world the glowing future of life in the Democratic People's
Republic. The National Library of Australia has bound volumes of the

English-language version of the journal *Korea*, which in the late 1950s was also published in Korean, Japanese, Chinese, Russian, and French and was widely distributed by *Chongryun* among the Korean community in Japan. It seems as though no one has looked at the Australian National Library's copies for many years.

Leafing through their pages, I am filled with unexpected waves of conflicting emotion—anger, sadness, but also something oddly like nostalgia. For between the unmistakably Cold War Communist headlines—"They Overfulfilled the Five-Year Plan!" or "Along the Road Shown by the Great Lenin"—so many of the images and articles stir memories of the magazines of my childhood on the other side of the world.

Here on the page are the dream homes of the 1950s—the sparkling new apartments by the banks of Pyongyang's Daedong River, with their net curtains and tartan tablecloths; their bookshelves adorned with rows of potted plants and family photographs, arrayed beneath discreetly placed portraits of Comrade Kim Il-Sung. The back covers of the magazines display the new commodities of postwar prosperity—from canned apple puree to sewing machines. The photographs show families treating themselves to tea and cakes in department store cafeterias. "More Foodstuffs and Daily Necessities," reads the heading above alluring images of electric irons and baby carriages.

It is, of course, the perfect embodiment of the 1950s dream of modernity, all the more appealing because it was promised not just to a lucky few, but to everyone. Even the villages depicted in the pages of *Korea* offer public bathhouses with laundries and barbers' shops attached. This material comfort, the journal's articles insist, is to be provided without the ruthless competition of capitalism. Life in the Republic is full of hard work, but it is also a life of dignity, communal cooperation, and innocent enjoyment; contributions to the Five-Year Plan are rewarded with visits to the fun fair and the thermal baths, skating on the frozen river, and shopping sprees in Pyongyang's new department stores.

Such was the future that the Democratic People's Republic of Korea laid out before its exiled compatriots, and even those who recognized skilful advertising copy when they saw it could be forgiven for thinking that at least part of the story must be true. But if the images evoke nostalgia, it is impossible not to feel anger at the gap between the promise of the images and the bitter realities that, as we now know, the returnees found waiting for them when they disembarked at the port of Cheongjin.

In September 1958, just after Nam Il's announcement welcoming returnees from Japan, *Korea* ran its first story on repatriation, featuring two

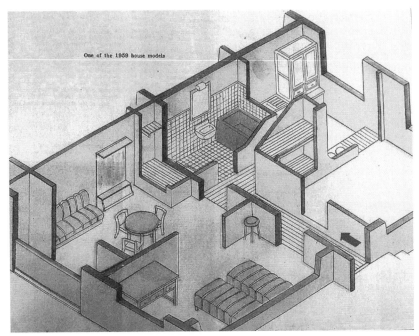

One of the 1959 house models

Figure 13.2.   Pyongyang dream home. One of the alluring images of planned workers' housing from the DPRK journal *Korea*, which was also published in Korean and Japanese and widely distributed among the Korean community in Japan

Zainichi Koreans who (according to the article) had returned from Japan in November 1957. It is difficult to establish just who they were and how they had returned. They were not among the forty-eight participants of the 1956 repatriation. Perhaps they had made their own way to North Korea with little public attention.

One of them, Kim Eung-Dai, tells readers:

> The Government of the DPRK provided me with everything I need: a new flat to live in and a job, as well as a large sum of money for immediate living expenses. My wife, a Japanese, is now working as a nurse in the maternity ward of the Pyongyang College Hospital. . . . The happier my life becomes in the fatherland, the more I think of my friends in Japan who are eagerly waiting for a chance to return home.

In the apartment above the Acacia Bookshop in Toyohashi, Yi Yang-Soo pored over magazines like this as he and his mother prepared to leave their familiar surroundings for this strange but exciting new world. "We believed them because we could see the photographs," he recalls. Although he was still in primary school, Yang-Soo was an avid reader, and as the repatriation movement gathered momentum, began eagerly to devour information about North Korea.

He particularly remembers, with anger, the series of articles *North of the Thirty-eighth Parallel* (*Sanjûhachi-do Sen no Kita*), published in 1960 in the *Asahi* newspaper, which ran many articles supporting the repatriation. Written by a left-wing Japanese journalist who visited North Korea just after the arrival of the first repatriation ship, it uncritically echoed the North Korean government's image of the happy life that awaited returnees in the homeland. Yi says,

> I remember reading about the North Korean hot springs. One episode in the series described these hot springs on the east coast, where work groups were able to stay for vacations. I looked up the map and found where those hot springs were.
>
> "Next year," I said to my Mum, "you and I will be able to go there."
> And then we started to plan where we'd go the following year, and so on.

Many thousands of other Koreans in Japan also began to think of embarking on the journey to North Korea as they encountered the flood of information that filled the media from the middle of 1958 into the first years of the 1960s.

One of these thousands was Oh Su-Ryong, who was then in his mid-20s. Born in Kobe of parents who had migrated to Japan from southeastern Korea, Oh Su-Ryong had been robbed of his chance of education by the events of the Pacific War.

Until the final stages of the war, his family had managed to get by, one way or another, largely through the hard work and determination of Su-Ryong's mother, who found ways to feed her family of five children on the meager income provided by her husband's work on construction sites. But the Oh family had lost their home and most of their possessions during the allied bombing of Kobe in the last year of the war. As Su-Ryong later realized, although his family had owned their own house, they did not own the land it stood on. They were forced to move into a cramped tenement nearby, and in the immediate postwar years, as Oh Su-Ryong simply states, "Finding food to eat was more important than going to school."

He dropped out of class and, in his early teens, began buying and selling on the black market—rice, vegetables, cigarettes, goods from occupation army stores—to supplement the family income. By the time the Japanese economy had begun to revive and life had become a little easier, it was too late for him to return to education, and his only future was in low-paid laboring jobs.

Although Oh Su-Ryong's mother was active in the women's section of *Chongryun*, he himself had never dreamed of going to live in North Korea until the end of the 1950s, when he began to see the appealing images in magazines and hear the stories of other Koreans who were setting off for new lives in the Republic.

Ironically it was his mother, the *Chongryun* activist, who begged him not to go. She knew enough to warn him against the propaganda images.

"Maybe the North really has developed, but after all it's only seven or eight years since the Korean War," she said. "Don't believe all the things they tell you."

For a while, her son was persuaded by her advice, but in the end, the lure of the images was too strong. Su-Ryong particularly remembers the moment in 1961 when he saw a Japanese magazine that carried a portrait of Kim Il-Sung on the cover.

"Kim Il-Sung: The Face That Moves the World," proclaimed the title above the photograph.

"I had no future in Japan. That was when I decided to leave. I'd go by myself to North Korea and get an education," says Oh Su-Ryong.

A crucial source of *Chongryun*'s power to spread the word about repatriation so quickly and effectively was its school network.

The question of ethnic education evoked strong feelings among Koreans in Japan, even among those who had little interest in the ideological battles between the Syngman Rhee and Kim Il-Sung regimes. Korean children who attended Japanese schools in the 1950s and 1960s faced an atmosphere heavy with prejudice. The regular school curriculum made no concession at all to the possible presence of non-Japanese in the classroom, and Korean children had no opportunity to maintain their Korean language. Many *Zainichi* Korean parents had a real longing for an alternative system of education that could give their children some knowledge of Korea and some confidence about their own origins.

After the forcible closure of Korean schools by the occupation authorities in 1948, community groups had once again begun the difficult task of rebuilding ethnic education, but with the advent of *Chongryun*, the system began to expand by leaps and bounds. Between 1955 and 1959, the number of students attending *Chongryun*-affiliated Korean schools rose from

17,604 to 23,425. The summit of these educational achievements was the founding of the community's very own Korea University. In 1956 the first handful of university students started classes in a group of rather ramshackle wooden buildings in one corner of the grounds of a Korean high school in Tokyo. The following year, however, *Chongryun* was able to purchase land for a campus, where in 1959 an impressive purpose-built university for Korean students in Japan was opened.

Korea University was a project in which Han Deok-Su took a particular personal pride. He himself became the university's president (*gakuchô*), and its successful completion greatly enhanced his authority within *Chongryun* and the wider Korean community.

The rapid growth of the *Chongryun* school system was the most visible and important result of the policy toward Koreans in Japan, which the North Korean government had developed from the mid-1950s onward. The key aim of this policy was to strengthen North Korea's connections to and control over the *Zainichi* Korean community (and also perhaps, as Foreign Minister Nam Il had indicated, to create a bridge for contact with South Korea). To achieve this purpose, the North Korean government was willing to invest very substantial sums of money in *Chongryun's* education system.

There is no clear evidence that this investment was originally intended as a way of promoting a mass return to the Fatherland, but from 1958 onward it served that purpose very well indeed.

The money from Pyongyang certainly helped *Chongryun* to develop innovative and widely welcomed school programs specially designed to meet the needs of Korean children growing up in a largely Japanese-speaking environment. But *Chongryun* ethnic education came inseparably packaged with other sorts of teaching. Above all, its school system gave *Zainichi* Korean children and their parents, many of whom had little previous knowledge about North Korea, a flood of detailed, vividly illustrated, and extremely rosy information about life in the Democratic People's Republic.

By the spring of 1959, *Chongryun's* Korean schools all over Japan had begun to organize "returnee brigades," and were providing special education and activities to persuade pupils and their parents that departure for the Fatherland was both their patriotic duty and their only chance of a brighter future. Pupils were encouraged to believe that all Koreans in Japan would eventually board the repatriation ships and go home to North Korea—it was just a matter of deciding who went first.

As an ICRC delegate to Japan was later told, between 1958 and 1961 the North Korean government had spent a total of some four hundred million yen on educational activities in Japan: "A large part of this sum was spent on encouraging the departure of Koreans by giving them an education that made them imagine life in North Korea in attractive colors."

In retrospect, the construction of the ethnic school network can be seen as a coproduction, in which the North Korean regime and *Chongryun* were clearly the key players, but some surprising participants also played valuable parts.

Since Japan and North Korea had no formal commercial or diplomatic relations, there was no regular way to send money between the two countries, and the large sums that North Korea wished to send to *Chongryun* for education could (under normal circumstances) only have been transferred with the express approval of the Japanese government. However, in the second half of the 1950s, such approval would certainly have evoked protests from South Korea, worsening the already strained relations with the Syngman Rhee regime.

Throughout 1956 and the first months of 1957, then, *Chongryun* struggled to find a way to transfer the promised funds from Pyongyang to Tokyo. Meanwhile, the North Korean Red Cross was also urgently cabling Geneva to ask for the ICRC's help in sending humanitarian assistance to the detainees in Ōmura. According to information given to Japanese parliamentary committees, it was the Japan Red Cross Society that generously helped to solve the problem.

By the end of 1956, the society had worked out a system by which money could be transferred from the North Korean government to the North Korean Red Cross, and thence (either via Geneva or directly) to the Japanese Red Cross for transmission to North Korean–affiliated groups in Japan. As Shimazu Tadatsugu explained in a highly confidential telegram to the ICRC, the advantage of such a money route was that it made it possible for funds to be transferred from Pyongyang to Tokyo without placing the Kishi administration in the "awkward position" of being asked to give its formal permission. However, as Shimazu was able to assure ICRC, if money was transferred using the route devised by the Japan Red Cross Society, "No objection would come from [the Japanese] governmental side."

Shimazu's telegram placed the issue of money transfers between Pyongyang and Tokyo in the context of the plight of Ōmura detainees, some of whom in 1957 were facing serious physical and mental health problems.

The North Korean Red Cross was eager to send a sum of over one million won to relieve their suffering. Shimazu's message implies that the Japan Red Cross Society's sudden interest in the problems of international financial transactions was prompted by the urgent need to send this humanitarian aid to Ômura.

But emergency funds to help ease the miseries of the Ômura detainees were not the only things that passed along this money route. According to parliamentary testimony by a *Chongryun* official, two payments with a total value of over two hundred million yen were made by the North Korean government to this organization for educational purposes in April and October 1957. Socialist Party parliamentarian Tanaka Orinoshin told the Diet:

> A sum of several hundred million yen was sent twice by the North Korean government to the General Association of Korean Residents in Japan for the education of North Korean affiliated *Zainichi* Korean children. It was sent via the Japan Red Cross Society and, according to my memory, via the International Committee of the Red Cross. I know this because we acted as intermediaries with the government about the matter. However, since these were after all said to be payments for the education of *Zainichi* Koreans, provided by their home government, and they passed through the International Committee of the Red Cross, I think that the Japanese government allowed them to be transferred to the people concerned.

Two hundred million yen was a very substantial sum: around US$700,000 in 1950s money, and the equivalent of tens of millions in today's terms. And over time, the sums increased. In October 1959, immediately before the mass repatriation began and at a time when the Japanese Red Cross and *Chongryun* were at loggerheads over repatriation procedures, the North Korean side began complaining to Tokyo about the Japan Red Cross Society's delay in handing over a further payment sent from Pyongyang to assist *Chongryun*-affiliated Koreans in Japan. On this occasion (as Inoue Masutarô explained) the sum involved was "1 billion yen, equivalent to 3 million dollars."

Oddly enough, I have so far failed to find any evidence in the archives of the International Committee of the Red Cross that these large payments passed through Geneva or were transferred with the prior knowledge of the ICRC. Of course, assisting the transfer of funds to help detainees or returnees and to develop ethnic education could be seen as a humanitarian venture. But did the funds, I wonder, in fact pass through International Red Cross channels? Was the ICRC aware of their scale and purpose, or even of their existence? And if it was, did the International Committee understand the power of these large flows of money between the North Korean government, the Red Cross, and *Chongryun* to recruit volunteers for the repatriation scheme—a scheme that (as Roger Gallopin had stressed in 1957) was supposed to be carried out "peacefully and entirely without political propaganda?"

Toward the end of my stay in North Korea, my guide Mr. Ri takes me to see the Tower of the Juche Idea—a 170-meter-high torch-shaped monument to Kim Il-Sung's political philosophy, which stands in the center of Pyongyang, on the banks of the Daedong River. Though the tower itself is designed in the worst traditions of revolutionary kitsch, the view from the top is breathtaking.

When we step out onto the balcony, whipped by a ferocious wind, the capital spreads out below, stretching toward distant blue-green wooded hills. As a side effect of its chronic energy shortage, Pyongyang has the clearest air of any metropolis I have even visited. The deep turquoise river, which curves through the city's heart, is lined by the willow trees for which Pyongyang is famous. Tucked away from the street fronts you can still see a surprising number of little tiled houses, overshadowed by the surrounding cliffs of modern apartment and office buildings.

On the side of the tower away from the river stand parallel rows of apartment buildings, built as part of a 1958 urban redevelopment plan that aimed to create housing for forty thousand families, as well as student dormitories, a hotel for eight hundred guests, and a massive theater, all to be completed in time for the sixteenth anniversary of Liberation in 1961.

The dream homes of Pyongyang were not a total myth. It is just that they were far too few, and they were built with a haste and lack of basic materials that made them hollow shells, empty of the promised vision of modernity. Today, their concrete is crumbling and streaked with grime.

Some of the very first returnees from Japan were indeed housed in these apartments by the Daedong; but they, as it turned out, were the lucky few.

14

THE DIPLOMATS' DIARIES

It is my last day in Pyongyang.

From my twenty-second-story hotel room I can see far below, in the first light of morning, streams of people converging on the city center. They walk in small groups along the broad avenues of the capital or gather on street corners and in the backyard of the little office building opposite the hotel, awaiting trucks to take them to their appointed places. The morning sky is pale and hazy, and there is a scent of approaching winter in the biting wind that whips through the crack of window that I have left open during the night.

The tiny figures of women in the street below wear cardigans or raincoats over their multicolored *chima jeogori* and carry plastic sprays of flowers in clashing shades of puce and pale pink. Today, 28 October 2005, Chinese leader Hu Jin-Tao arrives in the city on an official visit to North Korea. These human streams are flowing together to form the sea of smiling faces that will greet North Korea's most significant foreign friend as he is driven from the airport into the heart of Pyongyang.

The hotel elevator takes a long time to reach my floor, and as I wait for it in the large, silent, and dimly lit elevator hall, I suddenly become aware that I am not alone. At the opposite side of the hall is a western journalist—a tall man whom I guess to be in his late thirties. He stands with his back to me, facing the window, gazing intently at the landscape below through a pair of high-powered binoculars. When I greet him he half turns and gives the brief grunt of someone reluctant to be interrupted in the midst of an important mission, before returning to the absorbing task of Pyongyang watching.

Holding my breath while the elevator grinds its uncertain way down to the hotel's marbled entrance hall, I have to suppress the urge to laugh out loud. The scene upstairs says so much about the situation in which outside observers—journalists, passing visitors like myself—find themselves in this country. Trapped in our bubbles of globalized comfort—our twenty-something-story hotel rooms with their minibars and cable TV—whisked by attentive guides from one showplace monument to another, we are reduced to becoming voyeurs, eagerly peeking down alleyways and peering through the half-curtained windows of other people's houses in the desperate search for a glimpse of "the real North Korea."

And, as in all cases of voyeurism, what is seen is not the infinitely complex life that inhabits the alleyways or the rooms behind the curtains, but only fleeting views of nameless bodies, onto which we project our fantasies.

No wonder the resulting images so often seem grotesque. No wonder we swing from desire to loathing—from the naïve pictures of the socialist paradise that dominated the progressive foreign media of the 1950s, to the contemporary, one-dimensional caricatures of Kim Jong-Il's "rogue state."

In the hotel lobby the older of my two guides, Mr. Ri, is waiting for me, full of apologies. The arrival of the Chinese leader has made it necessary for us to change our itinerary for the day. The authorities are reluctant to have stray foreigners wandering around central Pyongyang in the midst of this important state occasion, so a planned trip to Kim Il-Sung University has been abandoned. Instead we will head out of town to visit more royal tombs, just beyond the outskirts of the city and dating back two thousand years to the time of the most ancient Korean kingdoms.

As it happens, our route out of the city takes us past one building that I had particularly hoped to see.

When I drew up a proposed itinerary at the start of my visit, I could think of no easy way of explaining my deep interest in the Russian Embassy in Pyongyang and, without an opportunity to wander around the city by myself, I had given up hope of seeing it. But now Mr. Ri casually points it out as we drive past the embassy district on our trip out of town. It is in a quiet avenue lined with imposing buildings in socialist neoclassical style. The avenue is overshadowed by tall trees, whose falling autumn leaves are being meticulously swept up by brigades of elderly women.

For the past three months, I have spent many hours reading and rereading the diary of the man who occupied this building in the late 1950s—Soviet Ambassador to North Korea A. M. Puzanov—scanning each entry in search of clues to the North Korean side of the repatriation story. It is a quest that has proved fascinating, sometimes revealing, and sometimes baffling.

At the heart of the repatriation story lies an unsolved enigma.

The newly declassified Geneva archives make it clear that sections of the Japanese establishment embraced the repatriation scheme as early as 1955. From then on, messages were repeatedly sent from Japan to North Korea via the Red Cross (and indirectly also via the Japan-Korea Association, *Chongryun*, and other groups), urging the DPRK to accept a mass inflow of ethnic Koreans from Japan and to arrange transport to carry them. But until the middle of 1958, the records show no sign that these approaches struck a responsive chord with the Kim Il-Sung regime.

Certainly, the North Korean government wanted to develop links to the *Zainichi* Korean community. It welcomed Koreans from Japan who wished to study at North Korean colleges, and it strongly supported the demands of Ōmura detainees who requested deportation to the North, rather than to the South, of the peninsula. North Korean officials also raised the issue of the free movement of people between Japan and the DPRK and showed a willingness to provide jobs and homes for the limited number of Koreans whom it had identified as being likely returnees.

But throughout the first two years of discussions about repatriation, I have found nothing to suggest a North Korean desire to promote a movement of tens of thousands of people across the East Sea from Japan.

Yet seemingly by coincidence, at the very moment when Japan and South Korea were on the brink of resolving the problem of the Ōmura and Busan detainees, Kim Il-Sung suddenly announced to the world that his country warmly welcomed the mass return of "the compatriots who, having lost the means of living in Japan, are desirous of returning to the bosom of their fatherland."

The commitment involved was enormous. Over a period of a little more than a year, the North Korea authorities were to arrange sea transport, reception, resettlement, housing, jobs, and welfare for some seventy thousand people, most of whom had no family or friends to support them in their new home. In fact, as soon became obvious, it was a project that taxed the country's resources beyond their limits.

Why did they do it?

Of one thing we can be certain: The North Korean government did not embark on this great undertaking to please Japan or to satisfy the enthusiasms of the *Chongryun* leadership. At some time in the months leading

Figure 14.1.   Kim Il-Sung (far left) addresses the tenth Anniversary reception, 8 September 1958. It was during this speech that he announced North Korea's welcome to a mass repatriation. (Source: *Korea*, no. 27, 1958, p. 1)

up to Kim Il-Sung's announcement, they must have decided that this policy was to their own benefit. In other words, they must finally have come to accept Inoue Masutarô's proposition that the point of dialectical synthesis between the conflicting interests of the Japanese and North Korean regimes was the mass repatriation of ethnic Koreans.

But the mountains of documents in Geneva provide no clue as to when or why this conclusion was reached.

There was, however, another source of information that I hoped might provide answers to the puzzle. I had almost given up hope of tracing Soviet documents about the repatriation, when a kind young Korean researcher pointed out that, soon after the collapse of the Soviet Union, the South Korean *JoongAng Ilbo* newspaper had purchased a large collection of Russian archival material related to Korea. This was now available on database. Among the material were diaries kept by Soviet Ambassador Puzanov in the second half of the 1950s, together with a large amount of other correspondence from the period.

The Puzanov diaries are remarkable documents. They are, of course, official records, sent home by the ambassador to his masters in the Soviet Foreign Ministry. Their pages cannot be expected to reveal the ambassador's private life and thoughts; but they paint a fascinating picture of the life of Pyongyang's political elite in the 1950s.

In search of an answer to the repatriation enigma, I first turned eagerly to the entries for the middle of 1956, when Shimazu Tadatsugu and Inoue

Masutarô were deep in negotiations about the forty-seven would-be returnees and when the North Korean government issued its first Cabinet order providing assistance for them. This, after all, was the time when the Japan Red Cross Society was (by roundabout routes) urging North Korea to negotiate with the Soviet Union about ships for the scheme.

Yet throughout these months, Puzanov's diary makes no mention of the repatriation issue at all. There is no sign that the North Korean Red Cross or government ever took up Shimazu's suggestion. What the diary does reveal is that (probably unknown to Shimazu and others in Tokyo) North Korea's political leaders had far more urgent issues on their minds that summer.

In 1956, Hungary was not the only place where Soviet denunciations of Stalin's "cult of personality" had been followed with keen interest. Like their counterparts in Eastern Europe, some intellectuals in North Korea thought they could glimpse a possibility for reform from within. While Inoue and Shin were holding their secret meeting in Tianjin, and immediately after the North Korean Cabinet had issued its order on assistance for the forty-seven would-be returnees, Kim Il-Sung left for a tour of Eastern Europe. In his absence, a group of prominent political figures in Pyongyang rallied forces for their own critique of Kim's increasingly authoritarian style of government.

Their chosen arena for the showdown with the Leader was the ruling party's plenum, to be held in August. But the reformers, many of whom came from either the Chinese-aligned faction or the Soviet Korean faction of the North Korean ruling party, had underestimated Kim's prodigious information-gathering and survival skills. The plenum was postponed, and after weeks of intense behind-the-scenes factional struggle, the reform group was defeated. Shrewd strategist that he was, Kim did not immediately expel all dissidents from the party or place them on trial. Instead, he waited until he was sure that his own position was secure before launching a series of purges that began with the pro-China faction, extended to the Soviet Korean faction in 1957, and gradually expanded to engulf many thousands of lower-ranking officials and others who had no connection to the original reform movement at all. Many were arrested and disappeared in the DPRK's expanding labor camps.

The events of the second half of 1956 sent tremors of unease through the relationship between North Korea and its two largest allies, the USSR and the People's Republic of China—countries whose relationship with one another was also becoming increasingly strained. In the wake of the failed North Korean reform movement, some prominent Soviet Koreans sought asylum in the USSR, and some students receiving training in the

USSR refused to return home. The aftershocks of the political crisis continued to reverberate through Ambassador Puzanov's diaries well into the late 1950s, and the Khrushchev regime's desire to rebuild its weakened relationship with North Korea seems to have been a key motive for the very active and enthusiastic support that the USSR would give to the repatriation scheme.

It is not until the summer of 1957 that repatriation makes an appearance in Puzanov's diaries, and even then, it appears only as a minor issue, raised almost in passing. *Chongryun* had approached the Soviet government (then in the midst of negotiating its treaty of commerce and navigation with Japan) to ask for help in transporting around sixty students from Japan to North Korea for college education. Although *Chongryun* indicated that it had already received the blessing of the North Korean government for this plan, Ambassador Puzanov wanted to hear Kim Il-Sung's views about this firsthand.

Kim's response was positive. North Korea was willing to accept the students, and he expressed his hope that Soviet transport could be provided for them. However, perhaps remembering the events of 1956, when the hostility of South Korea had persuaded Japan to avoid official endorsement of the repatriation, Kim also expressed doubts about the Japanese response to the scheme.

"How will the Japanese see this?" he asked Puzanov. "Will they give them exit permits? We have given our agreement to help Koreans living in Japan who want to study at colleges in the DPRK. We do this because we don't want the Association of Korean Residents in Japan to regard the DPRK in a bad light."

This rather bland response gives no sign of any grand plans for a mass inflow of compatriots from Japan. From August 1957 into the early part of 1958, indeed, there are no further entries about repatriation at all, and no indications as to whether the sixty students had ever reached North Korea.

Reading the entries from the first months of 1958 and approaching the date when Kim Il-Sung announced his welcome to returning *Zainichi* Koreans, I felt that I was on the brink of discoveries. Surely over the next page something would reveal the background to Kim Il-Sung's announcement of 8 September 1958.

Instead—exasperatingly—there was silence.

The collection of Soviet documents in the database is riddled with unexplained holes. The diaries are incomplete. It is impossible to tell why certain sections—some covering a week or two, some covering several months—are missing. Perhaps they were simply mislaid or misfiled in the archives. Perhaps they have been deliberately removed, but if so, there is no knowing why or by whom.

The entries for 1958 run smoothly from February until they reach 5 July, when Ambassador Puzanov is busy visiting a rural cooperative south of Pyongyang; then they abruptly stop. They resume for a few days, from 7 to 11 September, and after that there is again a prolonged and profound silence that lasts until the beginning of 1959, by which time plans for the repatriation are already in full swing.

My first reaction on reading these entries was one of intense frustration. And yet, as I went back and carefully reread the words that I had already skimmed over, the faint outlines of a story as seen from Pyongyang began to emerge.

And then, once again, chance intervened, in the form of some help from a generous fellow researcher. A reunion with my former colleague Andrei Lankov, who is now working in South Korea, prompted him to look once more through the cache of documents that he had extracted some years earlier from the former Soviet archives. Among them were extracts from the diary of Puzanov's deputy, V. I. Pelishenko, who (as it turned out) had been standing in for the ambassador while Puzanov took his summer vacation in July.

And there, finally, were a couple of pages whose contents cleared some of the fog surrounding the repatriation issue.

By the afternoon of my final day in North Korea, when my guides and I head back into Pyongyang after our visit to the royal tombs, the television screens of the capital are already filled with nonstop broadcasts of the arrival of Chinese leader Hu Jin-Tao. By evening, as I return to my hotel, the young women who work in its souvenir shop are gathered around the television screen. They have changed back into their trim blue uniforms now, but earlier that day, dressed in *chima jeogori* and waving plastic blossoms, they were part of the crowd on the screen. Like teenagers who have just attended a rock concert, they giggle and nudge one another as they scan the televised crowd for signs of their momentary brush with celebrity. "Look! That's us! That's us!" they cry.

The main reasons for Hu Jin-Tao's visit are no mystery. He is there to discuss China's rapidly growing economic commitment to the DPRK and to cajole North Korea back to the negotiating table in an effort to resolve the ongoing nuclear crisis on the Korean Peninsula.

But, as always in North Korea, history and memory keep intruding into the present. The newspaper headlines acclaim Hu's visit as reaffirming a "friendship forged in blood."

With fitting symbolism, Hu Jin-Tao has arrived in the week when North Korea is commemorating the fifty-fifth anniversary of the coming of the Chinese "volunteers" (more accurately, military recruits), whose entry into the Korean War in 1950 rescued the country from probable defeat at the hands of South Koreans and the United States–led United Nations forces. A few days earlier, a North Korean official ceremony was held at the memorial to Mao An-Ying, son of the late Chinese leader Mao Tse-Tung and one of the estimated five hundred thousand Chinese to die fighting in the Korean War.

The more I read of Ambassador Puzanov's diaries, the clearer it seemed that North Korea's sudden decision to welcome home the compatriots from Japan was prompted, not by a single motive, but by several major political factors that came together in the first part of 1958.

The most important factors were, first, the departure of the Chinese volunteers; second, North Korea's shortage of labor for its ambitious development plans; and third, rising North Korean concerns about the triangular relationship between Japan, South Korea and the United States.

After the end of the Korean War many Chinese volunteers stayed on to help with postwar reconstruction; some three hundred thousand were still in North Korea at the end of 1957. But the political upheavals of 1956 had placed strains on the friendship between China and North Korea, and by 1958 the North Korean economy was in any case well on the road to recovery. Meanwhile, the Chinese government was drawing up its own economic plan—better known to the world as the ill-fated Great Leap Forward—which was officially launched in January 1958. China needed to mobilize all available manpower for this extremely labor-intensive effort to propel the country toward modernity and prosperity, and it was at this point that the Chinese government decided to bring the volunteer force home from North Korea.

All over the country, during the first months of 1958, great farewell celebrations were being staged to thank the departing volunteers; Soviet Ambassador Puzanov himself attended several of them. To offset at least part of the loss of labor power caused by the volunteers' withdrawal, Kim Il-Sung repeatedly asked the Chinese to encourage a "return to the homeland" by ethnic Koreans living in northeastern China. Puzanov's diary notes that around the end of 1958, Kim managed to persuade the Chinese to promise a repatriation of some forty thousand ethnic Koreans.

The mass return of Koreans from Japan was obviously designed to help plug the same gap in the labor force.

But the withdrawal of the Chinese volunteers had other implications that caused even greater alarm in Pyongyang. It was indeed the source of an intense sense of vulnerability—a fear of the outside world—that has existed ever since and has grown to be the dominating feature of North Korean political thought.

For of course the departure of the Chinese meant that there were now no foreign troops on North Korean soil. But south of the thirty-eighth parallel (as North Korea's citizens were incessantly reminded) the United States showed no signs of withdrawing its troops and was indeed expanding its bases and importing newer and ever more high-powered weaponry.

Kim Il-Sung's immediate response to this alarming situation was to launch a new plan for Korean reunification.

On 5 February 1958, he issued a statement on the future of the Korean Peninsula that became the basis for a major DPRK diplomatic initiative. The main elements of Kim's proposal were the demand for a complete withdrawal of foreign troops from North and South Korea, to be followed by the development of economic and social ties between North and South, and later by free elections under international supervision throughout the peninsula. Needless to say, such proposals were regarded with intense suspicion in the South. In its efforts to win foreign sympathy for its position and gain the moral high ground in international politics, North Korea needed to enhance its own image as peace loving and progressive in contrast to South Korea, which it sought to depict as impoverished and oppressive.

In these strategic maneuvers, North Korea was deeply conscious of the relationship between the Kishi and Syngman Rhee regimes. Moves toward a rapprochement between Japan and South Korea at the end of 1957 had caused serious alarm in Pyongyang. Throughout the first half of 1958, as the Kishi and Syngman Rhee governments squabbled over the fate of the Ômura detainees, the North Korean government and Red Cross bombarded Tokyo and Geneva with messages on the subject—not (of course) out of pure humanitarian concern for the fate of the detainees, but above all because they recognized the issue as their best chance of driving a wedge between South Korea and Japan.

And the relationship between these two countries had implications that extended beyond the East Asian region itself. Japan and South Korea were the United States' most significant allies in the region. If the Japan–South Korea relationship deteriorated further, it would be difficult for the United States to maintain its regional influence. But if the relationship improved, it could greatly strengthen U.S. power in East Asia.

And just at that moment, in mid-1958, came that stream of signals from the Japanese Red Cross, apparently sent with the blessing of its government, indicating that Japan was preparing to open a door to the repatriation of Ômura detainees, and eventually perhaps of many others. North Korea was being asked to support and help arrange transport for this scheme, but to do so quietly, so as not to damage relations between Japan and South Korea. The opportunity to call Japan's bluff was obvious. By offering wholehearted support to the repatriation, but doing so with maximum publicity, North Korea could *both* claim the humanitarian high ground in the eyes of the international community *and* wreak havoc on Japan's relationship with South Korea and the United States. This was a temptation that the Kim Il-Sung regime seems to have found impossible to resist.

In July 1958 Ambassador Puzanov was on holiday. So too was North Korean Foreign Minister Nam Il, who had taken his wife and young son to Uzbekistan to do some fishing and visit the places where he had lived before his own return to the Korean fatherland. Nam was also planning to combine pleasure with some serious business meetings with leading Soviet politicians. It is likely that their discussions included the repatriation issue.

Meanwhile, Kim Il-Sung, on vacation at his holiday house near the Korea-China border, summoned Soviet Chargé d'Affaires V. I. Pelishenko to join him for two days of intensive discussions. The first day, 14 July, was devoted to the issue of Koreans in Japan, and it was there that Kim officially unveiled to the USSR North Korea's ambitious new policy on the problem of Koreans in Japan.

Kim was a strategic thinker who treated powerful allies like the USSR with considerable caution. There is no reason to suppose that his discussions with Pelishenko revealed his innermost thoughts about repatriation, but they provide a better indication of these thoughts than anything else available so far.

The six hundred thousand Koreans in Japan, Kim explained to Pelishenko, were living "in difficult material circumstances, and many of them are partially or wholly unemployed." From 1955, the North Korean government had developed a policy on the issue of Koreans in Japan that mainly involved lobbying the Japanese government "to provide normal living conditions and democratic national rights to these Koreans."

This, however, had produced little result, and now the DPRK was embarking on a new course. Kim told Pelishenko, "We will announce that the government and our people invite all compatriots living in Japan to return to their Native Land." He also added a comment that may have reflected recent information reaching North Korea from Tokyo: "On this question we hope to obtain the agreement of the Japanese government."

This change in strategy was partly prompted by optimistic (indeed, as it turned out, wildly overoptimistic) assessments of the future of the North Korean economy. Kim explained,

> Two to three years ago, our economic position did not make it possible for us to raise the idea that, for example, one hundred thousand families of Koreans living in Japan might return to the DPRK and be provided with homes and work. At the present time we have the capacity within a specific period to provide these families with work and one hundred thousand apartments. We could provide them work in residential and industrial construction in Pyongyang and the provinces, where there is a shortage of laborers, and in industry and above all in coal mining, as well as in our rural economy.

There is something deeply ironic in this. Koreans in Japan, many of whom had originally been brought there to satisfy Japan's wartime need for mine labor, were being invited to play the same role in the North Korean economy.

But as Kim's discussions with Pelishenko reveal, economic considerations were not the only motive for North Korea's new approach to repatriation. A successful mass repatriation, the North Korean leader stressed, would "bring great political, as well as economic, benefits" to the DPRK.

Repatriation could, after all, be used to claim the humanitarian ascendancy, not just over South Korea but even over the United States, a particularly appealing prospect at a time when (among other things) the United States was lobbying hard to have South Korea admitted to the United Nations. What more effective way could there be to counter these U.S. schemes than to present the world with the spectacle of tens of thousands of Koreans, almost all of them originally from the South, "voting with their feet" to return to the socialist North? As Kim observed to Pelishenko: "Even if the Americans do not allow the Japanese government to take a positive attitude to [the repatriation] proposal, this will mean that the political sympathy of global public opinion will be on the side of the DPRK. The great humanitarian concern of the Socialist state for its compatriots may be demonstrated."

In fact, it seems likely that the North Korean authorities were anticipating, and perhaps relishing, the prospect of resolute U.S. opposition to the repatriation plan. At this crucial moment in U.S.-Japan relations, United States opposition to repatriation could be expected to strengthen anti-U.S. and pro–North Korean sentiment in Japan. The South Korean archives contain a typescript copy of an intriguing English-language book, *On the Question of 600,000 Koreans in Japan*, prepared in 1959 by Pyongyang's Foreign Languages Publishing House, obviously for international propaganda purposes (though never widely distributed). The introduction to this book repeatedly refers to likely joint U.S.–South Korean resistance to the repatriation: "The wilder the U.S. imperialists and the Syngman Rhee clique run in checking the home-coming of the Koreans in Japan for political reasons, the more they will expose their fascist, terrorist rule in South Korea. Nothing can break the desire of Koreans in Japan to return to their fatherland."

But as was soon to become evident, in this the North Korean government had miscalculated. The United States had strategic considerations of its own. The Eisenhower administration would raise only mild and half-hearted concerns about the repatriation.

Kim's July 1958 conversation with Pelishenko concluded with a request to the Soviet Ministry of Foreign Affairs "through its channels in Japan to give us help in obtaining appropriate information about the situation of the Korean community in Japan, about the community's attitude to the advantages of returning to the DPRK, and about the possible positions of governmental circles and the Japanese public on the question of the return of Korean citizens to the DPRK." He also pointed out that his government expected to consult with "our Chinese comrades" about the matter.

In fact, both China and Mongolia eventually provided some assistance toward the repatriation scheme, although it is unclear how much or how this support was used. The Japan Red Cross Society played a role in transferring financial help for repatriation from China to Japan. The ICRC archives contain a copy of a telegram dated 28 November 1959 (just before the departure of the first repatriation ship), in which the Japan Red Cross Society acknowledges the receipt from the Chinese Red Cross of a sum of over fourteen thousand pounds sterling (some 14 million yen), that had been sent by the Chinese Red Cross and was duly transmitted by the Japanese Red Cross to Mr. Han Deok-Su, chairman of the General Association of Korean Residents in Japan (*Chongryun*).

But by far the most enthusiastic and generous response came from the Soviet Union. In the late 1950s, Khrushchev was attempting to carve out a place as a global statesman through his advocacy of "peaceful coexistence," a strategy that reached its climax in his widely publicized official visit to the United States in September 1959. Against a background of rising political rivalry between the USSR and Mao's China, diplomatic cooperation with Kim Il-Sung offered a valuable way of countering Chinese influence in North Korea and of promoting Khrushchev's image on the world stage. Like North Korea, the Soviet Union would benefit from worsening Japan-U.S. and Japan–South Korea relations. An added sweetener, from the Soviet viewpoint, was the prospect that, by providing ships for the repatriation, it could strengthen its newly created commercial and transport links to the booming Japanese economy.

One indication of the Soviet response to Kim's request is an interesting change of personnel took place at the Soviet Embassy in Tokyo in October 1958, when the prominent Soviet Korea expert and former chargé d'affaires in Pyongyang, S. P. Suzdalev, was appointed to the position of embassy counsellor. On his arrival, Suzdalev promptly approached the Japanese government about the repatriation issue. As well as providing information on developments in Japan and assisting in negotiations, the USSR also gave extensive material support for the repatriation, ranging from the repatriation ships and their naval escort to foreign currency to cover the expenses of the North Korean Red Cross negotiating team in Geneva.

During his discussions with Pelishenko in the summer of 1958, Kim Il-Sung made one further comment that gives a rather more sinister foretaste of events to come.

Pelishenko records Kim Il-Sung's prediction that "among such a massive entry of the Korean population from Japan various reactionary and espionage elements may be sent to our country." However, Kim assured the Soviet diplomat, "With correct work by our compatriot organs, we need not fear this,"

The meeting with Pelishenko marked the beginning of ongoing, intense consultation between the North Korean and Soviet governments over the repatriation.

Immediately after the arrival of the first repatriation ships in Cheongjin in December 1959, Kim Il-Sung was to offer his personal and fulsome gratitude to the USSR "for the immense support and help, provided both during negotiations with the Japanese and in carrying out the repatriation." Placing the issue firmly in its global Cold War context, Kim added that the repatriation of *Zainichi* Koreans would never have been possible without the thaw in international relations created by the "determined and consistent peace-loving policy of the Soviet Union and particularly by the great work achieved by comrade N. S. Khrushchev during his visit to the United States."

At that stage, the North Korean side clearly felt that their hopes for a propaganda victory on the world stage were being fulfilled. In mid-1959, for example, during a meeting with Soviet Deputy Premier Mikoyan, Foreign Minister Nam Il exultantly contrasted North Korea's international image with that of the South Korean government, which was developing plans to encourage emigration schemes for the rural poor. "The emergence of the repatriation issue," said Nam, "has brought political gains to the DPRK, while Syngman Rhee has lost out. He is not only unable to accept [returnees] to South Korea, but on the contrary is prepared to export unemployed people from South Korea to Latin America."

The following year, North Korea was busily producing multilanguage publications on the repatriation that it sent via the Soviet mission to be distributed to delegates at the UN General Assembly.

The propaganda's effect in Japan appeared to be particularly gratifying, as the head of the North Korean negotiating team, Ri Il-Gyeong, noted when he traveled to Japan with the first repatriation convoy in 1959.

Indeed, Ri Il-Gyeong's position as chief North Korean negotiator on the repatriation was itself a sign both of the significance that the DPRK attached to the project and of the importance of propaganda as a motive for repatriation. Ri (who is generally referred to in the ICRC records as Li Il Kyung) is often described as vice president of the North Korean Red Cross. But (as Puzanov's diaries make clear) he was simultaneously also the North Korean government minister of education and culture, and (as other Soviet documents show) before taking up this posts he had held the powerful position of head of the Central Committee's Department of Propaganda and Agitation.

Reporting back from Niigata at the end of 1959, Ri was to observe with delight that "the Japanese population, and even the Japanese police, are on the side of the DPRK. All steps were taken by the Japanese authorities to prevent provocation on the part of pro-Syngman Rhee elements. The repatriation has the support of Japanese society."

But if he believed that this was about to lead to a permanent improvement between North Korea and Japan, he was sorely mistaken. It was a mistake that cast its shadow over the fate of the Korean returnees from Japan; it was a mistake that may also have contributed to the ultimate fate of Ri Il-Gyeong himself.

My stay in North Korea has been only a short one; yet as I board my train for the twenty-four-hour journey back to Beijing, I feel strangely tired.

I am sharing a compartment with two men from the Ministry of Metal Industries on their way to trade negotiations in Beijing. As soon as the train has left the station, my companions remove their suits and spread themselves out comfortably on their bunks in their beige cotton undershirts. The younger of the two is a gentle-faced man in his twenties who speaks a little English. With a kindness that I have encountered again and again on this journey, he notices that I am not eating much and, when the train reaches Sinuiju, hurries off down the platform, returning with a bag full of apples and bread rolls, which he hopes will tempt a weary westerner's appetite.

Sinuiju's station is as empty as before. There are just two young women on the platform, walking up and down arm-in-arm and deep in conversation; perhaps they are sisters, perhaps best friends. One wears a frilly blouse and stylishly cut skirt. The other is dressed in the olive-colored uniform of the People's Army. The young woman in civilian dress has taken charge of her military companion's semiautomatic weapon and is, as they talk, dangling it casually from one hand like a fashion accessory.

Soldiers are an inescapable sight all over North Korea, but often (as here in Sinuiju) the image they project seems far removed from the clockwork precision of the military parades that I have seen on television.

Looking at the two women in Sinuiju station, I find myself thinking of the soldiers whom I saw a few days earlier when my guides took me to visit the thirty-eighth parallel. They were very young soldiers, walking in a line beside the dirt road. Their bodies were small and their faces looked like those of children. They had been helping with the harvest, and each was bent under a huge bundle of hay that he carried on his back.

That day, I was the only tourist on the north side of the border at Panmunjom, but from the other side, just a few hundred yards away, I could hear the voices and laughter of the crowd of visitors who stood on the viewing platform on the southern side of this last Cold War border.

More than thirty years ago, as a naïve young western traveler in East Asia for the first time, I had stood at precisely that spot on the southern side of the border, looking north. The little prefabricated hut where my fellow traveler and I photographed each other then still stands, just down the slope from the northern viewing point. Seeing it, I feel as though I could almost reach out, across space and across time, to touch both the past and the people on the other side of the line. But in fact, the line is still as impermeable as the barrier between present and past itself.

That line along the thirty-eighth parallel, which began as nothing more than a pencil mark on a map, has over the years carved itself deeper and deeper into the landscape and into human lives. The road where the hungry little soldiers carry their mountainous bundles of hay is just a few kilometers from the glittering new tourist center on the southern side of the border. But between them is an impassable wilderness littered with mines and tank traps, dividing a land in whose southern half thousands of foreign troops have remained for more than half a century.

At night, you can even see the thirty-eighth parallel from space, bisecting the Korean Peninsula into a southern sea of lights and a northern lake of darkness.

The gap between Kim Jong-Il's nuclear ambitions and the line of young soldiers trudging back to their barracks with their loads of hay seems both pathetic and ludicrous. But the laughter that had begun to rise within me when I first saw them suddenly died when, for a moment, I met the eyes of one of those young men as he glanced up at our passing car. It was a sad, fleeting, slightly questioning glance.

I cannot speak to him, and I know nothing of his life. But, rightly or wrongly, I read the look in his eyes as the expression of someone who faces all the hardships endured by past generations, but without past generations' confidence that they are building a better world—the expression of person who faces nothing but the long trudge down a dusty road into an uncertain future.

15

FROM GENEVA TO CALCUTTA

Toward the end of 2005, I make one more visit to Geneva. There are facts that need to be checked, unresolved questions nagging my mind, pieces of the jigsaw puzzle still to be found.

Winter is closing in, and Mont Blanc has retreated again behind its veil of clouds. The water of the lake is translucent grey, and the small boats moored along the embankment bob on the waves stirred by a sharp wind from the mountains. As I walk into town for some shopping, I pass the Hotel des Bergues, where Inoue Masutarô used to stay.

It is closed for renovations: the doors are boarded up, the façade is covered with scaffolding. Its windows have become sightless eyes.

At the start of April 1959, Kasai Yoshisuke, Inoue Masutarô, and their Red Cross team from Tokyo and Ri Il-Gyeong, with his team from Pyongyang, finally came here to Geneva to reach an agreement about repatriation. Their talks were slow to start, agonizingly prolonged and extremely arduous. The two sides were deeply suspicious of each others' intentions, a problem made worse by the fact (explained by Harry Angst to officials in Geneva) that Ri Il-Gyeong, for unknown reasons, had an intense personal antipathy toward Inoue Masutarô.

The result of their tortuous deliberations, as it turned out, would be one of the strangest dramatic performances in the history of international humanitarianism.

Heading back toward my hotel along the shores of Lake Leman, I think of those men—Inoue, Kasai, Ri Il-Gyeong—walking along this same shoreline, seeing the view that I am gazing at (for it has changed little since the

1950s). Although I have spent so much time recently reading and rereading their letters, telegrams, and reports, I feel as though I know nothing of what was going on in their minds.

What did they think of as they escaped from their meeting rooms to breathe in the fresh lake air or to see the sights of city? Did they convince themselves that they were truly pioneers of a great humanitarian project for which thousands would eventually thank them? Did they see themselves as patriots staunchly defending the interests of their nations? Propaganda chief turned Red Cross negotiator Ri Il-Gyeong had, I have discovered, five children. I wonder if they received cuckoo clocks and Swiss embroidery as souvenirs from the father's foray into international diplomacy.

In the three and a half years since Inoue Masutarô first visited the ICRC building on the hill above the lake, and tentatively raised the question of the repatriation of Koreans, the situation had been transformed. The International Committee of the Red Cross had officially offered to assist with the repatriation. The North Korean government had publicly welcomed the mass return of Koreans from Japan. The Koreans themselves had experienced the welfare cuts of 1956 and the growing mood of pessimism about the future of their life in Japan.

Meanwhile, since the summer of 1958, an almost hysterical wave of excitement about the prospect of life in North Korea had been sweeping through the minority community and the Japanese media. Everyone, from teachers in *Chongryun* schools to leading Japanese politicians and intellectuals, was assuring Koreans that a better life awaited them across the waters. The Soviet Union had promised to provide free transport. Now the targets first mentioned by the Japanese Red Cross in 1956 were indeed being fulfilled: Tens of thousands of would-be returnees were signing up for repatriation.

What happened in Geneva in the spring and summer of 1959 would determine the answer to some central questions: After all the backstage political intrigue of the past four years, could this still be a humanitarian project in any real sense of the term, or was humanitarianism about to be used as a cloak for yet more cynical power politics on both sides of the Cold War divide? Above all, what efforts would be made to confirm that the repatriation was voluntary?

The International Committee itself was expecting to be invited to send a mission to Japan to conduct a confirmation of free will. For this to have any real meaning, it would be necessary to interview returnees one by one in private, ensuring that each understood the path that he or she was taking and had made a properly informed choice to migrate to North Korea.

The North Korean side was adamantly opposed to this idea. At most, it was willing to allow the ICRC only a nominal role, providing (as it were) a humanitarian fig leaf for a repatriation to be carried out in practice by the North Korean and Japanese governments with the help of their two national Red Cross societies and *Chongryun*. Chief delegate Ri Il-Gyeong made clear that North Korea was particularly hostile to any arrangement that would allow the international agency to question returnees about their "political beliefs, place of birth, membership of organizations, etc." From the North Korean point of view, the only organization that should carry out any questioning or screening was *Chongryun*, whose task was to keep out the "reactionary and espionage elements" feared by Kim Il-Sung.

The North Korean government in fact expected to be able to negotiate a repatriation agreement directly with Japan without any ICRC involvement. When it became clear that Japan was insisting on a role for the international body, this triggered intense debate within the North Korean political elite. It was only after more than a month of hesitation, and considerable mediation and prodding by the Soviet Union, that in late March 1959 North Korea finally agreed to dispatch a delegation to Geneva for talks. There the North Korean and Japanese Red Cross delegations held negotiations behind closed doors without ICRC involvement, the Japanese delegation being given the responsibility of securing *post facto* ICRC approval of the agreement worked out by the two sides.

The Japanese authorities, meanwhile, were deeply committed to the repatriation project and extremely eager that this should be carried out under the imprimatur of the ICRC. To be precise, according to the information that leaked out to the ICRC from the negotiation room, the Japanese Red Cross soon agreed to "accept the position consistently taken by [North] Korea, confining the ICRC to a mere observer role." But the Japanese government, "probably at the instigation of the United States," urged an agreement that allowed more active ICRC screening of returnees.

This is a crucially important point. What mattered to the Japanese government, as it emerged, was not so much the *content* of any ICRC "confirmation of free will," but rather the fact that some semblance of confirmation took place. For this would allow the repatriation to be presented to the world as a humanitarian voluntary return; and the appearance of humanitarianism was the condition demanded by the United States, in return for which the United States would not actively side with South Korea on the repatriation issue.

In the circumstances, it was not surprising that the negotiations between the Japanese and North Korean Red Cross Societies acquired a rather surreal air.

In late April (according to Ri Il-Gyeong), the North Korean side proposed that the ICRC should be invited to make a radio broadcast confirming that the proposed repatriation was a purely humanitarian venture; it was a proposal that the Japanese delegation promptly accepted. Meanwhile, a core group of LDP politicians had become deeply involved in the process, holding discussions with Japan Red Cross Society officials in a convoluted search for an acceptable form of words to describe the ICRC's involvement in the process. Their deliberations took place against a background of widespread prorepatriation demonstrations by *Chongryun* and other groups and of elections for the Upper House of Parliament, in which the ruling Liberal Democratic Party gained ten seats. By early June agreement had been reached on the term advice—*jogen*—to describe the ICRC's function, and on 7 June the Central Committee of the North Korean ruling party approved a new proposal based on this formula. The North Korean side seems to have believed that this would allow the ICRC to endorse the process without carrying out the intrusive screening that North Korea so bitterly opposed. A compromise along these lines was accepted by both sides, and on the basis of this rather strained consensus, the Japanese and North Korean delegations then set to work to draft a written accord on repatriation.

Ri Il-Gyeong proclaimed this as a success that showed that "throughout the entire course of the negotiations, the initiative had been on the DPRK side." Although his assessment contains a good measure of self-congratulatory hyperbole, Ri was not the only person to feel that the North Korean side had done well from the proceedings. In early June, one senior ICRC official told the committee's plenary session that "at present, the Japanese government and Red Cross seem, in large measure, to have capitulated to the demands of North Korea by accepting that the ICRC will operate in the role of an observer with the ability to advise the Japanese Red Cross."

The wording of the draft accord, provisionally initialed by the heads of the Japanese and North Korean Red Cross delegations on 24 June 1959, did little to allay these concerns. It spelled out in detail the procedures for the registration and transport of returnees to North Korea, including the amount of luggage and money they could take with them. But Article 3 of the accord, which dealt with the role of the ICRC, was a masterpiece of vagueness. The crucial section stated that "the Japanese Red Cross will request the International Committee of the Red Cross to take the measures which the latter judges to be necessary and appropriate in order to guarantee an operation and organization which is impartial and which conforms to the principles of the Red Cross;" but it provided no indication as to what these measures might be.

By the time the draft agreement was presented to them for approval, some members of the ICRC had begun to feel serious unease at the turn that events were taking. The repatriation issue seemed to have acquired a momentum of its own, and there were fears that it was dragging the international Red Cross movement into some very murky waters indeed.

Already in early March, just before the Japan–North Korea negotiations began, Leopold Boissier had warned an ICRC Plenary Committee meeting that the issue had far-reaching implications that went beyond the fates of Koreans in Japan. It threatened, he said, to "disrupt the entire political stability of the Far East. It influences and will continue to influence the relations between the two Koreas and Japan, the United States, the USSR, and even China."

When it finally received a copy of the draft accord on 25 June, the ICRC's Presidential Council held a long discussion at which at least one member suggested that the organization should pull out of the scheme altogether. In the end, however, the council decided to consider the draft document carefully and seek further information before deciding whether or not the ICRC should endorse the accord and involve itself in the repatriation.

The task of persuading the ICRC to approve the scheme was entrusted jointly to Inoue Masutarô and the Japanese ambassador in Berne, Okumura Katsuzô, with support from the Japanese government and Red Cross. The Japanese side now began to lobby very vigorously for the ICRC to give its blessing to the draft accord. In the first week of August, ICRC president Boissier received visits from Kasai, Inoue, and Ambassador Okumura, all pressing him to see the merits of the agreement. A week later, Japanese Foreign Minister Fujiyama Aiichirô himself wrote to Boissier to tell him that "the Japanese government considers the Accord concluded between the Red Cross Societies of Japan and North Korea as conforming to its desires and its fundamental policy . . . and for this reason, the Accord is fully approved by the Japanese government, which will take final responsibility for its execution."

Vociferous demands for the ICRC to endorse the accord also came from the North Korean and Soviet governments, the Japanese Socialist and Communist Parties, and *Chongryun,* whose members were staging regular demonstrations on the subject outside Red Cross offices in Japan.

As the ICRC struggled to respond appropriately to the draft accord, it soon became obvious that the organization was severely handicapped by its lack of knowledge about East Asia. In July, for example, a group of officials from the Japanese Foreign Ministry called on Harry Angst to push for a quick decision on the issue. The officials, who had heard that the ICRC was hoping to interview each returnee in private, politely enquired whether the International Committee "had available in Geneva delegates speaking Japanese."

The answer, of course, was no. In the end, even the hunt for Japanese-speaking Swiss nationals who could interpret for the committee's delegates in Japan proved largely fruitless; other than missionaries (deemed inappropriate for this politically sensitive task), there appeared to be only one half-Japanese woman of Swiss nationality who was truly fluent in Japanese, and the ICRC mission was forced to rely heavily on interpreters provided by the Japanese government instead.

But without knowledge of the circumstances of Koreans in Japan, it was impossible to determine how far their departure was truly voluntary. People without welfare and residence rights, after all, are hardly in a position to make free choices in the full sense of the word. Neither are those who are being bombarded with misleading propaganda.

The ICRC was clearly uneasy, both with the vague wording of the draft accord and with the lacunae in its knowledge of the problem. The International Committee therefore decided to involve itself in the repatriation only if it received satisfactory assurances from the Japanese government and Red Cross on seven crucial questions.

For example, the ICRC wanted a clear statement as to whether it would be allowed to question returnees without witnesses, so as to verify whether or not each wanted to change his or her mind before embarkation. And would all potential returnees be free to speak to ICRC delegates, with ICRC delegates also being free to question any *Zainichi* Koreans they wanted?

In other words, the ICRC was demanding the right to carry out the very screening exercise that the North Korean side had insisted must be excluded from the accord.

The ICRC's memorandum to Japan also included two other particularly important questions: Was the Japanese government willing to publicly inform *Zainichi* Koreans of their status if they remained in Japan and to inform the ICRC in advance of the details of that status? And could the Japanese side promise to maintain order and keep unauthorized people away from the registration and embarkation centers? This last question obviously reflected concerns at the propaganda campaign being waged in particular by *Chongryun*, but also (from the opposite political angle) by the South Korean–affiliated *Mindan*.

The ICRC had perhaps hoped that these questions would force the Japanese side to think more carefully about the practical details of the repatriation, giving all involved some breathing space and enabling further debate to take place in Geneva. But in fact, the reply from Japan was remarkably swift and brief. Four days later, Shimazu, "after careful study with the Japanese government," replied to all seven questions in the affirmative.

The only answer that went beyond a bald *yes* was the answer to the question about the status of Koreans who remained in Japan. The status of those who had come to Japan before the end of the Pacific War, Geneva was informed, would be decided by negotiations between Japan and "the government representing Korea." Meanwhile, "a status of semi-permanent residence will be granted to them according to the laws and regulations of Japan as to date."

Behind the scenes, however, the Japanese authorities, in their eagerness to ensure ICRC involvement in the scheme, were providing the international body with a flood of intriguing if sometimes puzzling supplementary information. In early August, Inoue sent the International Committee a confidential statement on the treatment of Koreans in Japan. The statement, which had been authorized by the Japanese government, explained that "Koreans in Japan lost their Japanese nationality when the Peace Treaty became effective. Therefore, they should be treated as any other foreigners residing in Japan." However, the Japanese government had generously gone out of its way to accord them favorable treatment. For example, they were allowed to own ships and to attend state schools. They received livelihood protection benefits, and "lepers, mentally deranged persons, [and] needy people are not deported."

In response to specific queries from Geneva about *Zainichi* Koreans' right to work and welfare, the ICRC was also informed that Koreans in Japan were eligible to receive unemployment insurance and that both the

Labor Standards Law and the Law on the Stabilization of Employment "prohibit discrimination for reasons of nationality, etc."

The Japanese side was also particularly eager to dispel what it termed the public misunderstanding that many Koreans in Japan had arrived as forced laborers. A special press release on this problem was issued by the Japanese government on 11 July, and a copy was duly sent to Geneva. This stated that, of the two million Koreans who had been in Japan at the end of the Pacific War, those brought over as involuntary labor recruits accounted for "only a small proportion," and "needless to say, they were paid standard wages." Besides, almost all had left at the end of the war. As a result, a recent survey conducted by the government on the basis of the alien registration system was said to have shown that only 245 former Korean labor recruits were still living in Japan, and none of them wished to be repatriated to North Korea.

The ICRC, sadly, did not have the resources to conduct its own research in Japan. Its only representative there was Harry Angst, and he had neither the time nor the inclination to double-check the facts provided by the Japanese government.

Yet even a careful review of the ICRC's own files might have set a few alarm bells ringing.

On the forced labor question, for example, Inoue Masutarô himself had composed a long report that he had sent to Geneva three years before, with the express approval of the Japanese government. This informed the ICRC that one-quarter of a million Korean laborers had entered Japan "by enlistment" (that is, as labor recruits), and that there were also a further 365,263 Koreans who had been drafted as servicemen or auxiliaries by the Japanese armed forces: "It is presumed that many of them were in this country at the end of the war." In addition, 520,000 had been sent to Japan "under contract," between 1942 and 1945.

The test case whom Kasai Yoshisuke had hoped to send back to North Korea after the New Delhi conference had been, as Kasai himself explained to the North Korean Red Cross, a former conscript laborer who desired repatriation. Information that became available after the start of the repatriation would show that he was far from being the only returnee to have been involved in wartime forced labor.

On the employment and welfare issues, the information provided from Tokyo was technically correct but woefully inadequate. A relatively casual check of the facts would quickly have revealed that the Labor Standards Law and the Law on the Stabilization of Employment, though they might prohibit the payment of lower wages to foreigners, were completely powerless to prevent discrimination in the hiring of employees. Foreigners (including Koreans) were excluded by law from public employment, and in practice were almost always debarred from the better-paid, stable jobs provided by large Japanese firms. It was only after a major court case in the 1970s—in which a *Zainichi* Korean successfully sued the Hitachi Corporation for reversing its decision to employ him on learning of his Korean nationality—that the path to employment in large private companies began to become a little smoother.

The Unemployment Insurance Law, meanwhile, was a very limited measure introduced during the Allied Occupation whose coverage was restricted to firms with more than five employees (thus in effect excluding the large proportion of Koreans who were employed in tiny family concerns). By far the most significant postwar Japanese welfare measures, the national health insurance system and the national pension system, were actually being established at the very time when the Japanese government and Red Cross supplied this information to Geneva; the National Health Insurance Act (*Kokumin Kenkô Hoken Hô*) had come into force in January 1959, and National Pension Act (*Kokumin Nenkin Hô*) would be implemented from November 1959. As their Japanese titles made clear, the beneficiaries of these measures were "nationals" (*kokumin*). Foreigners, including Koreans, were explicitly excluded.

None of these facts, however, seems to have been known to the members of the ICRC when, on 7 August 1959, Leopold Boissier officially communicated to Shimazu Tadatsugu the International Committee's carefully worded response to the draft accord. "As a consequence of the replies which the Japanese Red Cross was good enough to provide to the questions we posed it on 24 July," the ICRC had decided to "give its assistance to the Japanese Red Cross with a view to the repatriation of those Koreans living in Japan who wish to return to the place of their choice in their country of origin." This offer, Boissier added, did not imply specific ICRC approval of the content of the draft accord. However, it did in practice provide the green light needed to allow the accord to be officially signed and put into effect.

Another remarkable aspect of the accord, though one that provoked much less discussion at the time, was the fact that it gave the ICRC absolutely no power to send representatives to North Korea to check the fate of the returnees once they arrived there. That task was to be left in hands of *Chongryun*.

The Accord Between the Japan Red Cross Society and the Red Cross Society of the Democratic People's Republic of Korea Relating to the Return of Koreans Resident in Japan was officially signed on 13 August in the Indian city of Calcutta, and thus became known by the more readily memorable title the Calcutta Accord. The signing ceremony itself, however, was a rather low-key affair—an indication, maybe, of the fact that many in the international Red Cross movement felt uncomfortable about the whole exercise.

This discomfort was evidently shared even by Leopold Boissier.

On the day after the July meeting at which the committee had provisionally decided to become involved in the repatriation scheme, Boissier wrote to a committee member who had missed the meeting. It is a rather curious and slightly sad letter, whose tone suggests a weary recognition that this was not going to be one of the high points in the ICRC's history. The committee, writes Boissier, had provisionally accepted the text of the accord "without enthusiasm."

The comments that follow suggest Boissier's own sense of remoteness from East Asia, which he describes as "a region of the world where human beings have never been in a position freely to determine their fate." If the ICRC managed to carry out its mission in Japan successfully, he adds, "It may perhaps be the first time that a little humanity appears in this world given over to violence."

His letter also expresses an awareness of the fragility of the humanitarian principles of the organization that he headed—an awareness, perhaps, that in this case those principles had been strained to cracking point. "Personally," he writes, "I do not believe that we can fly in the face of political opinion. . . . Our situation is always precarious, precisely because we can rely on nothing but the sympathy of individuals and, to a greater or lesser degree, on the tolerance of governments."

Sifting once again through the growing mountain of letters, minutes, and reports from Geneva and elsewhere, seeking to piece together this decisive moment of the story, I have become increasingly puzzled by one aspect of the Geneva negotiations: the fleeting, elusive references to the United States of America. Here and there, the United States appears momentarily in the narrative, only to disappear again. I am reminded of that famous moment in detective fiction, the curious incident of the dog in the night time:

"'The dog did nothing in the night time.'

'That was the curious incident,' remarked Sherlock Homes."

In this story, there is a silence, a lack of action, that grows more and more palpable as the negotiations reach their climax, and this silence is coming from Washington.

16

SILENT PARTNERS

In search of the source of the American silence, I spend long afternoons in the National Library of Australia in my hometown, Canberra, browsing microfilms and databases of declassified U.S. documents.

The National Library is one of my favorite places to read and think. It is quiet without being dauntingly hushed. Sunlight streams in through the windows. Just down the hill is the shore of Lake Burley Griffin, and between the library and lake lies one of Canberra's most beautiful and least-visited monuments—a small fountain, embedded in the grassy turf, where water bubbles up like a spring between stones engraved with the word *peace* in many languages—the French *la paix*, the Russian *mir*, the Japanese *heiwa*, and, in the language of the indigenous Ngunnawal people of this region, *narragunnawali*.

Having come this far in the journey, this seems as good a place as any to spread out the documents on the table once again and try to reach some tentative conclusions about the forces that shaped the repatriation to North Korea.

Reading through the ICRC's journal, *The International Review of the Red Cross*, I have come across a transcript of the opening address that Indian Prime Minister Nehru gave to the New Delhi Conference in October 1957. It is a surprisingly long and passionate speech, a heartfelt critique of the Cold War and of the limits of so-called coexistence between the communist and capitalist camps. All too often, said Nehru, coexistence was not a search for peace, but rather a hostile standoff, in which the fears and hatreds of one side amplified the fears and hatreds of the other.

Coexistence, it might be added, masked another sort of violence, too. In the interests of maintaining their own power, the powerful of both sides at times became in effect partners, tacitly collaborating in trampling on the rights of the powerless.

In tracing the repatriation story, I have been tempted to look for a single explanation, a single culprit to blame for the pain that followed. But the return to North Korea was ultimately shaped by a tacit partnership that spanned the Cold War divide. Not all partners were equally involved; not all bore equal responsibility for the outcome. But without their quiet collaboration, the events of December 1959 and thereafter could not have taken place.

The first push for a mass repatriation of tens of thousands of *Zainichi* Koreans clearly came from Japan—from the Japanese government and Red Cross, working in close collaboration. Their motives were economic and security concerns, enhanced by a large infusion of prejudice. They hoped to rid the country of those they saw as subversive and a welfare burden. But as time went on, another concern became increasingly important. In an era when Japanese politics were deeply polarized between right and left, repatriation brought both sides together. This issue was a vote winner, popular with media and the public alike. It helped sustain the popularity of the Kishi regime when other foreign policy issues—above all the deeply controversial renewal of the Security Treaty with the United States—were placing it under growing pressure.

The Japanese side was centrally responsible for the nature of the Calcutta Accord itself. In fact, eager to persuade the ICRC to endorse the agreement with North Korea, the Japanese Red Cross explicitly acknowledged this responsibility. In July 1959, as the international body was struggling to come to a decision about the contentious accord, Japan Red Cross Society vice president Kasai paid a visit to the ICRC's Tokyo representative Harry Angst and (in Angst's words) "went to some length in explaining to me that the role assigned to the ICRC in the present agreement was the one of an advisor and as such would not engage any responsibility on the part of the ICRC. Mr. Kasai was quite emphatic that the responsibility for the repatriation scheme rests squarely on the shoulders of the Japanese Red Cross and Japanese government."

But, as the vicissitudes of the 1956 repatriation had shown, Japan could not have implemented a scheme like this alone. *Chongryun* had also, from the first, been a very active campaigner for repatriation, and it was only after North Korea, with strong backing from the Soviet Union, threw its full weight behind the scheme in 1958 that mass repatriation became possible. Repeated messages about repatriation had been sent from Tokyo to Pyongyang in 1956 and 1957, but North Korea's wholehearted commitment to mass repatriation in 1958 was ultimately based on its own calculations of national self-interest. Repatriation served the Kim Il-Sung regime's need for labor, its grandiose dreams of spectacular economic progress, its desire to disrupt the triangular relationship between Japan, South Korea, and the United States, and its longing for propaganda victories on the global stage.

Meanwhile, in the South, efforts by the Republic of Korea's Rhee regime to block the scheme were undermined by that regime's own mistreatment of political dissidents, its reluctance to help Koreans from Japan return to the South, and its enthusiasm for using *Zainichi* Koreans as bargaining counters in its dealings with Japan. All of these placed South Korea on very shaky ground when it attempted to rally humanitarian world opinion against this violation of its citizens' rights.

So the wary collaboration between Right and Left in Japan was expanded into a wary collaboration between Cold War regional enemies Japan and North Korea. And by the second half of 1959, when Khrushchev traveled to the United States to present himself as a champion of Cold War coexistence, tacit collaboration on the repatriation issue was being extended again to the very highest levels—to the level of the superpowers.

The Soviet government saw active and well-funded support for repatriation to North Korea as a means to retain and strengthen its influence in the region, in opposition to its emerging rival, China.

The United States, on the contrary, had never favored or encouraged the repatriation plan. Indeed, North Korea had (reasonably enough) expected passionate opposition from Washington. But when the crucial moment came, the United States stayed largely silent.

And that silence was perhaps the final decisive factor that enabled the plans of all the others to become reality.

For any champion of liberal democratic principles, the repatriation issue (as the ICRC had already realized) raised challenging problems. There were indeed Koreans in Japan who wished to move to North Korea, and the right to choose one's place of residence was indeed a fundamental human freedom. The United States was at that very time trying to persuade Khrushchev to allow Soviet Jews to leave for Israel and elsewhere; it would have been contradictory to deny *Zainichi* Koreans the right to go to North Korea.

On the other hand, the Eisenhower administration knew that most Koreans in Japan came from the South of the country, that they were being subjected to an intense media and propaganda campaign in favor of repatriation to the North, and that the future that awaited them in DPRK was not rosy. As the self-styled leader of the free world and chief ally of South Korea, the U.S. government might have been expected to take a dim view of an agreement between Japan and North Korea to send tens of thousands of Koreans (most of them originally from the south of the peninsula) to be resettled in a reclusive Communist state. But for the United States, as for all the other nations involved in this story, the repatriation came to be inextricably embedded in wider Cold War strategies.

On 2 March 1959, shortly before negotiations between Japan and North Korea began, Henry Villard, who was both U.S. consul general and permanent delegate to the International Organizations in Geneva, telephoned ICRC president Leopold Boissier to explain the U.S. attitude to the problem. The State Department, Villard said, was "not opposed to the repatriation of individuals to their own country, on condition that this repatriation is preceded by a thorough screening." Although the United States did not, of course, recognize North Korea, Villard made it clear that the U.S. government knew that a substantial number of Koreans in Japan were likely to be "returned" to the DPRK. The State Department apparently had no problem defining this destination as the returnees' "own country," and in fact the overall impression conveyed to Boissier was that "the U.S.A. does not wish to get involved in this affair."

As events unfolded, however, the U.S. attitude to intervention seemed to be changing. A couple of weeks later, Villard requested a face-to-face meeting with a senior ICRC official, at which he passed on U.S. State Department worries about the notion of impending direct negotiations between the Japanese and North Korean Red Cross Societies. The United States was facing pressure to intervene from various sources—most powerfully, from South Korea, but also from sections of U.S. domestic opinion. Some Christian groups, alerted by coreligionists in South Korea, were sounding the alarm, and by the middle of the year the American Red Cross itself was expressing deep reservations about the scheme.

By June, as rumors of a Japanese capitulation to North Korean demands leaked out of the Geneva negotiation room, Henry Villard was again contacting the ICRC with the message that the proposed agreement between Japan and North Korea seemed to Washington to be inadequate. Only a fully fledged ICRC screening of returnees, he insisted, could ensure that the process was genuinely voluntary.

The U.S. State Department, in a confidential memo, warned the ICRC that "the communist controlled Chosen Soren [i.e., *Chongryun*], a powerful Korean residents' organization in Japan, is being given an opportunity and a cover to bribe or coerce Korean residents to agree to go to North Korea, because of the strong desire of the Japanese that as many Koreans as possible be repatriated voluntarily."

The memo also noted ominously that "it cannot be expected in this atmosphere that the JRC [Japan Red Cross] will be completely neutral."

Meanwhile, U.S. Ambassador in Tokyo Douglas MacArthur II (nephew of the general) was lobbying the Japanese government to incorporate a thorough screening process into the repatriation plan. The Japanese response was equivocal: Prime Minister Kishi, MacArthur reported, impressed him as being "vague on the entire matter."

A recently declassified top secret memo, signed by White House staffer John S. D. Eisenhower (the son of the president), shows that the U.S. government was above all anxious that the repatriation might hinder the normalization of relations between Japan and South Korea. The solution from Washington was to push for a clearer and more active ICRC role in the scheme, and Consul General Villard in Geneva was instructed to convey this view to ICRC officials.

"We desire the ICRC to realize," John Eisenhower's memo concludes, "that this matter has political ramifications of serious proportions."

These concerns from Washington may have been among the factors that encouraged the ICRC to pose its seven questions to Japan. However, once the rapid and uninformative replies came back from Tokyo, the United States took no firm steps to intervene or prevent the accord from being signed. Although Consul General Villard continued to complain that the accord would be a propaganda victory for North Korea, he expressed a somewhat grudging U.S. agreement that in the "last resort," the ICRC should announce "its decision in principle to participate subject to formal signature" of the draft agreement. This should be accompanied (as Villard's telegraphic message puts it) "by declaration ICRC determination to assure

Koreans in Japan full freedom real choice and that Jap authorities have agreed provide all necessary facilities." This indeed was the course that the ICRC took, and the U.S. reasons for adopting this compromise are, in the end, not difficult to fathom.

In the second half of 1959, the United States had strategic concerns in East Asia whose importance, from the perspective of Washington, far outweighed the significance of repatriation. At the end of the postwar occupation, the United States had signed a Security Treaty with Japan, firmly binding its former Pacific War enemy into the U.S. sphere of political and military influence. The treaty was due for renewal, and that renewal was bitterly opposed by a large section of Japanese opinion—particularly (though not exclusively) left-wing Japanese opinion.

Prime Minister Kishi was a firm supporter of the treaty—his commitment to its renewal, indeed, was ultimately to cost him his premiership. Repeated U.S. government reports warned that any replacement for Kishi was likely to be less sympathetic to the United States. While Japanese opposition to the Security Treaty mounted, there were growing fears in Washington of a leftward trend in Japanese politics. As Eisenhower himself put it, "We did not want to take any action in Japan that would have the effect of driving the Japanese further in the wrong direction." The second half of 1959 was no time for the United States to be opposing the one policy on which the Kishi administration and the Japanese Left saw eye-to-eye.

Indeed, U.S. concerns about the repatriation scheme had always focused less on the likely fate of returnees themselves than on the strategic impact of the project on Japan–South Korean relations. Rapprochement between Japan and South Korea was a core aim of U.S. policy, and the head of the State Department's Far East section, J. Graham Parsons believed that "the best chance to settle this matter was while Mr. Kishi was prime minister." By contrast, the aging and erratic South Korean president, Syngman Rhee, was increasingly being seen by his U.S. allies as a public embarrassment.

On 10 July 1959, just after the draft accord between Japan and North Korea was completed, Parsons wrote to U.S. Secretary of State Christian Herter, warning him that "in the next few weeks a major crisis in Japan-Republic of Korea [South Korea] relations is likely to occur" as a result of the anticipated ICRC decision on the repatriation accord. He attached a background paper, explaining the repatriation problem and the State Department's position on the subject.

This paper began with a statement that speaks volumes about the U.S. government's underlying approach:

> The Korean minority in Japan has always proved a troublesome problem to handle. The Koreans have never been integrated into Japanese society. They have been an underprivileged, economically poor group living in isolated communities within major urban areas. As a result, they have been a major crime problem and a drain on the national and local social services. The Japanese, beset by their own employment problems, have not welcomed this additional burden.

In discussing the current repatriation issue, the paper said nothing about any Japanese initiatives before 1959, but noted the Japanese government's 13 February 1959 decision to move forward with repatriation. "Given the attitude of the Japanese people toward the Korean minority," the State Department commented, "this decision was extremely popular."

After outlining the course of the Geneva negotiations, the paper concluded that repatriation was virtually a forgone conclusion. Consul General Villard had apparently already been told by ICRC staff that "the ICRC is so deeply committed to assisting the repatriation that it will probably not disapprove the agreement." As for Japan, it was even more firmly set on the idea of a mass return. The State Department explained,

> In view of the broader political implications of the repatriation issue, we have sought to discourage the Japanese government from conducting such repatriation and at a minimum urging [*sic*] that repatriation be entirely voluntary and under effective ICRC supervision. The Japanese Government, however, is politically so completely committed to repatriation that even ICRC disapproval of the Red Cross Societies' agreement would provide only a brief opportunity to block repatriation to north Korea. Under these circumstances, the Japanese government has indicated that it would be prepared to delay repatriation only if there were real promise of an overall settlement of its differences with the Republic of Korea.

Given this virtual fait accompli, it was suggested, the United States should focus on minimizing the damage to Japan–South Korean relations by encouraging the ICRC to become actively involved in supervising repatriation, while at the same time urging South Korea to acquiesce to the repatriation plan and open its own doors to an inflow of Koreans from Japan.

Shortly before submitting the background paper, at a meeting with the Japanese ambassador to Washington, Asakai Kôichirô, Parsons made a "helpful suggestion" about the repatriation, which Ambassador Asakai duly relayed to his government. The suggestion apparently outlined the form of ICRC involvement that the United States saw as the minimum necessary to secure its tacit support for the scheme. The State Department view was also conveyed personally by Herter to Boissier on 21 July. Meanwhile, the United States urged the Rhee regime to soften its stance on repatriation.

The U.S. approach seems to have produced some results, for in July Korea's Foreign Ministry began to suggest the possibility of a "positive program" to allow the repatriation of *Zainichi* Koreans to the South, and there were signs of a thaw in the economic relationship between Japan and South Korea, which had also been frozen in response to the repatriation issue.

In the end, however, the United States provided little practical support for repatriation to South Korea, and this idea seems to have quietly disappeared from the agenda. Instead, the State Department focused on dissuading South Korea from taking drastic measures to block the repatriation. As Secretary of State Herter wrote to South Korean President Syngman Rhee in September 1959:

> The United States fully endorses the principle of genuinely voluntary repatriation and I, personally, am convinced that faithful adherence to this principle has been and will be of great benefit to the Free World. In this connection I believe it is inevitable that, under the present circumstances, there will be some repatriation of Koreans in Japan to north Korea by mid-November. The Republic of Korea can scarcely fail to realize that the Japanese government is publicly committed to the point that it cannot withdraw from the repatriation arrangements which have been made, and which have the approval of the International Committee of the Red Cross. I need hardly say that any thought of resort to forcible interference with repatriation operations could lead to disastrous consequences to Korea's relations with the Free World.

In mid-1960, when South Korean Prime Minister Huh Chung met President Eisenhower, he complained about this U.S. attitude. During the early stages of the repatriation negotiations, Huh recalled, the United States had expressed objections, and these had had some effect, but later on, "When the United States kept silent, the Japanese were encouraged to reach the Calcutta Agreement." Eisenhower, without directly addressing the repatriation issue, responded that he "could see some justification in the grievances voiced by the prime minister." However, he stressed that the overriding issue was the "urgent problem of keeping Japan in the right camp." South

Korea's concerns, said Eisenhower, should be recognized and addressed, "but not at the expense of Japan."

Huh was probably right. The U.S. government, through its influence both on Japan and on the ICRC, was the one actor with the power to stop the repatriation plan. More importantly, it also possessed the power to pursue an alternative approach—an approach that was briefly raised in discussions, but never seriously pursued.

Immediately after the signing of the Calcutta Accord, Huh Chung (who was at that time South Korean foreign minister) urged the American government to put pressure on Japan to improve the lives of *Zainichi* Koreans by removing at least some of the many forms of discrimination that they faced in Japanese society. Such improvements, after all, would surely have helped to make repatriation a genuinely free choice in a way that no Red Cross screening program could ever do.

U.S. Ambassador MacArthur duly passed Huh's message on to Foreign Minister Fujiyama and leading Japanese bureaucrats. Fujiyama's reply was that there was "no discrimination" against Koreans in Japan. During and since the war, he said "they have been treated as foreigners, i.e. more favourably than Japanese. Furthermore, the Japanese government is spending much money to help their livelihood—poor Koreans are receiving government money. Legally or otherwise, there isn't any discrimination and if they feel so it must come from their sense of inferiority."

If there is any single statement of the attitudes that sealed the fate of the tens of thousands who would return to North Korea, it perhaps MacArthur's diplomatic and conciliatory response:

> "The Ambassador said that, obviously, there is some discrimination, even if it is not legal. It is social. For instance, Japanese employers understandably prefer to employ Japanese rather than Koreans. Such things cannot be corrected by laws. However, if there is no legal discrimination, perhaps it could be stated in writing, as a re-affirmation. This in itself might be helpful as a face-saving document. It would give the appearance that the South Koreans had obtained something."

When Prime Minister Kishi and Foreign Minister Fujiyama met the U.S. Secretary of State in Washington on 19 January 1960, three days after the revised Security Treaty was signed, Kishi took the opportunity to express his appreciation for "the U.S. attitude toward the repatriation of Koreans to North Korea."

In reply, U.S. Secretary of State Christian Herter

mentioned that the Department had received a telegram from Seoul setting forth a request of the Korean Government that we ask the [Japan-
ese] Prime Minister to stop further repatriation to North Korea. The
U.S., however, intends to maintain its past position on the repatriation
issue. The Secretary stressed that the U.S. continues to support the principle of voluntary repatriation to any part of Korea.

Five months later, amid the largest demonstrations seen in postwar
Japan and in the absence of the main opposition parties, who were boy-
cotting parliamentary sittings, the renewed United States–Japan Mutual Security Treaty was ratified by the Japanese Diet. But by that time, the repatriation program was already well under way.

17

A GUIDE FOR MR. RETURNEE

So the International Committee of the Red Cross found itself caught in the cross-currents of Cold War politics, constrained by its own lack of expertise on East Asia and its tradition of collaboration with national governments. The officials whom it dispatched to Japan to confirm the free will of returnees were in many cases dedicated humanitarians. They devoted great energy to the cause. Their letters and reports are mines of information on the everyday workings of the repatriation plan.

But from the first, they were up against insuperable odds. Nothing they could do prevented their work from becoming a strange masque, performed with meticulous precision before the eyes of the world, but utterly lacking the power to stop the tragedy unfolding before their eyes.

The Calcutta Accord unleashed a frenzy of activity in Northeast Asia and beyond.

A few days before the accord was even officially signed, the Japanese government, Japan Red Cross Society, and National Railways (who would provide the special trains to carry returnees to Niigata) had come together to create a Repatriation Coordination Committee. Their mission was to begin the massive task of registering and processing tens of thousands of people, and transporting them to the departure point of Niigata. By the following month, 3,655 Red Cross windows (as they were called) had been set up all over the country to register applicants for repatriation. Red Cross officials were also dispatched to Niigata to find an appropriate place to lodge the returnees as they waited for departure.

Chongryun, too, was busy setting up its own procedures for processing the departing *Zainichi* Koreans. Their task was to gather information on names, ages, dates of birth, social status, political affiliations, attitudes to the Democratic People's Republic of Korea, past contacts with the South Korean regime, and so forth, all of which was to be transmitted to Pyongyang. They were also to exercise their own very careful screening and control the flow of people, urging greater numbers to register or holding back the tides of returnees, as circumstances in the DPRK required.

In North Korea itself, the scale of the preparations was even greater. Already in February 1959 the North Korean cabinet had established a Returnees Welcoming Committee, headed by Deputy Premier Kim Il. As well as creating reception centers and education programs for returnees, preparing housing and jobs, and appointing local officials who would assist and supervise the new arrivals, the government was also conducting a campaign to inform the population about the impending inflow of compatriots from Japan. Posters began to appear across the country, depicting Mother Korea welcoming her returning children with open arms.

Meanwhile in the Soviet Union, the government was equipping the passenger ships *Kryl'yon* and *Tobol'sk*, as well as planning the discreet naval escort that would be used during early voyages to guard against the possibility of any attack or blockade by South Korea.

And in Geneva, the ICRC selected an emissary to Japan whose task would be to establish the International Committee's "confirmation of free will," preparing the ground for a team of delegates who would follow him to Tokyo soon after.

The man chosen for this task was one of the international Red Cross movement's most respected figures, ICRC vice president Marcel Junod, a person who had visited Japan once before, in the most dramatic of circumstances.

Sent on a wartime ICRC mission to investigate rumors of the maltreatment of prisoners-of-war in Japanese prison camps, Junod had first arrived at an airfield near Tokyo at the very moment of the Japanese surrender to the Allies in mid-August 1945. Within days of reaching Japan, he heard reports of the strange new weapon that had obliterated the cities of Hiroshima and Nagasaki and insisted on traveling to Hiroshima to witness the devastation for himself. Thus Junod, a trained doctor, became one of the first outsiders to witness the effects of the atomic bombing. His quick and compassionate response to the terrible suffering he saw had won him widespread respect in Japan.

In this sense, Junod seemed the ideal person to carry out the sensitive tasks of liaison with the Japanese government and Red Cross in the autumn of 1959. His disadvantage, however, was that he had not been closely involved in earlier negotiations about the repatriation scheme and seems to have been unaware of some important aspects of its background. Junod was also a very busy man, and could spend only one month in Japan—too short a period for a task that proved far more difficult and controversial than anyone had imagined.

He arrived at Haneda Airport on 23 August to be greeted by a demonstration of 2,500 South–Korean affiliated demonstrators, carrying placards saying, "Dr. Junod, Stay Home!" and "ICRC, Stay off Political Issue of ROK-Japan!" Ongoing protests from opponents of the repatriation scheme, indeed, were to provide a constant background to the rest of his stay in Japan.

After meetings with senior government figures including Prime Minister Kishi and Foreign Minister Fujiyama, Junod settled down to a routine of work that included regular attendance, as an observer, at meetings of the Japanese government's Repatriation Coordination Committee.

There he made an unwelcome discovery.

The ICRC had imagined that the whole repatriation process in Japan would actually be run by the Japan Red Cross Society. But instead, as Junod wrote to Geneva, he was "greatly surprised" to realize that the Red Cross had "declined responsibility for the execution of repatriation," claiming that the task exceeded in resources. Now, "except for the part consisting of the registration at [Red Cross] windows," the main work of the repatriation was to be controlled by government officials. Even in this, as it turned out, Junod was mistaken: ICRC delegates who followed him to Japan to oversee the repatriation soon realized that the Red Cross windows were actually rooms, or corners of rooms, set aside within local government offices. They too were staffed by local bureaucrats, many of whom were reported to have little knowledge of the fundamental principles of the Red Cross.

The documents that the Coordination Committee was preparing to guide the repatriation, however, seemed at first to provide reassurance that Red Cross principles would still prevail. They included a clear and simply worded guidebook, designed for the Korean returnees themselves. A beautifully presented English translation, entitled *A Guide for Mr. Returnee*, was provided to Junod, who also passed a copy to U.S. Ambassador MacArthur. It concluded with reassuring remarks about the absence of discrimination against Koreans in Japan. Perhaps this was the face-saving document which MacArthur had proposed to Foreign Minister Fujiyama.

Junod found the guidebook generally satisfactory; Ambassador MacArthur professed himself to be "very happy with its contents."

A Guide for Mr. Returnee (more blandly entitled *Repatriation Guide* in Japanese) was illustrated with attractive, cartoon-like drawings, showing a young Korean man choosing his path between three clearly marked roads—one leading to North Korea, one to South Korea, and one to a continued life in Japan. Above this were written the words that, on Marcel Junod's insistence, were to be posted in Japanese and Korean at every Red Cross window throughout the country: "You are free to stay in Japan, to go back to Korea, North or South, or to any place in the world where you are accepted. In so far as you observe Japanese laws and regulations, you are not forced to leave Japan."

The ensuing paragraphs walk the returnee through the registration process and onto the train to Niigata, where (he was informed) he would be "under the protection of the Red Cross," which would shield him from any form of political influence—a message graphically illustrated by a picture of a train encircled by protective arms emblazoned with the Red Cross emblem. At the Red Cross Center in Niigata, the guide informs, "The first person you meet . . . will be a representative of the [Japanese] Red Cross. You will meet him in a special room where there will also be a representative of the ICRC and an interpreter, but nobody else. As it will be practically your last chance to change your mind, if you want to do so, you should tell the Red Cross Representative about it."

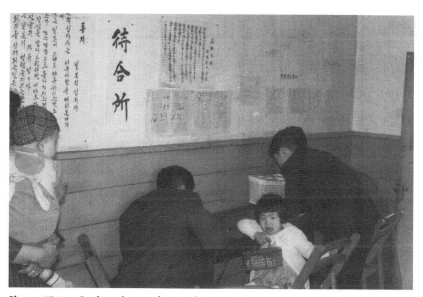

Figure 17.1. Registration at the "Red Cross Window," Ikuno-ku, Osaka (home to Japan's largest Korean community). A copy of the guidebook and of the statement on choices open to Koreans in Japan is displayed on the wall. (© ICRC)

When copies of *A Guide for Mr. Returnee* reached Geneva, this last passage provoked some raised eyebrows. The confident *yes* with which the Japanese authorities had replied to the ICRC's questions had led the committee to think that it was going to be allowed to confirm the free will of returnees by speaking to each person individually and in private, without Japan Red Cross officials present. Now, however, it seemed that the Japanese Red Cross would be playing the main role in the Special Rooms, with their foreign counterparts acting as mere observers.

But if the ICRC was somewhat uneasy at the wording of the guidebook, *Chongryun* and the North Korean government were furious.

The North Korean delegation had spent almost three months arguing over the wording of the accord. The whole purpose of these drawn-out negotiations (from their point of view) had been to ensure that no ICRC screening of returnees took place. Yet now this screening seemed to have reentered the process by the back door. While North Korea and its allies lobbied the Japanese government to abandon the guidebook, *Chongryun* demonstrated its power by launching a boycott of the whole repatriation project.

As a result, when the 3,655 Red Cross windows opened for business on 21 September, they were empty. On *Chongryun*'s orders, virtually no would-be returnees came to register, and in the course of the next six weeks, in place of the anticipated thousands, just 432 people signed up for places on the repatriation ships.

The Japan Red Cross Society tried to bring *Chongryun* back into the process, in part by mobilizing a powerful weapon of its own. It reportedly refused to transmit a sum of around one billion yen (about US$3 million, in the values of the time) that North Korea was trying to send to *Chongryun* for repatriation and relief activities, an action that evoked an outraged telegram of protest from the president of the North Korean Red Cross Society.

By then, the image of the repatriation as a humanitarian exercise controlled by the Red Cross was wearing rather thin.

It was perhaps not surprising that the solution to the conflict over the guidebook should be worked out neither by the Japanese Red Cross nor the ICRC, but by the Japanese Foreign Ministry, in consultation with Socialist parliamentarian and chairman of the Japan-Korea Association, Hoashi Kei, who was passing on the views of *Chongryun*.

Their strategy was to draw up a set of supplementary explanations to accompany *The Guide for Mr. Returnee*. These in effect revoked or significantly revised a number of statements in the guidebook. For example, rather than being isolated from outsiders during their travel to and stay in Niigata, returnees would now be allowed to receive visits from relatives, friends, and others on railway platforms and in the Niigata Red Cross Center. Returnees would enter the Special Rooms family by family, rather than as individuals, and the question to be posed to them there by a Japan Red Cross official would be simple, if not rhetorical, such as, "May I understand you have made up your mind to go to North Korea with full knowledge of the freedom choice of residence as indicated in this notice and there is no change in your decision?"

Most intriguingly of all, the supplementary explanations specified that the Special Rooms would not have doors.

In response to puzzled questions about this from ICRC representatives, an official of the Ministry of Foreign Affairs elaborated that the rooms would in fact "be ordinary office rooms with the doors taken off the hinges and screens, of course, put in their place; thus repatriates cannot be seen, but they can of course be heard." This, it was explained, was a compromise with *Chongryun*, which would have preferred the meetings to be held in a public hall where all around could hear the conversation between Red Cross delegates and returnees. The ministry official hastened to add that it was unlikely that eavesdroppers would be hanging around in the corridor outside the Special Rooms.

Perhaps he was right; but the knowledge that one might be overheard by unseen listeners beyond the screen would hardly have inspired confidence in any returnee who wished to discuss a last-minute change of heart with the Special Room officials. Reading his comments, I suddenly remember Mr. Yoon, the returnee whose silence in the Special Room so perplexed the ICRC delegates. All at once, his determination to write rather than speak all his answers no longer seems so strange after all: *My rights have been disregarded . . . I write because there is no other way to express my mind . . . surely you will understand . . .*

ICRC delegates' concerns about the repatriation process can hardly have been eased by an extraordinary meeting that took place on 24 October between Inoue Masutarô and a group of ICRC representatives including the committee's newly appointed chief delegate, Dr. Otto Lehner.

At this meeting, Inoue revealed that he was receiving very detailed briefings from the Japanese police, who were passing on intelligence that they had gathered through their clandestine infiltration of *Chongryun*. After giving the ICRC officials a summary of this intelligence, Inoue offered to introduce them to senior officers of the National Police Agency, who could fill in additional details.

An appointment was duly arranged, and two days later Lehner and his ICRC colleagues met the policemen at the Japan Red Cross headquarters in Tokyo's Shiba district. Among the information gleaned from these meetings was the police statement that "the current repatriation operation is being handled by Soren [*Chongryun*] in Japan, acting on behalf of the North Korean government. If individuals act contrary to the policy laid down by the Government of North Korea and applied by Soren they will compromise everything and therefore cannot expect good treatment from the authorities in North Korea or from Soren in Japan."

But the ICRC had come too far to turn back. In September, as the realities of the repatriation process had begun to become clear, the ICRC Presidential Council had indeed debated abandoning the process altogether. However, having very publicly accepted a role in the project, a retreat at this point would be extremely difficult and damaging. After some discussion, the council reached the unanimous opinion that "in the present state of affairs, it is not possible for the committee to withdraw completely from this action."

In late October, faced with consensus from the Japanese and North Korean governments, the ICRC reluctantly accepted the supplementary explanations to *The Guide for Mr. Returnee.* All that could be done was to encourage the team of ICRC delegates in Japan to achieve what they could within the given conditions—visiting Red Cross windows to make sure that posters were in place and procedures being followed; making themselves available in Niigata to listen to complaints and adjudicate on disputed cases.

The twenty-two ICRC delegates entrusted with this task (five of them recruited within Japan) worked in conditions that gave them only very limited power to influence the outcome of events. Most spoke no Japanese and had little background knowledge of the histories and societies of Japan and Korea. Apart from the fleeting and constrained encounters in the Special Rooms, they had no opportunity to talk directly to would-be returnees. They were accompanied everywhere by guide interpreters from the Japanese Red Cross, who booked their travel and paid for their hotel rooms, meals, and even their laundry. They were also a tiny group of people dealing with the mass movement of tens of thousands. Testimony by former returnees suggests that few remember seeing an ICRC representative or even being aware of their existence. One ICRC representative was rather startled to discover not only that the delegates from Geneva had little direct contact with the Korean returnees, but also that those they did encounter often took them to be "Russians or Americans."

Meanwhile, the guidebook itself seems largely to have disappeared from the scene. Although the Red Cross windows displayed posters setting out the choices open to Koreans in Japan and some apparently displayed full copies of the guidebook, I have yet to meet a former returnee or would-be returnee who recalls reading it or being aware of its contents.

In the first week of November 1959, *Chongryun* lifted its boycott of the repatriation, and thousands of applicants began flooding into the Red Cross windows all over the country. By 9 November, the Japan Red Cross Society was able to telegraph Pyongyang to say that they wished to "send as many repatriates as possible" by the end of December. "We should be obliged," they added, "if you could send ship three times before years end."

So they packed their bags, decided what to take and what to leave behind, and said farewells to families and friends—Shin Jong-Hae, whose sister was in the hospital with tuberculosis; the Pak family, who were to accompany her to North Korea; the young married couple who would soon become proud parents of baby Jo-Il.

The first trainloads of people to leave from Shinagawa Station in Tokyo, and from other stations around Japan, were seen off by massive crowds of people, shouting, cheering, singing songs, and waving North Korean flags. Along with the first returnees, others, too, traveled to Niigata. Inoue Masutarô went there to supervise proceedings at the Red Cross center. A substantial group of ICRC delegates went to witness the departure of the first convoy. From North Korea, Ri Il-Gyeong traveled to Niigata on one of the Russian ships. Having earlier nursed deep suspicions that the Japanese government was trying to sabotage the entire repatriation plan, Ri was now happy with the course of events.

Japan Red Cross Society president Shimazu Tadatsugu, too, was one of the many people who traveled to Niigata to bid farewell to the repatriation ships.

Shimazu in fact was to make this journey to Niigata several times, and (as he recalls in his memoirs) he always found it a deeply moving experience. Seeing the emotional scenes on the docks, as hundreds of people for whom Japan had been a second home left this land forever, he found himself reminded of the English phrase "the family of man."

On one of his visits, just as the ship was leaving, Shimazu looked up and saw a returnee leaning over the rail and waving to him. The excited, happy passenger had spotted the older man standing on the quay. Although the two were complete strangers, in this moment of departure, the returnee

**Figure 17.2.   Returnees boarding the repatriation ship, December 1959 (©
ICRC)**

called out a greeting to Shimazu, addressing him by the half-familiar, half-respectful term "uncle."

When the vessel drew away from the dock, the two men waved to one another, and the returnee raised his voice above the clamor of those around him for one final farewell.

"Ojisan, genkide naa!"—*All the best, uncle!* he shouted to Shimazu as the Niigata shoreline receded and the ship headed out toward North Korea.

V

ARRIVALS

18

TOWARD THE PROMISED LAND

In April 1961, as he and his mother Miyo prepared for the journey to their life in North Korea, ten-year-old Yi Yang-Soo left his primary school in Toyohashi and enrolled in a local Korean school affiliated with *Chongyrun*. Adjusting to the new school environment and unfamiliar language was a bewildering experience.

"When I changed schools," he recalls, "about the only words of Korean I knew were *kimchi* [Korean pickles] and *hangeul* [the Korean script]. I don't think I even knew how to say *abeoji* and *eomeoni* [father and mother]."

But he was not alone. In that year, many Korean children were moving to *Chongyrun* schools—others, too, like Yi, in preparation for their "return home."

"For the first hour of every day," says Yi, "the new students who had just changed schools were in a separate classroom. We were taught by the head teacher, who introduced us to basic Korean. But after that, from the second hour of the day, all the classes were in Korean, so we were plunged right into it. Kids of that age learn quickly, and after three months, I could read simple texts and greet people in Korean."

In fact by June, when they were due to leave for Korea, Yang-Soo's Korean was good enough for him to be chosen to give a little speech at a party held for the children who were departing for North Korea: "There were four or five other families with children at my school who were being repatriated at the same time. I think I said something about how wonderful it was to be returning to the Fatherland. Afterwards I remember my classmates praising me for having learned to speak such good Korean in such a short time."

Yang-Soo's father had a theoretical belief in the socialist future but had spent almost all his life in Japan, spoke no Korean, and had no desire to experience the realities of life in North Korea. His grandfather, who was an official of the South Korean–affiliated community association *Mindan*, was appalled to learn that Yang-Soo and Miyo were planning to leave for North Korea, and "there was a big row about it."

But by then, mother and son were convinced that this was the only path to a better future. Because Yang-Soo was still a child, he was not involved in the process of registering for repatriation, but he vividly remembers the preparations for departure. The Japanese government provided them with their free rail tickets to Niigata, and they started to pack their bags for the journey. Like others setting off on this migration, they tried to go well prepared. "Ordinary suitcases and cardboard boxes weren't strong enough for this move," he says. "We had large wooden packing cases made. The biggest things in our luggage were bicycles—I had a kid's bike, and Mum had an adult-sized one."

Since there were particularly large numbers of people leaving for North Korea in 1961, a special night train for returnees from Nagoya was provided. On the day of their departure, Yang-Soo and his mother made their way to Toyohashi Station, where a crowd of people was waiting to see them off. They arrived at Nagoya early in the evening and then had some

Figure 18.1.   An elderly returnee waits at the "Red Cross Window," Ikuno-ku, Osaka (© ICRC)

five or six hours to wait for the train for Niigata. Before the train left, there was a simple ceremony at the station, where the local *Chongyrun* leader and a representative of the returnees made short speeches, and they all sang *The Song of General Kim Il-Sung*.

Yang-Soo's school friends had given him a puzzle to keep him occupied on the journey.

About half an hour before midnight on Sunday, 25 June 1961, mother and son boarded the special train for Niigata. Yi recalls,

> There was a woman who had been teaching Mum Korean language once a week. Of course, she was a *Chongyrun* member. She came all the way to Nagoya to see us off. When we opened the window of our carriage to say our farewells, she said, "Do your best when you get over there. We'll be joining you soon, too." So I asked her, "How soon?" But she didn't reply. And at that moment, when I looked at her face, I knew that she wasn't telling the truth. She didn't really intend to go to North Korea at all.

Still, the train trip was full of hope and excitement. Yang-Soo loved steam trains, with their smell of smoke billowing though the carriage windows, and the start of the long journey to Niigata was beautiful. The train ran along the upper reaches of the Kiso River, whose fast-flowing water swirled around rocks and boulders, all illuminated by a long line of lights. He vividly remembers the excitement of the journey.

> It was summer and hot, and being a kid, I'd open the window to look at the view. Then a tunnel would come along and all the smoke would blow into the carriage, so I'd slam the window shut, but as soon as some more beautiful scenery appeared, I'd open it up again.
>
> The young men in the carriage were all drinking *sake* and getting excited. I remember them saying, "Next year we're going to go cherry blossom viewing in Pyongyang!" I guess they thought I was just a rather annoying little kid.
>
> But then at one point we passed some rocks sticking up in the midst of the river. I said in my best Korean, "Those rocks there look like the traitor Pak Heon-Yeong and Heo Ka-I, disrupting the unstoppable flow of our glorious Korean revolution."* Well, that really amazed them.

---

*The prominent Korean Communist politician Pak Heon-Yeong was purged by Kim Il-Sung in 1953; Heo Ka-I, another senior Communist Party figure, allegedly committed suicide in the same year after being criticized for his "mistakes." Both were frequently depicted in North Korean writings of 1950s and 1960s as archetypal traitors to the cause.

None of the young men could say anything like that in Korean, and they just looked at me open mouthed with astonishment.

Around one o'clock in the morning I started to feel sleepy. And then the next thing I knew, it was getting light, and through the train window I could see something that looked like a temple.

"What's a temple doing here?" I thought. You see, the old Nagano station, which was pulled down when the bullet train line was built, was designed to look like the Zenkôji temple. What I was looking at was actually the station building.

Then we arrived at Naoetsu and could see the Japan Sea, or the East Sea as they say in Korean. But after that, somehow the journey seemed to go on forever. Even though we'd reached the sea coast, it still took a really long time—three or four hours, I think. All the people who'd been drinking all night kept going to the toilet to throw up. I got bored and played with my puzzle.

Then, somewhere along the way, someone suddenly cried "Look! There's Korea!" So we all stared out of the window. But of course you can't really see Korea from there. It was just the outline of Sado Island.

Around the time when Yi Yang-Soo and his mother were planning their departure from Japan, Yamada Kumiko, too, was preparing to set off on the same journey. As the moment to leave home approached, she was assailed by doubts and anxiety.

A few years earlier, Kumiko could hardly have imagined in her wildest dreams that she might spend most of her life in the Democratic People's Republic of Korea. At that time, she was just an ordinary Japanese teenager on the brink of becoming a young woman, living in a small city in central Japan. While the prolonged secret dealings between Tokyo, Pyongyang, and Geneva were unfolding, her schooldays came to an end, and she started work as an assistant in a local office. Her life was much like those of other young Japanese people living in a small town in the 1950s—reasonably comfortable and rather uneventful.

In the provincial towns of 1950s Japan, the choices of entertainment after work and on weekends were limited. Television was still an expensive novelty, and the craze for bowling that would sweep Japan in the 1960s had yet to take off. But the town where Kumiko lived did boast a dance hall where the young (somewhat to their elders' disapproval) could meet, flirt, and listen to the latest American-style music. A friend persuaded Kumiko to go along with her to the dance hall, and it was there that she met a young man who soon became her boyfriend.

Kumiko's boyfriend had a skilled job in a local manufacturing company. He had been born in Japan and spoke perfect Japanese. It was only when Kumiko was invited to his home for the first time to meet his parents that she noticed that his mother spoke Japanese with a foreign accent and realized that her boyfriend was Korean.

His extended family had moved to Japan from the southern part of Korea during colonial times, although members of the family had crossed back and forth over the border many times since.

Yamada Kumiko married just as the repatriation agreement between Japan and North Korea was being drawn up, and the following year her first daughter was born. As she later realized, her parents-in-law were members of *Chongyrun*. Her husband possessed precisely the sort of technical skills that North Korea sought from returnees, and the whole extended family was soon persuaded to join the repatriation. "Originally, the idea was that my husband and father-in-law would go over first," Yamada recollects. "But then they thought, 'Life in North Korea seems to be good. Rather than splitting up the family, let's all go over together.'"

Kumiko herself was not involved in registering for repatriation—all that was taken care of by her husband and father-in-law. She had little information about life in North Korea and has no memory of ever seeing or hearing of *The Guide for Mr. Returnee*, or any posters explaining the choices facing Koreans in Japan. She says, "My parents were very strongly opposed to my going. But I had my daughter to think about. And after all, I was a married woman and I'd left home. I reckoned that when a woman marries, that's the way it always is."

Besides, like many returnees, she had heard a story that Japanese wives would be allowed to come back to visit to their families after three years in North Korea. The origins of this story are uncertain. It had no factual basis.

About a month before Kumiko was due to leave, her mother began to beg her not to go. Caught between conflicting loyalties and inclinations, Kumiko recalled a snippet of information she had picked up about the repatriation process, which suggested that there might still be a chance to change her mind: "I'd heard that we might all be asked one-by-one whether we really wanted to go to North Korea. One of my in-laws was Japanese, too, and we promised each other that, if we were asked about our decision individually, we'd say we wanted to stay in Japan."

Their big family group traveled by train to the nearest big city, en route for Niigata. It was the middle of the day when Kumiko left her hometown. Most people were at work, and Kumiko's mother was the only person who came to the station to see her off.

By the time Yi Yang-Soo and Yamada Kumiko left for Niigata, some disturbing fragments of news were starting to trickle back to Geneva about the return process. The reports sent back by delegates suggested that visible conflicts and overt instances of pressure on returnees were rare. Most people, it seemed, left Japan willingly, many with obvious enthusiasm. And yet, undercurrents of unease about the nature of this free choice kept disturbing the smooth surface of the repatriation operation.

Commenting on the overall progress of the repatriation early in 1961, ICRC delegate Max Zeller wrote, "Soren [*Chongnyun*] generally do not retaliate against refusals, cancellations or recalcitrant Koreans but try to form an obedient, closely knit community, equally closely watched by agents, i.e., commissars of their own." On the original copy of this report in the Geneva archives, someone has underlined the word *generally* in red pencil.

And if there was concern over events in Japan, there was even greater anxiety about the situation of returnees once they reached North Korea. In August 1960, staff of the Public Security Investigation Bureau from the western Hyôgo district of Japan passed on to Max Zeller and to Inoue Masutarô secret intelligence gathered from their surveillance of *Chongnyun*, which suggested that all was not well with the repatriation scheme. According to the intelligence report, until April or May of 1960, North Korea had managed reasonably successfully to resettle around one thousand new arrivals per week. This number seemed to be the maximum, as it was necessary "to allow gradual adjustment to the new way of life [and] different surroundings, giving the new arrivals also a fair chance to acquire better knowledge of the Korean language . . . which a great many of the returnees are not sufficiently conversant with." But by the summer of 1960, as the cumulative number of returnees grew, the strains were beginning to show.

The intelligence report noted that early letters home, sent back to Japan by the very first returnees, often contained positive news of the conditions they found waiting for them in their new home. But more recently, the flow of letters seemed to be drying up, and the messages that did arrive often contained nothing but platitudes, or included cryptic but worrying references to such things as hard work: "Koreans here interpret that their relatives must either be on guard as to what they say or have been assigned to far-away working places."

All of this would help to explain why, in the course of that year, the flood of applications for repatriation seemed to be subsiding, and North Korea itself was using events such as an outbreak of the flu in Japan to demand a temporary halt to the movements of the repatriation ships.

Similar worrying reports were discussed on several occasions by ICRC representatives, Japan Red Cross Society officers, and government officials. In late January 1961, for example, representatives of the national headquarters and Osaka, Kyoto, and Hyôgo chapters of the Japan Red Cross Society had a special meeting with Japanese government officials to discuss the problem of the falling number of departures. The problems reported by returnees were raised, and the meeting was told that "according to letters received by those who have repatriated already, it seems that life in the North is really quite hard."

Inoue Masutarô, however, had a ready answer to such concerns. After presenting a talk to U.S. servicemen in Tokyo in February 1960, he was questioned about the harsh conditions that returnees might face in the DPRK. His reply was simple and confident: "I presume," he said, "that if the situation of North Korea was intolerable, the ICRC would not have made a recommendation to the JRC [Japanese Red Cross] to repatriate Koreans to North Korea."

Meanwhile, the U.S. government, concerned that repatriation was hindering progress in the normalization of relations between Japan and South Korea, urged Japan to complete the return process as quickly as possible and terminate the Calcutta Accord. The Japanese government, however, resisted pressure to bring the accord to an end, telling the United States that repatriation was "extremely important in terms of Japanese domestic opinion." It did try, however, to speed up the rate of departures, in the hope that this might soon enable it to put repatriation behind it and focus its energies on mending fences with South Korea.

The initial Calcutta Accord ran for one year and three months, and when the time came to renew the agreement in the second half of 1960, despite the mounting evidence of bad news from those who had returned already, the Japanese side strongly urged the North Korean Red Cross to increase the capacity of transports from one thousand people a week to 1,500. North Korea resisted, eventually and reluctantly accepting a compromise figure of 1,200.

Even this more modest increase meant that during the period when Yi Yang-Soo traveled to Niigata, the weekly number of departures for Cheongjin was running at well over one thousand.

Yi Yang-Soo and his mother arrived at the Red Cross Center in Niigata early on Monday morning in the last week of June 1961. Along with other returnees, they spent four nights there, sleeping alongside dozens of strangers in one of the center's big dormitories.

Yang-Soo explored the duty-free shop looking for a good map of North Korea and a timetable of North Korean trains, and was puzzled to be told that, for security reasons, no such things existed. Other than that, there was little to do in the center but play cards; time passed slowly. Like others who flowed through the center on their way to North Korea, he vividly remembers meals in the refectory, and particularly the delicious *kimchi* pickles that were served there. Returnees believed that these *kimchi* had come over with the ships from North Korea. They seemed an appetizing foretaste of life to come.

In the mornings, announcements were made over a loudspeaker, sometimes offering general information, sometimes summoning individual returnees for special consultations with officials. Yang-Soo's mother's name repeatedly echoed through the corridors of the center. *Chongryun*, it appeared, was puzzled and unhappy about the circumstances of her return. The North Korean government had agreed to accept the Japanese wives of Korean repatriates, but a Japanese woman traveling with her Korean son and no husband was another matter altogether.

Unable to explain that she was going to North Korea specifically to escape from a violent marriage, Miyo instead told the *Chongryun* officials that her husband would be joining them later—he was simply staying on for a couple of months to wind up his business affairs in Japan. Yang-Soo's father had in fact arranged to arrive in Niigata on the day before his wife and son were due to leave, to say goodbye to them for the last time. When he arrived, he too was questioned by the *Chongryun* officials, and backed up his wife's version of events.

By now, Yang-Soo and Miyo had already handed back their alien registration cards. Yang-Soo remembers how the Japanese migration officers carefully stamped each card submitted by the departing repatriates with the word *Sai-Shukkoku*—Re-Exit.

The aliens, having come into Japan for a while, had now gone away again.

"But how could it be 'Re-Exit,' when I'd been born here?" he asks. "I'd never 'entered' in the first place."

Their ship was due to leave on Friday. On Thursday, *Chongryun* informed Miyo and Yang-Soo that they would not be allowed to board it. North Korea was refusing to accept them. Instead, while all the other returnees embarked on the two repatriation ships, they would be taken to a *Chongryun* hostel, where they would be given one night's accommodation. Then they were to find their own way back to Toyohashi.

Unbelieving, devastated, his cherished dream in ruins, Yang-Soo remembers crying, "Then I'll swim to North Korea by myself!"

The *tanka* poetic style, which both Yi Yang-Soo's parents loved, condenses a world of experience and emotion into a few syllables.

In the official records of the repatriation program, too, lives, dreams, and human tragedies are reduced to a few words of black print on a page. But here, there is no poetry—only a dust-dry and cryptic prose. The stern language of the bureaucratic report, however, has as much power as any work of literature to mix fact with fantasy. The Immigration Control Bureau's Report Number 18 for 1961 (translated into English for the ICRC) contains this terse paragraph:

> Will-changers at the 65th ship:
>
> A Korean woman (ex-Japanese) of 35 years old who came from Aichi Prefecture with her second son of 10 years old was persuaded by the chief of the returnees to repatriate with her husband, who had not yet presented the application. After talking with her husband who came to the Centre to see her, she decided to leave Japan only with her son and finished the confirmation of will. But after that she changed her mind just before the departure and went back to Tokyo.

And when the story was passed on to the ICRC, as though in some game of Chinese whispers, it became briefer still, and the facts became ever harder to discern: "Op. 295—One woman and her child asked, at the last moment, to remain in Niigata for personal reasons, and travel to North Korea with the 66th ship. Her request was granted."

The Japanese government paid for travel to Niigata, but there was no provision for those who failed to leave for North Korea. Miyo and Yang-Soo had to pay their way back to their old home in Toyohashi. Yang-Soo's father had actually hoped to take a holiday with a young woman friend as soon as his wife and son departed, and despite the change of plans, he insisted on making their return to Toyohashi into something that resembled a vacation trip around hot spring resorts of Japan. For Yang-Soo, it was a miserable reversal of the journey of hope he had made from Toyohashi and Niigata—made worse by the fact that his father was in a sour mood, and that this was a journey by diesel train and bus, whose fumes made him feel sick.

Back in Toyohashi, he returned to his Korean school, where other children looked askance at this student who had been seen off to North Korea with such ceremony, only to return ignominiously a few weeks later. The process of regaining his alien registration card was also long and tortuous. By the time Miyo and Yang-Soo returned to the Acacia bookstore, another woman had already moved in to live with their father in the apartment above the shop. Mother and son moved out, and went to live with relatives of Miyo's for a while, before settling in a tenement in an impoverished Korean district of the town.

Yang-Soo continued to attend Korean school, and six years later, when he reached the age at which people were allowed to join the repatriation scheme as independent migrants, he applied again to go to North Korea. His teachers eagerly urged him to return to the Fatherland, but his request to take his mother with him was denied. "They said, 'You're a good student and have high marks in your classes. You can contribute to the building of Socialism. But your mother is of different blood. Leave her behind.' That was when I gave up the idea of returning to North Korea. From then on, I no longer saw North Korea as a homeland. I couldn't regard a state which said such things as my country."

Yi has spent the rest of life in Japan, where he became an outspoken campaigner for the rights of *Zainichi* Koreans, and also for the rights of returnees to and refugees from North Korea.

Yamada Kumiko and her extended family spent just a couple of days in the Red Cross Center in Niigata. In the bus from the station to the center, she recalls that they sang songs like "Red *Chima Jeogori*":

> *When we work wearing a red chima jeogori*
> *Our voices join in harmony across the tranquil fields . . .*

She also remembers the encounter in the Special Room.

"It was not a very big room," she recalls. "There were fifteen or sixteen of us, and we could just about fit in there, so it can't have been very big." For, as it turned out, they were interviewed, not individually, but by family group. "Father [her father-in-law] was our representative. He did everything," she says with a little laugh, "He just said a couple of words, and then it was all over." Neither she nor the other Japanese member of her family had the courage to raise their voice.

> I was only young at the time. I can't say that I wanted to go. I don't really
> know what I felt. If I'd said I didn't want to go, my husband would have

Figure 18.2.   A family of returnees in one of the "Special Rooms," Niigata Red Cross Center (© ICRC)

dragged me along with him in any case. And then there was my child. Wives always leave their parents when they get married; I thought it was better to be separated from my parents than be separated from my daughter. They said life in Korea was good, so I thought maybe it would be OK when I got there. I'd heard again and again that we'd be allowed back to Japan in three years time. In the end, it turned out to be forty years."

The family was given two cabins on the bottom deck of the repatriation ship. There was a big dining room on the ship, but Kumiko found its smell nauseating, and couldn't eat there. "Father went to eat in the dining room several times," she says, "but my husband and I just went once. We tried going out on the deck, too, but there were Russian soldiers there carrying rifles, so we beat a hasty retreat."

After two long days at sea, around midday on the third day, they approached the North Korean port of Cheongjin and were finally allowed out onto the deck so that they could see the approaching shoreline, and the crowds of North Koreans carrying bouquets of flowers who had gathered there to welcome them.

Oh Su-Ryong, on the other hand, seems to have missed his confirmation of free will altogether. After seeing the glowing reports on Kim Il-Sung—

"the face that changed the world"—in the Japanese media, Oh made up his own mind to leave for the DPRK in 1962. But when he reached the Niigata center, he felt a longing to say one last goodbye to his brother and sister, who were living in Tokyo, so instead of registering his arrival at the center, he quietly slipped out again and boarded a train to the capital, where he remained until shortly before he was due to board the repatriation ship.

Oh has no memory of the Special Room and thinks that he must have been away on his unauthorized outing when that part of the proceedings took place.

19

RETURN TO NOWHERE

Oh Su-Ryong, however, has vivid memories of the arrival in Cheongjin on the morning of 25 February 1962:

> The ship didn't enter the harbor right away. It seemed to wait in the off-ing for a long time. We could dimly see the shoreline in the distance. Little boats went to and fro between us and the shore.
>
> Then we sailed in towards the docks. There were people standing there to greet us—crowds of people. When I saw the port and those people, I thought, *oh no!*
>
> I think everyone felt that when they saw the scene in front of us— *oh no!*
>
> There was a row of grim-looking warehouses. The wind was blow-ing hard and it was still cold. The people waiting on the dock for us were all wearing shabby, padded cotton jackets. We thought, "This isn't right. This isn't how it's supposed to be." I think everyone felt disillu-sioned when they saw it.

Memories are complex things, colored by subsequent experience and shaped even as they are told, in counterpoint to the questions and responses of listeners. Writing about other people's memories is more complex still.

The experiences of the "returnees" are overwhelming, unimaginable. Whether they began with hope, anxiety, or a mixture of both, all their journeys seem to have involved extraordinary pain. Above all in their rec-ollections of the past fifteen years, they speak of absolute hunger and the fear of imminent death. (As a consequence of the hunger, I notice, they all have uncannily accurate memories of food.) My words, and my awkward transcriptions of theirs, cannot do them justice.

The more I listen, the more I realize, too, how multifaceted these recollections are. There is no single story of the experience of repatriation. There are ninety thousand different stories, and each one has many twists and turns, for it extends over half a lifetime or more. The pain is mixed with survival and laughter, hopes entertained and dashed, paradox and mundane ordinariness.

For historians or journalists seeking a compelling conclusion to the narrative that they construct, it is tempting to try to smooth out the contradictions, to adjust the balance between light and darkness. I am trying to resist the temptation but am unsure whether or not I have succeeded.

These stories urgently need to be heard, and I want to help pass them on in all their complexity. But the very act of writing, quoting, editing, and cutting seems itself like a certain sort of violence.

Words on the page cannot convey the quality of voice and expression.

Before speaking face-to-face with Oh Su-Ryong, Yamada Kumiko, and others, I had read interviews in which returnees described their instant disillusionment at the sight they encountered on their arrival in Cheongjin. I found these accounts difficult to believe. It seemed hard to imagine that the hope and anticipation of returnees could so swiftly have turned to despair. I assumed that the remembered images of the moment of arrival must have been darkened by subsequent experiences of suffering in North Korea.

Indeed, I do not think that all returnees experienced the same disillusionment. But the testimonies of a bleak homecoming are frequent and powerful enough to cast deep shadows over the repatriation story.

The voices of Oh Su-Ryong and of Yamada Kumiko, and the vivid detail of their accounts, carry a conviction that the printed word can only faintly reproduce.

Yamada Kumiko recalls the wave of disappointment that swept through the passengers on the repatriation ship as the scene on the Cheongjin docks came into clear focus. At first, from the distance, all they could see were the crowds of people waving flowers, but,

> When we went out on the deck, and saw what the people were wearing, well, I think everyone felt disheartened. The moment I saw them, I felt that, too. I really didn't want to get off the ship. The people were wearing these really baggy trousers, and their faces . . . they were just a

completely different color, sort of blackish, and the children all had
these red faces . . . I can't really explain it in words.

If those people had come to meet their own relatives, they probably
would have been genuinely excited. But they'd all been mobilized to
greet us, so I don't think many of them felt really happy."

One of the other Japanese women on the ship tried to stay on board,
crying, "Take me back, take me back!" But of course it was useless. They
were ushered into a sports hall, where they stayed all day, until 10:00 p.m.,
when it was time to board the train that would take them to the city of
Hamheung, where they were to spend the next week. It was a long day, and
they were only given a few biscuits to eat. Otherwise, they shared the remains of the food that they had brought with them from Japan.

Kumiko says, "Once we were in the sports hall, we were by ourselves.
People started saying 'I didn't think it was going to be like this,' or getting
all upset and shouting that they wanted to go home. . . . Everyone was so
worried about what they should do now."

Yamada Kumiko and her family traveled to Hamheung at night, and
could see nothing but darkness outside the train windows, but those who
traveled by day later told her about the scenery: "There were a lot of big
holes which had been made when the American military dropped bombs.
The holes were full of rainwater, and women were in there naked, washing
their hair."

In Hamheung they were given lectures and taken on tours of the
town, including one of the showpieces of the current development plan—
a vast synthetic fabrics factory that was then under construction. They were
told that "when this factory was up and running, life for Koreans would no
longer be so hard, and everyone would be able to wear nylon clothes." In
the meanwhile, however, the shelves of Hamheung shops were largely
stocked with decorative but empty boxes. Kumiko and her family could
find virtually nothing to buy except a drink made from the fruit of a tree
that grows on the slopes of Mount Paektu (Korea's highest mountain), so
they bought three bottles of that to console themselves.

On the advice of relatives who were already living there, the family asked
to be sent to a place near the Chinese border. Kumiko's husband had
brought his own manufacturing equipment with him, but when they arrived at their new home, the factory where he could use his skills had not
yet been completed, so for the first few years he worked on a production
line making household goods and then in a shoe factory. As the years

passed, he worked his way up from manual labor to his own skilled trade, eventually becoming a supervisor.

Her husband found life in North Korea hard, but seldom complained, and her father-in-law, who had made the decisive choice to bring his family there, said nothing—his disappointment expressed only by a deepening silence. But Kumiko and her sisters sometimes talked quietly together about their shock at the poverty of the life they had come to.

"My eldest sister-in-law and I generally got up at the same time," says Kumiko. "We were supposed to make breakfast, but Mother [her mother-in-law] said she'd take turns with me. . . . I think she felt sorry for me."

Kumiko's second child, a son, was born in December of the year they arrived in Korea. Winters in the far north of the peninsula are bitterly cold, and she vividly remembers that first winter:

> First of all, we had to make *kimchi* to see us through the cold months. My husband's factory gave us the raw materials—fifty kilos per person, 150 kilos for the three of us—cabbage and radishes, it was. We had to chop and pickle them. We couldn't carry them up to our fourth-floor apartment, so we dug a hole for them below the apartment window and made the pickles there.
>
> Making the *kimchi* over that hole and putting them into the jars was the worst thing. It was so cold. We made three fifty-kilo jars full. We had to wash the vegetables in the river, and in December the shallows of the river were frozen solid. We'd boil the water, but in ten or twenty minutes it would be stone cold again, so we'd have to plunge our hands into the cold water to make the *kimchi*. It was really hard.

It was difficult, too, to face childbirth in a strange land. When they arrived, Kumiko spoke little Korean, though she learned fast. Her only opportunity to use her native language was the one day per month when the twenty or more Japanese women from her district gathered at the local government offices to receive the special allowance paid to Japanese wives.

But although she was a "foreigner," a child of the much-reviled former colonizers, Kumiko remembers little hostility or discrimination from the people around her. Later on, her children were sometimes teased at school for being "*kuibo*" (a colloquial term for returnees), but the memory that she chooses to put into words is one of the warmth of the people who shared this harsh existence. The hospital where Yamada gave birth to her son was primitive and poorly stocked, but she says, "The people around me were kind. You know, people in Japan can sometimes be cold. But those Korean people were really good to me. If the neighbors had something a bit special, they'd always bring some over to our place to share. Things like that. We suffered together."

The Calcutta Accord on repatriation to North Korea was renewed annually until 1967, but from 1962 onward, the early flood of returnees slowed to a steady trickle. In 1960, after massive public demonstrations in South Korea, the Rhee government fell from power, and the following year, former army officer Park Chung-Hee seized power in a coup. The ascendancy of Park, who in colonial times had served in the Japanese military in Manchuria, raised new hopes for the normalization of relations between Japan and South Korea.

Meanwhile, during the first three years of the 1960s, trade and economic connections between Japan and North Korea gradually expanded, and in 1963 the North Korean government, via *Chongryun* and the North Korean Red Cross, began a campaign for the free movement of people between Japan and the DPRK.

Chongryun and Japanese Communist Party representatives approached the Japanese Red Cross and the ICRC, asking them to take up the issue. But (as ICRC representative Michel Testuz reported to Geneva) Inoue Masutarô's response to this appeal was unenthusiastic. The problem of the free movement of people between the two countries, Inoue serenely told the representatives, was "above all political," and the Japan Red Cross Society, "basing itself on the Principles which forbid it to engage in all political action, could not accept their request."

During a meeting with a senior ICRC official in Geneva soon after, however, Inoue put the reluctance to discuss this issue in different terms, explaining the position of the Japanese government "which wishes to get rid of as many Koreans as possible and is not inclined to favor these comings and goings." This government attitude was reconfirmed in 1966, when a Korean returnee from Japan, who was a member of the North Korean team participating in an international sporting contest in Cambodia, fled to the Japanese embassy in Phnom Penh, where he sought political asylum. The embassy handed him over to the Cambodian authorities, who returned him to North Korea.

The North Korean motives for raising the issue of free movement remain unclear. A large-scale "re-return" of disillusioned Koreans to Japan would have been a propaganda disaster that it surely could not have allowed. There are clear signs, however, that by 1962 or 1963 the authorities in Pyongyang were aware that many returnees were experiencing great difficulties in adjusting to life in North Korea. It is possible that they may have hoped to ease the problem by allowing the short- or long-term return of (for example) some Japanese wives. On the other hand, it is also possible (as some in Japan suspected) that their proposal was simply a propaganda exercise, made in the knowledge that it would be rejected by Japan. The truth cannot be known, because neither Japan not the ICRC was prepared to take the issue further.

In 1965, Japan and South Korea signed a treaty normalizing their relations and establishing formal diplomatic ties. As part of this accord, Koreans in Japan who possessed South Korean nationality were finally able to obtain full permanent residence rights in Japan, though not full rights to welfare (which started to improve only after Japan ratified the international refugee convention in the early 1980s). Growing numbers of *Zainichi* Koreans now began to opt for South Korean citizenship, and the numbers seeking repatriation to North Korea declined still further.

As a result, the Japanese authorities decided that continued renewal of the Calcutta Accord was unnecessary. In August 1967, eight years after it had been signed, the accord came to an end.

But this was not the end of the repatriation story. After pressure from North Korea to create a channel for the small number of people who still wanted to migrate from Japan to the DPRK, the Japanese and North Korean Red Cross Societies reached an informal agreement in Moscow in December 1970, and in 1971 repatriations began again on a small scale. They were to continue until 1984. This time, the International Committee of the Red Cross was not directly involved.

Meanwhile in North Korea, political purges of returnees had begun.

At first, the North Korean government clearly made some serious attempts to help returnees settle into their new lives, and in some respects the compatriots from Japan constituted a privileged group.

Oh Su-Ryong recalls that those who came on the first three or four ships were particularly fortunate, because they were generally given homes and jobs in Pyongyang: "One of my mother's friends had come on the first ship and was given a home in Pyongyang. His son appeared in that photo with Kim Il-Sung, the one taken in a theatre. They were the lucky people, the ones who were greeted by Kim Il-Sung."

Oh himself was sent to work in a machinery factory in the garrison town of Dongnim and, like Yamada Kumiko, recalls the shock he experi-

Figure 19.1.   Kim Il-Sung Greets Returnees from Japan (Source:
***Korea,* no. 43, 1960)**

enced at the grinding material poverty of his new homeland during his first
few months there. But on the advice of his *Chongryun* activist mother, he
had arrived well prepared, his luggage filled with clocks and even a glass
cutter, which he knew to be readily saleable items in North Korea. When
this supply ran out, his mother sent him more.

"Life was hard, for sure," he recalls, "but it was easier for us returnees
than it was for the natives, particularly if we had goods that we could sell."
A clock could be sold for the equivalent of a month's wage or more. Those
who suffered most were returnees who brought nothing with them or
whose family in Japan did not continue to help them after their arrival. In
the early months, however, all were given special returnee registration
cards that, among other things, enabled them to travel around the country
more easily. "In those days in North Korea," says Oh Su-Ryong, "you
practically had to queue for the whole day to get a rail ticket, but if you

had a returnee's card you could jump the queue, and you got better seats on the train, too."

Inevitably, though, this special treatment stirred resentment among some local people. There were rumors that returnees were being given all the best new housing, even that local people were being turned out of their homes to make room for the compatriots from Japan. Returnees' homes were specially redecorated on the occasions when delegations from *Chongryun* visited them from Japan to check on their well-being.

Some North Koreans soon began to express unease and suspicion about the alien values that the returnees were bringing with them into North Korean society. As a Hungarian diplomat stationed in Pyongyang reported in 1960, "The Korean workers particularly often say that if so many people return home, they also include a number of people who are not motivated by patriotism and the desire to work, but by 'other aims.'" Having been targets of discrimination as an ethnic minority in Japan, returnees rapidly became an identifiable social minority in North Korea.

At first, returnees not only enjoyed material privileges, but also had a degree of political latitude. It was understood that they had grown up in a capitalist society, and their ideological mistakes were more readily forgiven. But this indulgence did not last long. Yamada Kumiko recalls that "after we'd been there for about two or three years, there was this growing feeling that you mustn't say anything bad. There started to be a belief that returnees shouldn't get let off so easily. That was around 1964 or 1965."

For some, this tightening of controls had drastic consequences. One returnee, who later crossed the border into China and has published an account of his experiences, tells of a casual conversation he had in 1965 with a group of fellow repatriates, in which he half-jokingly said that he wished he could go back to Japan. Until then, it had been quite common for returnees to make such remarks to each other. But on this occasion, the comment was reported to the authorities, and he was arrested and spent several months in prison as a suspected spy.

A major wave of purges seems to have begun around the beginning of the 1970s, and it was during this decade that large numbers of returnees were rounded up. The targets of the purges were often those in elite positions, whose status made them subject to particularly rigorous ideological scrutiny and whose relative prosperity attracted envy.

Among the victims of the 1970s purges was the family of Kang Cheol-Hwan, whose book describing his experiences has attracted widespread international attention. Kang's grandparents, prewar migrants to Japan from Jeju Island, had run a successful business in Kyoto, where Cheol-Hwan's grandmother was a prominent *Chongryun* activist. They and their adult children joined the repatriation to North Korea in its early stages, and Cheol-Hwan was born in Pyongyang in 1968.

His parents and grandparents were among the lucky ones. They were given prestigious white-collar jobs in the capital, and lived in a newly built apartment "a few dozen steps from the Soviet embassy."

Kang's memories are of a happy and comfortable childhood in Pyongyang. He writes that the area around his home seemed more like a park than an urban neighborhood, and says, "My family enjoyed a level of comfort foreign to most North Korean homes, even in Pyongyang. We had a refrigerator, washing machine, vacuum cleaner, and even the most sought-after of all luxury goods, a color television set, on which, to our great delight, we could watch the dramatic political crime series *Clean Hands*."

This peaceful and prosperous world fell apart, however, in 1977, when Kang's grandfather was arrested for treason, and most of family (including Cheol-Hwan himself) were sent to Yeodok, one of the most feared of the rapidly expanding zones (enclosing whole villages, factories, and farms) that were set aside for the punishment of the politically suspect. Particularly large numbers of former returnees are known to have been held in Yeodok. According to another former Yeodok prisoner, the first contingent of around six hundred returnees arrived there in 1970, and by 1988 there were over five thousand in Yeodok alone (with substantial numbers also incarcerated near Cheongjin and in other punishment zones). Kang Cheol-Hwan's harrowing account of the starvation, beatings, gruesome killings, and routine brutality that he witnessed during his ten years in Yeodok did much to draw international attention to the problem of gross human rights abuses in North Korea.

The number of returnees who fell victim to political purges is unknown but is clearly very considerable. The arbitrariness of the North Korean system, which grew more marked as the economy fell apart from the end of the Cold War onward, meant that misdemeanors that might be overlooked by the authorities in some circumstances could attract the most terrible of punishments in others.

Returnees from Japan were disproportionately represented among the victims of North Korean political purges, but they were, of course, neither the only nor the most numerous victims. Many other North Koreans, both ordinary people and members of the political elite, encountered equally terrible fates.

Among them was North Korea's chief negotiator at the Geneva talks on repatriation, Ri Il-Gyeong. By 1964 Ri had become North Korean trade minister, but in April of that year he was arrested, put on trial, and hanged. His wife and five children were exiled from the capital, and two of his brothers were sent to work in the mines. According to one report, his offense had been a failure to negotiate a satisfactory trade deal with the Soviet Union, but I cannot help wondering whether his role in the repatriation of Koreans from Japan may also have been among the crimes for which Ri Il-Gyeong paid with his life.

For those returnees who were not directly affected by the purges, the greatest hardships have come from the collapse of the North Korean economy since the early 1990s. After the end of the Cold War and the breakup of the Soviet Union, much of the DPRK's already overstretched and crumbling economy became a wasteland. From the early 1990s onward, Oh Su-Ryong recalls, factory production began to fall sharply. Workers from nonessential industries were recruited to work on farms or in mines, but "People who didn't want to go would bribe the bosses, and just stayed at home, or went to trade on the black market instead."

By then, Yamada Kumiko was approaching old age. Her children had grown up, and she had separated from her husband. As rations ceased and shortages turned into famine, she found the search for food becoming a growing daily struggle:

> Every morning I'd get up and walk about an hour to the bottom of the mountains, and then another half an hour into the mountains to the place where I'd made fields. I cut down the trees in a couple of places and planted maize, soy beans, and azuki beans. I didn't have official permission, of course, but everyone did it. It was the only way to survive.
>
> When autumn harvest-time came, there were people who'd sneak around and steal the crops, so you had to guard them. I built a little hut next to my fields, and from July to the end of August I'd stay there all the time, day and night. It was scary being alone in the mountains at night, so I got my little grandson and granddaughter to come along with me. I'd grind up the maize into flour and make noodles with it, and we lived on that. My grandson was young, but somehow having a boy around made me feel better.

Soon after, Yamada Kumiko began to cross the border into China to trade; it was the start of the journey that would ultimately bring her back to Japan.

Taniguchi Hiroko is Korean but uses a Japanese name in her everyday working life. I met her at a busy suburban station in Japan. A petite, cheerful, stylishly dressed woman in early middle age, she blends in easily with the evening crowds. The only distinctive thing about her appearance is her slight build. As she remarked in passing, she stopped growing on the day in her teens when she boarded the repatriation ship to North Korea.

Hiroko and her family joined the repatriation in its later phases, after her father became chronically ill and, without savings or welfare to fall back on, was persuaded by a neighbor that his best hope was return to the DPRK.

By the time they traveled to Niigata, the Red Cross Center had been closed down, and they and other returnees stayed in a guesthouse until it was time for them to board their ship. Hiroko would have much preferred to stay behind with her friends and felt only anxiety about the journey ahead of them. "It seemed like a dream," she says, "I couldn't believe that this was happening to me."

They traveled on a North Korean ship that took three days to make the crossing to Cheongjin.

> It was early morning when we arrived. We could see mountains along the coastline—dark mountains. There were slogans painted on them: "Long live the Korean Workers' Party!" and "Long Live the Great Leader Kim Il-Sung!" I thought it seemed really strange. That was when I truly knew I'd arrived.
>
> People from the town had come out to meet us. All the returnees on the ship started crying and shouting, "Hurrah!" I cried, too. After all, it would have looked odd if I was the only one who didn't.
>
> I said to one boy, "Why are you crying?"
>
> "Because I'm so happy," he said.
>
> "You're really happy?" I asked. And he said, "Yeah."
>
> They all started singing the Song of General Kim Il-Sung, and I sang along too. This boy was one class below me in school. I just couldn't understand how he could be crying for joy.

Hiroko and her family were sent to a small farm village. Her father tried to do his share of work, but there was virtually no medical care, and his health grew steadily worse. "He didn't complain," says Hiroko, "All he said was, 'it's hard.'" Two years after they arrived in North Korea, his stomach had swollen and he was becoming mentally confused. Even then it was a struggle to get hospital treatment. It was only after the local official in change of returnees appealed specially on their behalf that that they were able to get him a hospital bed. But by then it was too late: he had terminal cancer.

After a little while, the hospital said that they could nothing more for him, so the family put him on an ox cart and took him home where, two months later, he died.

Hiroko's mother, who was born in Japan to Korean parents and spoke almost no Korean language, suffered a nervous collapse. At night, she would suddenly wake with a start and begin shouting aloud but in the morning would have no memory at all of these episodes.

Meanwhile, Hiroko was attending the local high school. "I was surprised," she says, "During classes, the kids would pretend to be studying, but actually they'd be reading novels or knitting or writing notes to each other, just like Japanese schoolchildren." After class there was "social labor"—tasks such as clearing snow in the winter. The bitter cold was hard to bear, but summer, she says, was the worst. The evenings were so long. When study and social labor were finished, the hours stretched ahead interminably with nothing to do. They listened to the ubiquitous radio—every North Korean home has a speaker tuned to the state broadcasting station, but theirs didn't work very well—and sometimes she played table tennis with her classmates. "We did Japan-versus-Korea table tennis matches," she recalls.

As a teenager, used to life in high-growth Japan, Hiroko found it hard to adjust to the little things as well as the big. There was no running water in the house, no toothpaste, and no shampoo to be had in the village. She and her sisters and brother tried washing their hair with the blocks of hard laundry soap, but it didn't remove the grease. Very occasionally, they managed to buy Soviet-made soap powder, which they used as a substitute for shampoo. "It was really bad for your hair," she says, "but at least it felt clean and grease free for a little while after you'd washed it."

It was, she says, "heaven" when she finally married and moved to the nearby city, where their apartment had running water. There were shops selling basic necessities, and you could "travel on a bus and walk on paved streets."

For a while things grew a little easier, but after the birth of her children, Taniguchi Hiroko and her husband separated. And then the food shortages came, and after that the famines. As one system fell apart, another began to take root among the rubble:

> Up until that time, there had only been peasant markets, where they sold handicrafts or things like cabbages that they grew themselves. But then people started coming over the border from China. Life was hard in China, too, but not as difficult as in North Korea, so Chinese people started bringing bundles of goods across the frontier to sell. They brought all sorts of things that hadn't been available before, like detergent and scented soap. Of course, once people saw things like that, they wanted to buy them, so the trade began to grow and grow. Some people borrowed money and set up groups to start trading themselves. Then they got into debt. There are all sorts of problems like that in North Korea nowadays. But without that trade, things would have been even worse."

Like Yamada Kumiko, Taniguchi began to cross the border into China, buying black-market goods to exchange for food. "I was really scared the first time I crossed the frontier," she recalls. "It was pitch dark. I don't know how long I walked, and I lost track of the time. I couldn't tell whether it was still the middle of the night or almost dawn. My shoes had got washed away in the river, so I had to walk barefoot. Luckily I was wearing socks, so my feet weren't cut. But still, I'm not sure how I managed to get to my destination."

Taniguchi completed this first crossing successfully, but later she was arrested by the Chinese police and handed over to the North Korean authorities. The Chinese prison, she says, was not so bad. Life there was "relatively normal," and you could say what you liked; the only trouble was that "the Chinese women used to insult us Koreans terribly." But the prison in North Korea where she spent more than a month was terrifying. The cells were freezing cold and the inadequate blankets full of lice. Guards would shout and swear at the prisoners, and force them to sit in silence in their cells for long periods of "self-criticism." In Hiroko's case they did not use physical violence. But the fear of violence hung over them every day. "We had no idea what punishment would be inflicted on us," she says. "I would wake in the mornings with my heart pounding, unable to breathe. There were a number of times when people fainted from the terror of their situation."

She was, however, released, and out of sheer necessity once more crossed the border to China to trade. It was on this occasion that someone suggested to her that she should try to go to Japan or South Korea. In South Korea, she knew, refugees from the North were given welfare and government support. In Japan she would receive nothing. But Japan was the country where she had been born and brought up, and she chose to make the perilous journey there, seeing this as the best way to secure a future for her children. The children themselves, however, were still in North Korea, and she was unable to take them with her.

She did not talk in detail about the route she used. But now she is back in Japan—still a foreigner, still receiving no government assistance, working from morning to night six days a week to send money to her children in North Korea.

I talked to her in a karaoke box—one of the few places in a Japanese city where you can be sure that your conversation cannot be overheard. We sat in our booth, eating rice omelets (standard karaoke box fare) while all around the pounding bass notes from neighboring booths resounded through the imperfectly sound-proofed walls. As our allotted time in our booth drew to a close, Taniguchi Hiroko began to talk about the present and future.

Just as the experiences of the returnees from Japan vary, so too do their perceptions of North Korea today. Oh Su-Ryeong, who crossed the border into China in the 1990s and now lives in Seoul, still feels a certain appreciation of the original egalitarian ideals of socialism: "If they'd tried it in one of the most developed countries of the world, perhaps it might have worked," he says. "The problem was that they tried it in a terribly poor country." But for the Kim Jong-Il regime, he has only distain and distrust, and he favors a tough line toward North Korea from the outside world.

But Taniguchi Hiroko sees things a little differently. North Korea will change for sure, she says, but it will take time—a long time. Meanwhile, her great anxiety today is that sanctions will be imposed on the country; for without trade and aid, how will her children survive? At the end of our long conversation, she says,

> When I was there, there was a time when the price of rice doubled. There was rice to buy in the market, but it was so scarce that the price went right up. Well, when that happens, ordinary people can't afford it, so they try to make do with rice gruel. And then the gruel becomes more water than rice. If you eat that for long enough, you starve.
>
> But just before I left, rice was starting to come in from China, so things got just a little better.
>
> During the time when I was there, if it hadn't been for UN aid, we wouldn't have survived. I remember the big bags of maize—fifty-kilo or one hundred-kilo bags, I think they were—heavy paper sacks with the

American flag and "U.S.A." written on them. They were distributed by the UN. We were just so happy when we saw those! North Korea may have been mad at America and said that the U.S. has done all sorts of wicked things, but at least they let that in. And then there was South Korean rice. Maybe only a bit of it gets distributed as rations. Maybe the rest gets siphoned off along the way. But anyhow, some of it gets onto the market, so if you can make a little bit of money, at least there's something to buy. The real disasters begin when there's nothing to buy, even if you have money.

If just some of the food gets into the hands of ordinary people, that's the only thing that matters. Without it, we wouldn't be alive today."

20

THE WILLOW TREES OF NIIGATA

The Niigata docks lie still and empty under a hazy sky. In the gray-green waters where the *Kryl'ion* and the *Tobol'sk* once anchored, a solitary small fishing boat floats on the calm sea. Around me are the port offices where Shimazu Tadatsugu, Inoue Masutarô, Ri Il-Gyeong, and others came to witness the departure of the repatriation ships. Some of the buildings that stood around the dock in the 1950s have now been replaced by larger and newer concrete structures, but otherwise, little has changed since the days in 1959 and 1960 when throngs of people crammed this wharf to say goodbye. This is the place where Yamada Kumiko, Oh Su-Ryong, Taniguchi Hiroko, the parents of baby Jo-Il, and ninety thousand other people embarked on their journey into life in North Korea.

Today there is only one other person here: a youngish man in a white cotton sweater, who has set up his fishing rod on the quay. His company car is parked at the far end of the docks, and he appears to be popping back and forth between business appointments to see whether his line has snared anything.

I first came here in the company of Chang Myeong-Su, who showed me the way to the docks and pointed out the *Chongryun* offices where he once worked helping returnees to pack their baggage for the journey home. But this time I wanted to come here by myself.

The road that leads from downtown Niigata toward the docks, and beyond to Niigata Airport (where the Red Cross Center once stood) is called Botonamu Street, a Japanized version of the Korean word *beodeunamu*—willow tree. All along its length is the great row of willows, planted to celebrate the start of the repatriation to North Korea.

On a quiet street corner between the city and the docks stands a small engraved plaque, erected by the city authorities in the year 2000. Its margins are decorated with designs of willow leaves, and the text explains the origins of the name Botonamu Street. The monument briefly recounts the history of colonization and the coming of Koreans (including forced laborers) to Japan. Then it tells of the repatriation project, and opposition that it evoked from some quarters. At that time, reads the inscription, the mayor of Niigata City, remembering prewar connections that his city had had to Asia and "looking forward to future connections with the land across the water, decided that Niigata should be the exit port for the repatriation." In honor of the event, 305 willow trees were planted along the road that became known as Botonamu Street.

Although it is less than ten years old, the plaque has a forlorn and neglected air. The plastic coating that covers its surface has begun to blister, making parts of the inscription difficult to read.

On the way from the station to the city, curious to discover how this history is remembered in Niigata, I asked the taxi driver if he knew the story behind the name Botonamu Street. The driver—a friendly, garrulous man—paused for a long time. "I'm sure someone told me once," he said, "But . . . No, sorry. It's gone . . . Botonamu. That's not Japanese is it? Maybe it's Russian?"

Figure 20.1.   Plaque commemorating the repatriation, Botunamu Street, Niigata (author's photograph)

Having reached this point in my journey, I realize how many holes are still left in the story I am trying to tell.

Entire books could be written, for example, about the role of the Japanese Communist Party, the Japanese Socialist Party, and the Japan-Korea Association in encouraging and promoting the repatriation, and about the role of local governments like the Niigata authorities. Here I have mentioned them only briefly, choosing instead to focus on the role of national governments, the Red Cross movement, and *Chongryun*, for—however much others may have lobbied for repatriation—it was these groups (I believe) who possessed the power to make the plan reality.

The complex South Korean dimension to this history is another narrative that remains to be told, and others will be able to tell it far better than I could.

Much more still remains to be discovered, too, about the role of *Chongryun*. Some day soon, perhaps, more will be known; for, shaken by the kidnapping revelations since 2002, the organization's power and role in Japanese society have been changing.

In fact, though the Korean Peninsula remains divided, in the Korean community in Japan a remarkable reunification has been taking place. Today, younger members of the South Korean–affiliated *Mindan* and the North Korean–affiliated *Chongryun*—organizations that were until recently sworn enemies—play friendly soccer matches and organize Korean cultural festivals together.

The precise apportionment of blame for the tragedies of the repatriation could be debated endlessly. But now it is time to confront its legacy, and to try to ensure that such things do not happen again. Many forces came together in the making of the repatriation movement: most notably, the Japanese and North Korean governments, the Red Cross Societies of both countries, *Chongryun*, the Japanese opposition parties and media, the ICRC, and the governments of both the Soviet Union and the United States. All share the responsibility to right the wrong. But the story traced here from newly released documents begins with the actions of Japanese bureaucrats, LDP politicians and the Japanese Red Cross. The acceptance of responsibility and the process of righting wrongs should surely begin in the same place.

After fifty years of concealment, the true outlines of this story are finally beginning to come to light. Very few of the individuals directly involved in drawing up the repatriation plan are still alive. Their successors have a choice. They can, once again, pursue a path of secrecy, prevarication and denial of responsibility, or they can choose to work openly across national borders to ensure that the truth is told and that everything possible is done to recompense the victims of this policy of deceit. The second choice is the only conscionable option.

As it leaves the downtown area, Botonamu Street enters a straggling portside district of small offices, petrol stations, and warehouses. The willow trees stand like brave sentinels along its verges—a line marching toward the sea, toward the continent of Asia. When they were planted, they were seen as a symbol of the link between Niigata and the "city of willows," Pyongyang.

But, like all frontier cities, Niigata is Janus-faced—both the point of contact with, and the defensive shield against, the outside world. Since the willow trees were planted, and particularly in the past decade, it is the defensive face that has appeared most frequently in public discourse and the national media. The city has become the focal point of anger about the kidnappings by North Korea and of demonstrations against North Korean ships.

Today, the willow trees have come to symbolize the repatriation in a different way.

Many are now old and gnarled. Some have lopped limbs and are struggling to survive. Elsewhere, trees seem to have died or been cut down and have been replaced by new, spindly saplings. Just here and there a sturdy survivor spreads its shade across the roadside.

My journey through the Cold War has been unable to do justice to the multiplicity of the experience of returnees. I have not, for example, spoken to any of the former returnees now living as refugees across the border in China, many of whom are in desperately difficult circumstances: undocumented, exploited, vulnerable to the depredations of people traffickers. Former *Zainichi* Koreans make up a disproportionate share of North Korean refugees in China, whose number is probably around one hundred thousand (although some put the figure as high as three hundred thousand).

The fate of these refugees, caught in the power politics of the post–Cold War world, seems disturbingly to echo that of the returnees themselves. Like the returnees in the 1950s and 1960s, North Korean refugees in the twenty-first century are convenient pawns on the chessboard of global politics, mobilized when grand strategy requires them, forgotten when it does not. In the interests of international politics, their small, diverse, human needs are all too easily rendered invisible.

To the North Korean government, they are renegades and traitors, imprisoned, sometimes tortured, and even executed. To the Chinese authorities, they are illegal migrant workers, to be handed back to North Korea in the interests of good relations with the Kim Jong-Il regime. Much of U.S. political opinion, meanwhile, defines them all as political defectors, eagerly seeking liberty, democracy, and the American way. U.S.–North Korea human rights policy, which sees refugees as a potentially useful agent of "regime change," encourages people to make the exodus across the border, an act that exposes vulnerable people to terrible risk. On the Chinese side, meanwhile, a host of Christian religious groups devote energy and money to the refugee crisis, seeing in it a future harvest of souls.

None of these approaches takes real account of the diversity of the refugees who (like the returnees from Japan to North Korea in the Cold War days) include the politically committed and the utterly apolitical, people with big ambitions for a better future, and people simply struggling to buy a few bowls of rice for their families. They need help from groups who can attend to that diversity without ulterior motives, but (as in the case of the return movement) such groups are hard to find.

Greatest of all the holes in this story is the fact that I have been unable to speak to any of the returnees who still live in North Korea. On my visit there, I made no attempt to contact any of them. I knew that they would be unable to talk openly about their experiences and feelings, and approaches from inquisitive foreigners might cause them embarrassment or danger.

There was just one curious encounter, on the train back from Pyongyang to Beijing, that reminded me of what the repatriation movement might have been but tragically was not.

Struggling to make conversation with my fellow travelers in a combination of my rudimentary Korean and their hesitant English, I suddenly became aware that one of the passengers in the carriage spoke perfect Japanese. The man—I shall call him Mr. Kim—had not been part of the regular return movement, but he had been born and grown up in Japan before going to North Korea after completing high school, at the time when the repatriation was drawing to its close. After living there for a while, he moved to another Asian country, where he is now engaged in international trade. Unlike any other person I have met or heard of, Mr. Kim was able to obtain a visa that enables him to travel back and forth between North Korea, Japan, and other parts of the region, developing commercial relations that span many borders.

Ebullient, confident, multilingual Mr. Kim sees himself as a bridge between his multiple homelands. On the Chinese side of the border, he picked up the late-model mobile phone that he had left with friends (for mobile phones are banned in North Korea) and began proudly displaying its functions to the men from the North Korean Ministry of Metal Industries, with whom I shared a compartment. They sighed and exclaimed in wonder at this marvel of technology, and then entered into a lively conversation with him about the education and health care systems of North Korea and Japan.

In other circumstances, the returnees of the 1960s and 1970s might have played a similar role, opening windows from North Korea into a wider world. Instead, the walls of the Cold War closed in around them. Could there still, I wonder, be a role for them in a future opening of North Korea? After all, many of the older generation are bilingual, or at least retain some memory of Japanese. They are among the very few North Koreans who have maintained continuous personal contacts with relatives and friends outside the nation's borders.

Sitting on the seawall with my feet dangling over the opaque waters of Niigata Harbor, I look out toward the misty horizon, beyond which lies North Korea. The solitary fisherman on the dock has now been joined by another man. They seem to be old friends. The newcomer is a squarely built middle-aged man with the weather-beaten face of a sailor. You rarely see such faces in Tokyo, but in Niigata they are common.

As I watch the horizon, I find myself thinking not just about the returnees to North Korea, but also about a much-loved fellow researcher, Hokari Minoru, known as Mino to all his many Australian friends. Mino was born and brought up here in Niigata. A remarkable young scholar, he left Japan as a postgraduate student and spent years in Australia, where he traveled the desert, learning the history of Australian Aborigines. To the heartbreak of his family and friends, he was stricken by cancer, and died in 2004 at the age of 32. But he left behind a remarkable account of the history and the philosophy that he had learned from his encounters with Aboriginal elders.

Mino also wrote a series of articles for a local Niigata newspaper, and in these he spoke about his complex relationship with his home city. Niigata the provincial city was a place from which he felt the need to escape. But this port city, battered by the wild winds that blow in from the Asian continent, was also the place that gave him his openness to the outside world.

As a child, he recalled, he loved to go fishing:

From the beach or the seawall, away from the cramped houses and class-rooms and narrow city streets, I could see the ocean all the way to the horizon and beyond. I was still in elementary school, and at that age, it was not the subtle give-and-take of fishing that I enjoyed; rather, facing the ocean, I was physically experiencing the world and the meaning of freedom.

Remembering Mino, with his unruly mop of hair and his big, irrepressible laugh, I think that the fearlessness and warmth that he brought to his encounters with strange worlds were in part a legacy of this city and its people. And if that is so, perhaps the line of willows along Botonamu Street may some day again become a path toward the Asian continent. Not a path linking governments, not one paved with political intrigues and ideologies, but a causeway reaching out fearlessly to the uncertain, complex, painful lives of the people across the water—to those returnees who seek to "return" again to Japan, to the refugees on the Chinese border, and to the ordinary, suffering people of North Korea who, as their country faces its perilous future, are going to need all the good neighbors they can get.

Glancing at my watch, I suddenly realize how much time has passed while I have been sitting here on the quay. It is getting late, and I have a train to catch and a long journey still ahead of me.

I am halfway across the great empty expanse of the docks, heading back toward the avenue of willows, when I hear a shout from behind. The man on the quay has caught his fish at last. It is not a particularly impressive fish, but he seems as delighted with it as any schoolboy. His line sways in the wind, and the fish soars over the dark waters of Niigata Harbor with a flash of silver as his friend helps him reel it in.

NOTES

CHAPTER 1 - MORNING SUN

For reasons of privacy, the names of some returnees have been replaced by pseudonyms. In these cases, the names are placed in quotes when they first appear in the text. The description of the train journey to Niigata (immediately before the departure of the second convoy of repatriation ships to North Korea) is based on the account given by ICRC delegate Max Zeller. See memo by Max Zeller, 19 December 1959, Archives of the International Committee of the Red Cross (hereafter ICRC Archives), file no. B AG 232 105-015, *Problème du rapatriement des Coréens du Japon, dossier XIII: les premiers départs vers la République démocratique populaire de Corée*, 3.9.1959–28.1.1960; see also *Asahi Shimbun*, 17 December and 18 December 1959; and Letter from André Durand, "Opération de Rapatriement à Niigata du 18 au 21 Décembre 1959," 23 December 1959, ICRC Archives, file no. B AG 323 105-015.

On South Korean military alert, see *Sankei Shimbun*, 14 December 1959, evening edition. On Soviet naval maneuvers, see official diary of the Soviet ambassador to the Democratic People's Republic of Korea, A. M. Puzanov, *Dnevnik posla SSSR v KNDR A. M. Puzanova* (hereafter Puzanov Diaries), 8 December 1959, *JoongAng* Russian archive (hereafter JRA), file no. RU-secret 1959-3-3, *JoongAng Ilbo*, Seoul; see also *Asahi Shimbun*, 21 December 1959.

Descriptions of events at the Niigata Red Cross Center between 18 and 21 December 1959 are based on a letter from André Durand, "Opération de Rapatriement à Niigata du 18 au 21 Décembre 1959," 23 December 1959, ICRC Archives, file no. B AG 323 105-015, Geneva; *Asahi Shimbun*, 19 December 1959, evening edition; and 21 December 1959; *Sankei Shimbun*, 24 December 1959; *Yomiuri Shimbun*, 26 December 1959.

Interviews with returnees are quoted from *Tokyo Shimbun*, 14 December 1959.

Statistics for the number of returnees are cited from Kim Yeong-Dal and Takayanagi Toshio, eds., *Kita Chôsen kikoku jigyô kankei shiryôshu* (Tokyo:

Shinkansha, 1994), 341. For information on the return of overseas Chinese to the People's Republic of China, see Michael R. Godley, "The Sojourners: Returned Overseas Chinese in the People's Republic of China," *Pacific Affairs* 62, no. 3 (Fall 1989): 330–352.

CHAPTER 2 – HOSTAGES TO HISTORY

On Koizumi's visit to Pyongyang, see Gavan McCormack, *Target North Korea*, (New York: Nation Books, 2004), chap. 6.

"Yamada Kumiko's" story is taken from interviews conducted by the author with Ms. Yamada on 26 May and 3 June 2005.

For 351 people repatriated to North Korea, see Kim Yeongdal and Takayanagi Toshio, *Kita Chôsen kikoku jigyô kankei shiryôshû* (Tokyo: Shinkansha, 1995), 350. On the Korean community in Japan and the role of the occupation forces, see Kim Tae-Gi, *Sengo Nihon seiji to Zainichi Chôsenjin mondai: SCAP no tai-Zainichi Chôsenjin seisaku 1945-1952* (Tokyo: Keisô Shobô, 1997); Miyazaki Akira, "Senryô shoki ni okeru Beikoku no Zainichi Chôsenjin seisaku: Nihon seifu no taiô to tomo ni," *Shisô*, no. 734 (August 1985): 122–139; Tessa Morris-Suzuki, "An Act Prejudicial to the Occupations Forces: Migration Controls and Korean Residents in Post-Surrender Japan," *Japanese Studies* 24, no. 1 (May 2004): 4–28.

Takemae Eiji, *Inside GHQ: The Allied Occupation of Japan and Its Legacy*, trans. Robert Ricketts and Sebastian Swann (London: Continuum, 2002), 447–454 also includes a substantial section on policy towards Zainichi Koreans.

The cited words on the "last gasp of empire" are from historian Peter Bates in George Davis, *The Occupation of Japan: The Rhetoric and Reality of Anglo-Australian Relations, 1939-1952* (Brisbane: University of Queensland Press, 2002), 299–300.

CHAPTER 3 – GENEVA: CITY OF DREAMS

Material on the Red Cross Principles is cited from Comité International de la Croix-Rouge, *Les Principes fondamentaux de la Croix-Rouge et du Croissant-Rouge*, Geneva, Comité International de la Croix-Rouge. Other material on Red Cross history is derived from Ian Reid, *The Evolution of the Red Cross* (Geneva: Henry Dunant Institute, 1975) and Caroline Moorhead, *Dunant's Dream: War, Switzerland and the History of the Red Cross* (New York: HarperCollins, 1998).

Kang Sang-Jung's quotations are from his autobiography *Zainichi* (Tokyo: Kodansha, 2004), 24, 26–27. For an English translation of sections of the autobiography, see Kang Sang-Jung (trans. Robin Fletcher), "Memories of a *Zainichi* Korean Childhood," *Japanese Studies, 26, no. 3,* (December 2006), 267–281.

Newspaper headlines about the repatriation movement are cited from *Chôsen Sôren*, 21 November 1958 and *Sankei Shimbun*, 12 December 1959.

For reference to the Japanese ruling party's plan to "start a movement to support the repatriation," see letter from Inoue Masutarô to Leopold Boissier, 18 January 1956, ICRC Archives, file no. B AG 232 105-002, *Problème du rapatriement des Coréens du Japon, dossier I: généralités,* 17.2.1953-11.10.1957, Geneva; for consensus of the governing board of the Japanese Red Cross, see letter from Inoue to Boissier, 31 March 1956, ICRC Archives, file no. B AG 232 105-002, Geneva (this letter also refers to the need to repatriate "Koreans who cannot earn a living in Japan"); for description of Koreans being "very violent," see letter from Inoue to Boissier, 11 January 1956, ICRC Archives, file no. B AG 232 105-002; for "acting as a fifth column," see Inoue Masutarô, "Recognition of Korea: An Essay from the Standpoint of Geneva Conventions," ICRC Archives, file no. B AG 232 105-006, *Problème du rapatriement des Coréens du Japon, dossier VIII: année 1958,* 13.11.1957-15.12.1958, Geneva; for "Japan has had no experience hitherto," see confidential essay by Masutaro Inoue, "Fundamental Principles on the Solution of Question of North Koreans in Japan," appended to letter from Inoue to Boissier, 18 January 1956, ICRC Archives, file no. B AG 232 105-002, Geneva.

Quotations from returnees' letters are cited from ICRC Archives, file no. B AG 232 105-017, *Problème du rapatriement des Coréens du Japon, dossier XIV: Généralités concernant l'année 1960, deuxième partie,* 12.04.1960-21.12.1960; the story of "Mr. Yoon" appears in A. Dunant to ICRC, 26 January 1960, ICRC Archives, file no. BAG 232-016, *Problème du rapatriement des Coréens du Japon, dossier XIV: Généralités concernant l'année 1960, première partie.* 05.01.1960-08.04.1960, Geneva.

Titles of books on North Korea are Koh Se-In, *Rachi: Kita Chôsen no kokka hanzai* (Tokyo: Kodansha, 2002) and Mike Bratzke, *Kita Chôsen 'rakuen' no zankoku,* translated by Kawaguchi Azumi (Tokyo: Sôshisha, 2003).

For further details of Kawashima Takane's research see Kawashima Takane, "Tsuihô seisaku to shûdanshugi no hazama de," *Ronza* (April 2005): 240–248; also cited is Takasaki Sôji, "Kikoku undô to wa nan datta no ka," pt. 1, *Ronza* (May 2004): 114–143. See also Okonogi Masao, ed., *Zainichi Chôsenjin wa naze kikoku shita no ka* (Tokyo: Gendai Jinbunsha, 2004). Chang Myeong-Su's account of the repatriation story is given in Chang Myeong-Su, *Bôryaku: Nihon Sekijûji Kita Chôsen 'kikoku jigyô' no shinsô* (Tokyo: Satsuki Shobô, 2003).

CHAPTER 4 - ACROSS THE EAST SEA

The story of Yang I-Heon is told in the documentary film *Ama no Ryan-san (Ryang the Diving Woman),* directed by Haramura Masaki (Tokyo: Sakura Film Corporation, 2004).

A detailed history of the Busan *Waegwan* is given in James B. Lewis, *Frontier Contact between Chosŏn Korea and Tokugawa Japan* (London: Routledge Curzon, 2003). On Jeju diving women and the impact of Japanese colonialism, see Koh Sunhui and Kate Barclay, "Re-Reading the Region from the Perspective of a Traveling Society: A History of Jeju Island's Economic, Politics and Culture" (paper presented at the conference *Regional Integration in the Pacific Rim: Imagining the Pacific*, University of Guadalajara, Mexico, 28–30 January 2004)..

The account of the division of Korea and the Korean War is based on Bruce Cumings, *The Origins of the Korean War: Liberation and the Emergence of Separate Regimes* (Princeton: Princeton University Press, 1981), particularly 118–122; Bruce Cumings, *Korea's Place in the Sun: A Modern History* (New York: W. W. Norton, 1997), chap. 7; Bonnie B. C. Oh, ed., *Korea under the American Military Government, 1945–1948* (Westport, CT: Praeger, 2002); Steven Hugh Lee, *The Korean War* (Harlow, UK: Pearson Education, 2001).

CHAPTER 5 - TO THE FIELD OF DANCING CHILDREN

On postwar Jeju and the history of the Jeju 4/3 incident, see Moon Gyong-Su, *Chejudô gendaishi* (Tokyo: Shinkansha, 2005), 19–83; Kim Seong-Nae, "Sexual Politics of State Violence: On the Cheju April Third Massacre of 1948," *Traces*, no. 2, (2001) 259–291; Seong Nae Kim, *Chronicle of Violence, Ritual of Mourning: Cheju Shamanism in Korea* (unpublished Ph.D. dissertation, University of Michigan, 1989).

On the 1 March 1947 demonstration, see letter from D. W. Kermode, "Korean 'Independence Day' Disturbances," *Quelpart Island – Cheju Province*, 27 March 1947, National Archives of Australia, series no. A1838, control symbol 506/1, Canberra; Allan Raymond, "Police Brutality Held Cause of Cheju Civil War," *New York Herald Tribune*, 30 April 1948.

On the postwar migration of Jeju Islanders to Japan, see Koh Sunhui, *20 seiki no Tainichi Chejudôjin: Sono seikatsu katei to ishiki* (Tokyo: Akashi Shoten, 1998); see also "Certified Official Translation – Control of Illegal Entry into Ehime Prefecture" 25 October 1948, Australian War Memorial, file no. "[Intelligence – Reports, Post War Japan:] BCOF CSIDC – Translation, Illegal Entry into Japan," 1948 series no. AWM 114, control symbol 423/10/42, Canberra.

The description of the Korean War as "one of the most devastating of modern conflicts," and the details of casualties in the Korean War are cited from Steven Hugh Lee, *The Korean War* (Harlow, UK: Pearson Education, 2001), 9 and 124–126. Information on the "disappeared" can be found in Jo Eun, *Chinmoku de tateta ie: Chôsen sensô to reisen no kioku*, translated by Nakamura Fukuji, Jin Hwa-Su, and Murakami Naoko (Tokyo: Heibonsha, 2004).

The description of Busan after the Korean War is cited from "Déroulement de la visite des délégués du CICR en Corée du Sud," 27 May 1956, ICRC Archives, file no. B AG 121 056-001, *Généralités. Correspondance au sujet d'un possible rapatriement des prisonniers japonais en Corée-du-Nord via la Corée-du-Sud, correspondance relative à la création d'un syndicat du personnel de la Croix-Rouge coréenne*, 11.07.1955-03.12.1960. MacArthur's refusal to allow Korean refugees into Japan is cited from

S. J. Sebald, top secret telegram, 8 January 1951, "Entry and Departure," Jan. 1951–March 1951, National Diet Library microfiche, file no. GHQ-SCAP Records box AG-12(16), fiche no. TS-00117, Tokyo.

CHAPTER 6 - THE BORDERS WITHIN

For the story of Yi Yang-Soo (Rika Hiroshi), Yi Yang-Soo, interview with author, 2 June 2005; A serialized account of Yi Yang-Soo's experiences has been published under the title "Aru oyako no sengo," *Kyodo Tsûshin*, 7 August, 10 August, 13 August, and 14 August 2003; see also Yang-Su Lee, "The Repatriation of Koreans from Japan to North Korea," *Life and Human Rights*, no. 4 (1997) 10–25; Yi Yang-Soo, "Honrô sareta jinsei ni shûshifu o utsu!" *Kurio*, nos. 5–7, 1987–1988.

On the demonstrations surrounding the closure of ethnic schools and the dissolution of the League of Koreans, see Hiromitsu Inokuchi, "Korean Ethnic Schools in Occupied Japan, 1945–1952," in *Koreans in Japan: Critical Voices from the Margin*, ed. Sonia Ryang (London: Routledge, 2000) 140–156.

Yoshida Shigeru's request to MacArthur to deport all Koreans is discussed in Takemae Eiji, *Inside GHQ: The Allied Occupation of Japan and Its Legacy*, trans. and adapted by Robert Ricketts and Sebastian Swann (London and New York: Continuum, 2002) 497. On the 1950 plan to deport "subversive Koreans," see "Communist Koreans May Be Ordered Deported," Jiji press reports, 24 December 1950, evening edition, and "Korean Mission Releases Statement on Deportation of Koreans," *Immigration – February 1950–March 1952*, 13 January 1951, National Diet Library microfiche, GHQ-SCAP Records, Box 2189, fiche no GS(B) – 01603, Tokyo; comment on execution, untitled GHQ-SCAP memo, *Immigration – February 1950–March 1952*, 13 January 1951, National Diet Library microfiche, GHQ-SCAP Records, Box 2189, fiche no GS(B) – 01603, Tokyo.

For deportation plan evoked a united response from Koreans, see memo from Chief, Liaison Section, MPD, "Re Movements of the Koreans Centering around the Enforcement of the Emigration Control Ordinance," *Immigration, April 1951–Oct. 1951*, 30 October 1951, GHQ/SCAP archives, box no. 353, folder no. 8, reproduced on Korean National Library database, Seoul.

For deportations likened to the "Jewish expulsion conducted by Hitler," see memo from Matsumoto Hideyuki, Liaison Chief, MPD, "Protest against the Attorney General around the Compulsory Deportation of the Koreans," *Deportation, October 1951–November 1951*, 23 October 1951, GHQ/SCAP records, box no. 353, folder no. 6, reproduced on Korean National Library database, Seoul. For U.S. occupation authorities voice concerns about deportation plan, see untitled memo outlining GHQ/SCAP's views on deportation, initialed "MU," *Immigration, February 1950–March 1952*, National Diet Library microfiche, GHQ/SCAP archives, box no. 2189, microfiche no. GS(B)-01603, Tokyo; memorandum for Colonel Napier, "Deportation of Korean [sic] Issue," *Immigration, February 1950–March*

1952, 9 March 1951, National Diet Library microfiche, GHQ/SCAP records, box no. 2189, microfiche no. GS(B)-01602, Tokyo.

On the problems of the nationality of Koreans in Japan, see Kim Tae-Gi, *Sengo Nihon seiji to Zainichi Chôsenjin mondai: SCAP no tai-Zainichi Chôsenjin seisaku 1945–1952* (Tokyo: Keisô Shobô, 1997); memorandum for Chief, Diplomatic Section from Alva C. Carpenter, Chief, Legal Section, "Japanese-Korean Nationality Conference," 22 October 1951, National Diet Library microfiche, GHQ-SCAP records, fiche no. LS 24687-24688, Tokyo; Kim Il-Hwa, "Zainichi Chôsenjin no hôteki chii," in Pak Chong-Myeong, ed., *Zainichi Chôsenjin: Rekishi, genjô, tenbô* (Tokyo: Akashi Shoten, 1995), 205–207.

For Okazaki Katsuo's involvement in the nationality issue, see answers by Health and Welfare Minister Yoshibe to the Welfare Committee of the Lower House of the Diet, 2 April 1952. Okazaki Katsuo's statement in the Diet on the nationality status of Koreans in Japan was given to the Foreign Affairs Committee of the Lower House on 14 May 1952, *Kokkai Gijiroku* at http://kokkai.ndl.go.jp (hereafter KG).

For welfare status of Koreans after the loss of nationality, see Shin Yeong-Hon, "Zainichi Chôsenjin to shakai hoshô," in Pak Chong-Myeong, ed., *Zainichi Chôsenjin: Rekishi, genjô, tenbô* (Tokyo: Akashi Shoten, 1995), 286–289; Social Affairs Bureau, Ministry of Health and Welfare, "Public Assistance for the Koreans Resident in Japan," 30 April 1956, ICRC Archives, file no. B AG 232 105-002, Geneva; "Treatment of Koreans in Japan," 3 August 1959, ICRC Archives, file no. B AG 232 105-011.06, *Notes et procès-verbaux d'entretiens avec Masutaro Inoue, directeur du Département des Affaires etrangères de la Croix-Rouge japonaise, lors de son séjour à Genève*, 10.07.1959-13.08.1959, Geneva.

CHAPTER 7 - THE SHADOW MINISTRY

For article cited at the start of this chapter, see "Nisseki Gaijibuchô ni natta Inoue Masutarô," *Asahi Shimbun*, 2 July 1955. Other details of Inoue's life and career come from "Gaimushô shokuin haizokuhyô," *Japan, Ministry of Foreign Affairs Archives 1868–1945*, various years, National Library of Australia, BM series, reel 3, Canberra; *Daijinmei jiten*, vol. 5 (Tokyo: Heibonsha, 1954) 342 (on Horikoshi Zenjirô) and Chang Myeong-Su, *Bôryaku: Nihon Sekijûji Kita Chôsen 'kikoku jigyô' no shinsô* (Tokyo: Satsuki Shobô, 2003).

On the career of Shigemitsu Mamoru and his role in peace negotiations, see Shigemitsu Mamoru, *Shigemitsu Mamoru gaikô kaisôroku* (Tokyo: Mainichi Shimbunsha, 1958); Shigemitsu Mamoru, *Shôwa no dôran*, reprinted in Shigemitsu Mamoru, *Shigemitsu Mamoru chosakushû*, vol. 1 (Tokyo: Hara Shobô, 1978), translated by O. White as *Japan and Her Destiny: My Struggle for Peace* (London: Hutchinson, 1958); on Okazaki, see Okazaki Katsuo, *Sengo nijûnen no henreki* (Tokyo: Chûô Kôronsha, 1999).

See also Gar Alperovitz, *Atomic Diplomacy: Hiroshima and Potsdam—The Use of the Atomic Bomb and the American Confrontation with Soviet Power* (London and East Haven, CT: Pluto Press, 1994).

For OSS memorandum to President Truman, see "Memorandum for the President," in *Memoranda for the President: Japanese Feelers*, 31 May 1945, compilation of documents approved for release under the CIA historical review program, 22 September 1993, athttp://www.cia.gov/csi/kent_csi/docs/v09i3a06p.

For article on the views of the "Japanese security establishment," see "Zainichi Chôsenjin no dôkô: Chian tôkyoku no kenkai," *Asahi Shimbun*, 2 July 1955.

Details on Shimazu Tadatsugu and on the old Japan Red Cross building are cited from Shimazu's memoirs, *Jindô no hata no moto ni* (Tokyo: Kodansha, 1965), especially 11–17. The official Red Cross account of the repatriation is given in Nihon Sekikijûjisha, ed., *Nihon Sekijûjisha shashikô*, vol. 7 (Tokyo: Nihon Sekijûjisha, 1986), 178–265.

CHAPTER 8 - THE TIP OF THE ICEBERG

On Inoue's visit to Geneva, see letter from de Weck to Angst, 7 October 1955, ICRC Archives, file no. B AG 121 105-006, *Visites au CICR de prince Tadatsugu Shimadzu, de Mme Kimi Kotani, de Masutaro Inoue et Mlle Shio Hayashi*, 07.05.1955-18.08.1959, Geneva; E. de Weck, "Procès-Verbal d'entretiens avec M. Masutaro Inoue," 27 September and 29 September, ICRC Archives, file no. B AG 232 055-001, *Ressortissants japonais en Corée-du-Nord*, 22.01.1954-11.05.1956, Geneva. The personal background of Leopold Boissier is outlined in ICRC, "The ICRC and Its Departments," in *International Committee of the Red Cross Annual Report 1955* (Geneva: ICRC, 1956) 6–7.

For Japan Red Cross Society's January 1954 telegram to Pyongyang and the response from North Korea, see Secretary General, League of Red Cross Societies, Geneva, telegram to Red Cross People's Republic, Pyongyang, 6 January 1954; and Li Dong Yung, Red Cross Society of the Democratic People's Republic of Korea, Pyongyang, telegram to League of Red Cross Societies, Geneva, 6 February 1954, ICRC Archives, file no. B AG 232 055-001, Geneva.

For Inoue's first long letter to Boissier, see Inoue to Boissier, 14 November 1955, ICRC Archives, file no. B AG 232 055-001, Geneva.

For Shimazu's request of 13 December 1955, see Shimazu to Boissier, 13 December 1955; Inoue to Gallopin, 11 January 1956; and Inoue to Boissier, 19 January 1956, ICRC Archives, file no. B AG 232 105-002, Geneva.

For Inoue suggests that ICRC should send representatives to East Asia, see Inoue to Boissier, 22 December 1955, ICRC Archives, file no. B AG 232 105-002, Geneva. For Boissier's response, see Boissier to Inoue, 29 December 1955, ICRC Archives, file no. B AG 232 055-001, Geneva.

For "North Koreans . . . preparing to hold nationwide rallies," see letter from Inoue to Boissier, 11 January 1956, ICRC Archives, file no. B AG 232 105-002, Geneva; for similar warnings of impending violence, see letter from Shimazu to Gallopin, 23 July 1956, ICRC Archives, file no. B AG 232 105-004, *Problème du rapatriement des Coréens du Japon, dossier III – Rapatriement de 48 Coréens en Corée-du-Nord*, 28.05.1956-03.12.1956, Geneva; letter from Inoue to Boissier, 10 September 1956, ICRC Archives, file no. B AG 232 105-004, Geneva. For "An indication that the Japanese Governmental party. . . would start a movement to support the repatriation," see Inoue to Boissier, 19 January 1956, ICRC Archives, file no. B AG 232 105-002, Geneva; for Ashida Hitoshi's diary entry, see Ashida Hitoshi, *Ashida Hitoshi nikki*, vol. 6 (Tokyo: Iwanami Shoten, 1992), 68.

For ICRC's request for information "however approximate" on likely number of returnees, see Gallopin to Shimazu, 21 December 1955, in ICRC Archives, file no. B AG 232 105-002, Geneva. For Japan Red Cross Society's response, estimating of numbers of Koreans in Japan, and numbers of potential returnees, see "Exposé synoptique du télégramme de la Croix-Rouge japonaise" 13 January 1956, ICRC Archives, file no. B AG 232 105-002, Geneva. This figure is repeated in a letter from Inoue to Gallopin, 26 March 1956; and letter from Inoue to Boissier, 31 March 1956, ICRC Archives, file no. B AG 232 105-002, Geneva. Statements by the senior officials of the General Association of Korean Residents in Japan are cited from "Déroulement de la visite des délégués du CICR au Japon," 27 May 1956, ICRC Archives, file no. B AG 232 105-002, p. 7, Geneva.

Transcript of the Diet Lower House Foreign Affairs Committee Meeting of 14 February 1956 can be found in KG, Shûgiin Gaimu Iinkai, 14 February 1956, http://kokkai.ndl.go.jp.

CHAPTER 9 – THE PYONGYANG CONFERENCE

Except where otherwise stated, details of the Japan Red Cross Society's mission to North Korea are derived from Masutaro Inoue, *Report of the Phyongyang* [sic.] *Conference held by Japanese and North Korean Red Cross Societies (January 27th–February 28th 1956)*, 17 March 17 1956, ICRC Archives, file no. B AG 232 055-001, Geneva.

For Miyakoshi Kisuke's role in mission to Pyongyang, see secret note exchanged between the Representatives of the Japan Red Cross Society and the Japan-Korea Association (signed by Kasai Yoshisuke and Hatanaka Masaharu), 17 December 1955, ICRC Archives, file no. B AG 232 055-001, Geneva. On the history of the Japan-Korea Association, see Yi Sang-Jin, "Nicchô Kyôkai no seikaku to yakuwari," in Takasaki Sôji and Pak Jeong-Jin, eds., *Kikoku undô to wa nan datta no ka* (Tokyo: Heibonsha, 2005) 235–267.

For description of the delegation's arrival in Pyongyang and visit to the North Korean Red Cross headquarters, see *Asahi Shimbun*, 29 January 1956. Details of the destruction of North Korean housing during the Korean War are cited from "Spravka o Polozhenii v Koree," p. 9, JRA, file no. RU–secret 1955-4-3, Seoul.

For Japan Red Cross delegation meets Japanese returnees, see *Asahi Shimbun*, 31 January 1956.

Inoue's advice about conditions in North Korea was passed on to the ICRC by Harry Angst in letter from Angst to de Weck, "Your Mission to the Far East," 12 March 1956, ICRC Archives, file no. B AG 232 055-001, Geneva.

For details of Nam Il's background, see Andrei Lankov, "The Soviet Faction in the DPRK, 1945-1955" at http://www.fortunecity.com/meltingpot/champion/65/sov_fact.htm, accessed 22 April 2006. For Nam Il and policy toward Koreans in Japan, see Pak Jeong-Jin, "Kikoku undô no rekishiteki haikei: Sengo Nicchô kankei to kaisho," in Takasaki Sôji and Pak Jeong-jin, eds., *Kikoku undô no wa Nan datta no ka* (Tokyo: Heibonsha, 2005), 54–92.

Nam Il's comments to Ambassador Ivanov are quoted from Ivanov Diaries, 1 October 1955, JRA, file no. RU–secret 1955-2-2, Seoul.

For Nam Il's message to Japan, see Li Byung Nam, telegram to Shimazu Tadatsugu, 31 December 1955, ICRC Archives, file no. B AG 232 105-002, Geneva.

For North Korean assistance to *Zainichi* Korean students, see Takasaki Sôji, "Kikoku mondai no keika to haikei," in Takasaki Sôji and Pak Jeong-Jin, eds., *Kikoku undô to wa nan datta no ka* (Tokyo: Heibonsha, 2005); see also "Statement of the Vice-Minister of Education of the DPRK in Connection with the Full Preparations for Ensuring the Democratic National Education of the Foreign Students in Japan," in *On the Question of 600,000 Koreans in Japan* (Pyongyang: Foreign Languages Publishing House, 1959), June 1959, South Korean Declassified Documents on Korea-Japan Negotiations (hereafter SKDDKJR), 723.1 JA, file number 177, pp. 437–440, Seoul (also available on the database of the *Dong-A Ilbo* newspaper).

For details of the June 1956 meeting between Inoue and Shin, Inoue, letter to Boissier, 2 July 1956, ICRC Archives, file no. B AG 232 105-002, Geneva.

For Inoue's report on "certain Koreans,"see Inoue Masutarô, *Fundamental Conditions of Livelihood of Certain Koreans Residing in Japan*, Japanese Red Cross Society, November 1956, ICRC Archives, file no. B AG 232 105-002, particularly pp. 24–25 and 35–37, Geneva.

For twenty-one additional Japanese in North Korea identified, see *Asahi Shimbun*, 23 March 1956.

For Inoue and Shin's final conversation in Pyongyang, see Inoue to de Weck, postscript to "Report of the Phyongyang Conference," 9 April 1956, ICRC Archives, file no. B AG 232 105-002, Geneva.

CHAPTER 10 - SPECIAL MISSION TO THE FAR EAST

For Michel's illness in China, see "Après une mission en Extrême-Orient," *Revue Internationale de la Croix-Rouge*, no. 452 (August 1956): 443–450 (particularly 444).

Except where otherwise specified, the account of Michel and de Weck's visit to Japan is derived from "Déroulement de la visite des délégués du CICR au Japon," 27 May 1956, ICRC Archives, file no. B AG 232 105-002, Geneva. For account of the mission's visit to North Korea, see "Déroulement de la visite des délégués du CICR à la C.R. de la République démocratique populaire de Corée," 29 April 1956, ICRC Archives, file no. B AG 232 105-002, Geneva.

Comments on terrible "dusty roads" and "seeing the speed with which the bricks were laid" are from "Déroulement de la visite des délégués du CICR à la C.R. de la République démocratique populaire de Corée," 29 April 1956, ICRC Archives, file no. B AG 232 105-002, Geneva. Details of Michel and de Weck's meeting with the North Korean Red Cross are given in "Entretien du 7/IV/56 avec le C.R. Coréenne," Annex 4 of "Déroulement de la visite des délégués du CICR à la C.R. de la République démocratique populaire de Corée," 29 April 1956, ICRC Archives, file no. B AG 232 105-002, p. 4, Geneva.

For Michel's comments on varied estimates of numbers seeking repatriation, see Michel to ICRC Geneva, 9 May 1956, ICRC Archives, file no. B AG 232 105-002, Geneva.

For Harry Angst's career, see "Angst to Leave Nihon Siber Hegner," *Daily Yomiuri*, 12 June 1974.

For Angst's ability to "move with ease in all the social circles of the capital," see letter from Marcel Junod to Boissier, 26 August 1959, ICRC Archives, file no. B AG 232 105-011.02 *Rapports du Dr Marcel Junod, délégué au Japon, 26.08.1959-06.10.1959*, Geneva. Criticisms of Angst's attitudes to prisoners-of-war reported by long-time Australian resident in Japan, Harold Williams; see the note "Angst," in the Harold Williams Collection, Australian National Library, Canberra.

For meeting with officials of the Police and Public Security Agencies, see "Séance de travail du 7.v.1956," annex 4 to "Déroulement de la visite des délégués du CICR au Japon," 27 May 1956, ICRC Archives, file no. B AG 232 105-002, Geneva; for Shigemitsu Mamoru's comments on repatriation, see W. H. Michel, "Gouvernement Japonais," 27 May 1956, annex 8 to "Déroulement de la visite des délégués du CICR au Japon" 27 May 1956, ICRC Archives, file no. B AG 232 105-002, Geneva; for Inoue's comments on "total absence of humanitarian considerations," see letter from Michel to ICRC, "Mission Michel et de Weck," 23 May 1956, ICRC Archives, file no. B AG 232 105-002, p. 2, Geneva.

Information on the Ministry of Health and Welfare's crackdown is derived from Social Affairs Bureau, Ministry of Health and Welfare, "Public Assistance for the Koreans Resident in Japan," (English-language report given to Michel and de Weck during their visit to Japan), 30 April 1956, ICRC Archives, file no. B AG 232 105-002, Geneva; see also Social Affairs Bureau, Ministry of Health and Welfare, "On the Struggle of Koreans in Japan for Livelihood Protection," (English translation), 3 May 1956, ICRC Archives, file no. B AG 232 105-003, *Problème du rapatriement des Coréens du Japon, dossier III*, 16.01.1956-25.10.1957, Geneva. On the number of welfare claimants, see also Zenkoku Shakai Fukushi Kyôgikai, ed., *Nihon no shakai fukushi* (Tokyo: Zenkoku Shakai Fukushi Kyôgikai, 1958), 242. On the effect of welfare cuts on the Tôhoku community, see Pak Jae-Il, *Zainichi Chôsenjin ni kansuru sôgô kenkyû chôsa* (Tokyo: Shin-Kigensha, 1957), 149, 151.

Japanese press articles on welfare cuts are "Chôsenjin no seikatsu hogô – Nihonjin no nibai ijô," *Asahi Shimbun*, 26 April 1956; "Nen ni yaku 5 oku-en o sakugen – Chôsenjin no seikatsu hogôhi," *Asahi Shimbun*, 25 May 1956; "Yen 470,000,000 a Year Received Illegally by Koreans as Livelihood Protection," *Nihon Keizai Shimbun*, 24 May 1956 (English translation), and "Reduction of Livelihood Protection for Koreans," *Tôkyo Shimbun*, 24 May 1956 (English translation), ICRC Archives, file no. B AG 232 105-002, Geneva. On the drop in the number of Korean welfare recipients, see also Pak Sang-Deok, ed., *Zôho Zainichi Chôsenjin no minzoku kyôiku* (Tokyo: Ariesu Shobô, 1984), 137.

For Shimazu's letter on cuts to "the total amount of livelihood relief fund," see Shimazu to Boissier, 19 July 1956, ICRC Archives, file no. B AG 232 105-004, Geneva.

"Taniguchi Hiroko's" story is from author's interview with "Ms. Taniguchi," 10 June 2005.

CHAPTER 11 - THE FIRST "RETURN"

Information on Michel and de Weck's visit to Ômura is from "Ômura Immigration Center" (report by E. de Weck), 18 June 1956, ICRC Archives, file no. B AG 232 105-002, Geneva.

For the official Japan Red Cross Society account of the demonstration by the forty-seven returnees, see Nihon Sekikjûjisha, ed., *Nihon Sekijûjisha shashikô*, vol. 7 (Tokyo: Nihon Sekijûjisha, 1986), 178–179. See also note de dossier, "Remise des titres voyage à 48 Coréens résident au Japon," 20 November 1957, ICRC Archives, file no. B AG 232 105-004, Geneva.

For Therng Ik-Sam's letter, see Therng Ik-Sam to International Committee of the Red Cross, 23 July 1956, ICRC Archives, file no. B AG 232 105-004, *Problème du rapatriement des Coréens du Japon, dossier III: rapatriement de 48 Coréens en Corée-du-Nord*, 28.05.1956-03.12.1957, Geneva. For Shimazu's letter to North Korean Red Cross, including reference to the "next step," see Shimazu to Li Byung Nam, 6 June 1956, ICRC Archives, file no. B AG 232 105-004, Geneva.

For five of the forty-seven were detainees, see "Chronology Concerning Attempts of Korean Residents in Japan to Proceed to North Korea since August 26, 1955," SKDDKJR, 723.1 JA, file number 177, p. 118.

For Inoue's letters about transport of repatriates, see Inoue to Gallopin, 26 March 1956, and Inoue to Boissier, 31 March 1936, ICRC Archives, file no. B AG 232-002, Geneva.

For requests to Butterfield and Swire and Hong Kong colonial government, see Shimazu to Carey, 11 June 1956, and Shimazu to Sir Alexander Grantham, 11 June

1956, ICRC Archives, file no. B AG 232 105-004, Geneva; For Inoue plans second and third groups, see Inoue to Boissier, 16 June 1956, ICRC Archives, file no. B AG 232 105-004, Geneva; For response from North Korea, see copy of telegram from Central Committee of Red Cross Society of Democratic Republic of Korea to Japancross, 8 July 1956, ICRC Archives, file no. B AG 232 105-004, Geneva.

For Inoue's secret meeting with Shin, see Inoue to Boissier, 2 July 1956, ICRC Archives, file no. B AG 232 105-002, Geneva. For DPRK Cabinet Order No. 53, see English text contained in typescript *On the Question of 600,000 Koreans in Japan,* SKDDKJR, 723.1 JA, file number 177, Seoul, pp. 426–427.

For Inoue and Shin's secret discussions, see Inoue to Boissier, 2 July 1956, ICRC Archives, file no. B AG 232 105-002, Geneva.

For telephone call from Butterfield and Swire, see Shimazu to Boissier, 19 July 1956; Butterfield and Swire (Japan) to Ota, Japan Red Cross, 9 July 1956, ICRC Archives, file no. B AG 232 105-004, Geneva.

For Michel and de Weck's discussions in South Korea, see "Déroulement de la visite des délégués du CICR en Corée du Sud," 27 May 1956, ICRC Archives, file no. B AG 121 056-001, *Généralités. Correspondance au sujet d'un possible rapatriement des prisonniers japonais en Corée-du-Nord via la Corée-du-Sud, correspondance relative à la création d'un syndicat du personnel de la Croix-Rouge coréenne,* 11.07.1955-03.12.1960, Geneva.

For South Korea's 27 June 1956 contact with Japanese Foreign Ministry, see "Chronology Concerning Attempts of Korean Residents in Japan to Proceed to North Korea since August 26, 1955," SKDDKJR, 723.1 JA, file number 177, p. 113. For South Korean statement on "indirect declaration of war," see Shimazu to Boissier, 23 July 1956, ICRC Archives, file no. B AG 232 105-004, Geneva.

For numbers of Japanese fishermen detained in Busan, see Gaimushô Jôhô Bunka Kyoku, "Hokusen jiyû kikan mondai ni tsuite," *Sekai no ugoki,* special issue 10, March 1959, reprinted in Kim Yeong-Dal and Takayanagi Toshio, eds., *Kita Chôsen kikoku jigyô kankei shiryô* (Tokyo: Shinkansha, 1994), 105–135, particularly 123–127.

For condition of forty-seven returnees, see Inoue to Boissier, 10 September 1956, ICRC Archives, file no. B AG 232 105-004, Geneva.

For request for Harry Angst to carry out repatriation procedures, see Shimazu to Boissier, 5 July 1956, ICRC Archives, file no. B AG 232 105-004, Geneva. For Shimazu's letter to Tikhvinsky, see Shimazu to Tikhvinsky, 11 July 1956, ICRC Archives , file no. B AG 232 105-003, Geneva. For Inoue's meeting with Tikhvinsky, see Information to ICRC from JRC, "Conversation between Director Inoue and Minister Dr. Sergei L. Tikhvinsky, Head of the USSR Mission in Tokyo," 14 July 1956, ICRC Archives, file no. B AG 232 105-004, Geneva; for Soviet Navy reluctant to provide escort, see copy of telegram from Inoue to Shin Koreacross Pyongyang, 22 July 1956, ICRC Archives, file no. B AG 232 105-004, Geneva. For Tikhvinsky's private assurance to Inoue, see Inoue Masutarô, "Report: Visit to the Omura Detention Camp, June 28, 1958," 1 July 1958, ICRC Archives, *Problème du rapatriement des Coréens du Japon, dossier VIII: année 1958*, 13.11.1957-15.12.1958, p. 8, Geneva.

For Boissier's letter of 16 July 1956, see correspondence, ICRC Archives, file no. B AG 232 105-005.06, *Proposition du CICR aux trois parties de 16 juillet 1956 et réponses*, 16.07.1956 – 15.08.1956, Geneva. For letter proposing meeting in Geneva and responses, see correspondence, ICRC Archives, file no. B AG 232 105-005.05, *Invitation à une rencontre à Genève lancée par le CICR aux trois parties le 15 août 1956 et réponses*, 15.08.1956 – 04.09.1956, Geneva.

For Shimazu Tadatsugu's concrete proposals to Boissier, see Shimazu to Boissier, 12 January 1957, ICRC Archives, file no. B AG 232 105-005.04, *Mémorandum du 12 décembre 1956 adressé aux trois parties et réponses*, 12.12.1956 – 12.01.1957, Geneva.

For threat of riots, see Inoue to Boissier, 10 September 1956, ICRC Archives, file no. B AG 232 105-004, Geneva; for forty-eight protestors were a "nuisance," see Angst to ICRC, 7 September 1956, ICRC Archives, file no. B AG 232 105-004, Geneva. Return of first 20 on Norwegian ship – Inoue to Gallopin, 6 February 1957, ICRC Archives, file no. B AG, file no. B AG 232 105-005.01, *Généralités: Correspondance avec les Sociétés nationales de Japon, de la République démocratique populaire de Corée et de la République de Corée au sujet du rapatriement des Coréens du Japon et du retour des pêcheurs Japonais détenus en République de Corée*, 01.08.1956-29.12.1957, Geneva. For their arrival in Pyongyang, see English translation of "News through the New Asia News Agency," Pyongyang Broadcast, 14 December 1956, ICRC Archives, file no. B AG 232 105-004, Geneva.

For departure of remaining protestors to North Korea, see Nihon Sekijûjisha, ed., *Nihon Sekijûjisha shashikô*, vol. 7 (Tokyo: Nihon Sekijûjisha, 1986), 179. For Japan Red Cross Society did not inform ICRC about return of remaining twenty-eight although the twenty-eight returned in March 1957, see the ICRC document "Remise des titres voyage à 48 Coréens résidents au Japon," 20 November 1957, ICRC Archives, file no. B AG 232 105-004, Geneva, which states that after a report from Pyongyang about the arrival of the first twenty in December 1956, "We have not had any news on the subject of the repatriation" of the forty-eight Koreans.

CHAPTER 12 - RESOLUTION 20

For Red Cross Principles, see Comité International de la Croix-Rouge, *Les Principes fondamentaux de la Croix-Rouge et du Croissant-Rouge*, Geneva, Comité International de la Croix-Rouge, n.d.; see also "The Fundamental Principles of the Red Cross: Commentary," 1 January 1979, at http://www.icrc.org/Web/eng/siteeng0.nsf/htmlall/5MJE9N.

For Inoue's translation of Pictet's *Principles*, see "Une Édition Japonaise des Principes de la Croix-Rouge," *Revue Internationale de la Croix-Rouge*, no. 468 (December 1957): 676–678.

For February Memorandum, see ICRC Archives, file no. B AG 232 105.03, *Mémorandum du 26 février 1957 adressé aux trois parties et réponses*, 26.02.1957-28.03.1957, Geneva.

For Gallopin's comments on propaganda, see Gallopin to Inoue, 16 April 1957, ICRC Archives, file no. B AG 232 105-005.01, Geneva.

For LDP and Ministry of Foreign Affairs attitudes to repatriation issue in 1957, see Inoue to Boissier, 31 May 1957, ICRC Archives, file no. B AG 232 105-005.01, Geneva. For political popularity of repatriation, for example, Vice Foreign Minister Yamada told the U.S. Ambassador in Tokyo that repatriation was "extremely important" to the Japanese government in terms of "Japanese domestic opinion," see telegram from the Embassy in Japan to the Department of State, Tokyo, 22 July 1960, in Madeline Chi, Louis J. Smith, and Robert J. McMahon, eds., *Foreign Relations of the United States 1958–1960*, vol. XVIII (hereafter FRUS XVIII), Washington D.C., Department of State, document no. 477, p. 389, Tokyo. For Japan Red Cross Society's response to the February Memorandum, see Shimazu to Boissier, 13 May 1957, ICRC Archives, file no. B AG 232 105-005.01, Geneva. For Shimazu's letter to Kishi and other ministers and Kishi's reply, see Annexes A and B to Shimazu to Boissier, 1 October 1957, ICRC Archives, file no. B AG 232 105-005.01, Geneva; see also Nihon Sekikjûjisha, ed., *Nihon Sekijûjisha Shashikô*, vol. 7 (Tokyo: Nihon Sekijûjisha, 1986), 187–188.

For the New Delhi Conference, see "XIXme Conférence Internationale de la Croix-Rouge," *Revue Internationale de la Croix-Rouge*, no. 471 (February 1958): 88–105; For Conference Resolution 24, "Campaign Against Prejudice and Discrimination," see *Revue Internationale de la Croix-Rouge* 11 (Supplement), no. 2 (February 1958): 48; For Conference Resolution 20, "Reunion of Dispersed Families," see *Revue Internationale de la Croix-Rouge* 11 (Supplement), no. 1 (January 1958): 20.

For Japan Red Cross Society's "energetic insistence" on ICRC intervention, see Michel to Durand, 8 November 1957, ICRC Archives, file no. B AG 232 105-005.01, Geneva.

For correspondence between Japan Red Cross Society and ICRC about proposed resolution for the New Delhi Conference, see "Note sur le problème de la libération et du rapatriement de Coréens internés ou résidant au Japon et des Japonais internés en Corée," 9 October 1957, and Kasai to Boissier, 5 November 1957, ICRC Archives, file no. B AG 232 105-005.01, Geneva.

Inoue's interpretation of Resolution 20 is quoted from Inoue Masutarô, "Why Is the Question of Repatriation an Urgent Humanitarian Issue?" document for circulation to national Red Cross Societies, 29 January 1959, Archives of the International Federation of Red Cross and Red Crescent Societies, file no. 22/3/4, *Coréens au Japon*, p. 4, Geneva.

For Kasai's letter to North Korean Red Cross, see Kasai to Li Byung Nam, 10 December 1957, ICRC Archives, file no. B AG 232 105-003.01, Geneva.

For ICRC letter to Japanese and South Korean Foreign Ministers on Busan and Ômura detainees, see Gallopin to Fujiyama, 3 December 1957, ICRC Archives, file no. B AG 232 105-005.01, Geneva. (This letter refers to the resolution on the reunion of families as "Resolution 8." It was in fact Resolution 8 of the conference's Humanitarian Law Commission, and Resolution 20 of the conference as a whole.)

For disputes over interpretation of 31 Dec. 1957 Accord, see "Chronology Concerning Attempts of Korean Residents in Japan to Proceed to North Korea since August 26, 1955," SKDDKJR, 723.1 JA, file no. 177, pp. 120–147. See also Inoue to Gallopin, 28 January 1958, and other letters; ICRC Archives, file no. B AG 232 105.006.01 *Généralités*. 01.01.1958-15.12.1958, Geneva.

For role of Inoue Takajirô in negotiations between Japan and South Korea, see Memorandum of Conversation between Ambassador Inoue, Minister Shimada, Howard P. Jones and Howard L. Parsons, Department of State, Washington, 12 February 1958, held in National Archives and Records Administration (hereafter NARA), section, RG95, CFDF 1955–1959, box 2722, document no. 694.95B/2-1258, Washington D.C.; also telegram from U.S. Ambassador MacArthur to State Department, Washington, 12 February 1958, in NARA, section RG95, CFDF 1955–1959, box 2722, document no. 694.95B/2-1258, Washington D.C.

For Angst and Inoue's communications with Ômura detainees, *Chongryun*, Japan-Korea Association, and Miyakoshi Kisuke, see Inoue Masutarô, "Report: Visit to Omura Detention Camp," 28 June 1958, 1 July 1958, ICRC Archives, file no. B AG 232 105-006, *Problème du rapatriement des Coréens du Japon, dossier IV: L'Année 1958*, 13.11.1957-15.12.1958, p. 6, Geneva; see also report by Harry Angst, "Distribution of Monetary Relief from the North Korean Red Cross Society among Inmates of the Omura Immigration Center on June 28, 1958," 3 July 1958, ICRC Archives, file no. B AG 232 105-006.04, Geneva.

For Shimazu's highly confidential telegram, see Shimazu to Li Byung Nam, 5 July 1958, ICRC Archives, file no. B AG 232 105-006, Geneva. For information sent by Inoue to the ICRC about the repatriation plan, see Inoue Masutarô, "Report: Visit to Omura Detention Camp," 28 June 1958, 1 July 1958, ICRC Archives, file no. B AG 232 105-006, Geneva.

For Foreign Minister Fujiyama's statements on repatriation, see *Mainichi Shimbun*, 31 January 1959; *Asahi Shimbun*, 31 January 1959; and telegram from U.S. Ambassador MacArthur to Secretary of State, Washington, 7 February 1959, in NARA, section RG95, CFDF 1955–1959, box 2722, document no. 694.95B/759, parts 1 and 2, Washington D.C.

For Japanese Cabinet's statement on repatriation, 13 February 1959, see Nihon Sekikjûjisha, ed., *Nihon Sekijûjisha shashikô*, vol. 7 (Tokyo: Nihon Sekijûjisha, 1986), 191.

For South Korean demonstrations against Japanese Cabinet statement on repatriation 13 Feb. 1959, see "Chronology Concerning Attempts of Korean Residents in Japan to Proceed to North Korea since August 26, 1955," SKDDKJR, 723.1 JA, file no. 177, pp. 166–172.

CHAPTER 13 - DREAM HOMES ON THE DAEDONG

For Han Deok-Su's background, see Sonia Ryang, *North Koreans in Japan* (Boulder: Westview Press, 1997), 91, 140–141; see also Kim Chan-Jong, *Chôsen Sôren* (Tokyo: Shinchô Shinsho, 2004), 51, 64–66.

For Inoue's preference for dealing with *Chongryun*, see Inoue to Boissier, 19 January 1956, ICRC Archives, file no. B AG 232 105-002, Geneva. For Han Deok-Su's meeting with Michel and de Weck, see "Déroulement de la visite des délégués du CICR au Japon," 27 May 1956, ICRC Archives, file no. B AG 232 105-002, pp. 7–8, Geneva. For August 1957 *Chongryun* approach to USSR, see Puzanov Diaries, 19 August 1957, JRA, file no. RU Secret 57-2-1-2, Seoul.

For 11 August 1958 meeting, see Takasaki Sôji, "Kikoku mondai no keika to haikei," in Takasaki Sôji and Pak Jeong-Jin, eds., *Kikoku undô to wa nan datta no ka* (Tokyo: Heibonsha, 2005) 22.

For statements by Kim Il-Sung and Nam Il, see "An Extract from Premier Kim Il Sung's Speech Made on the 10th Anniversary of the Founding of the People's Democratic Republic of Korea," 8 September 1958, in *On the Question of 600,000 Koreans in Japan*, SKDDKJR, 723.1 JA, file number 177, Seoul, p. 422; see also "Statement of the Foreign Minister of the DPRK in Connection with the Question of the Return Home of the Korean Nationals in Japan," 16 September 1958, in *On the Question of 600,000 Koreans in Japan*, SKDDKJR, 723.1 JA, file number 177, Seoul, p. 449–450.

For *Chongryun* response to North Korean announcement, see, for example, *Chôsen Sôren*, 1 October 1958 and 1 January 1959. For Japanese press reports on the prorepatriation movement, see for example, *Yomiuri Shimbun*, 22 Oct 1958; *Asahi Shimbun*, 30 November 1958; *Tokyo Shimbun*, and 16 December 1958; see also Takasaki Sôji, "Asahi Shimbun to Sankei Shimbun wa kikoku undô o dou hôjita no ka," in Takasaki Sôji and Pak Jeong-Jin, eds., *Kikoku undô to wa nan datta no ka* (Tokyo: Heibonsha, 2005), 286–305. For reptriation cartoon, see *Yomiuri Shimbun*, 5 February 1959, evening edition.

On the activities of the *Zainichi* Korean Repatriation Cooperation Society, see Yi Sang-Jin, "Nicchô Kyôkai no seikaku to yakuwari," in Takasaki and Pak, *Kikoku undô to wa nan datta no ka* (Tokyo: Heibonsha, 2005), 251–252; see also "Chôsenjin kikoku sokushin no dai-undô," *Akahata*, 15 December 1958. For Koizumi Junya's role in the society, see *Chosun Ilbo* [Joseon Ilbo] (English online edition) 19 October 2005.

For growth of *Chongryun* schools and founding of Korea University, see Kim Deok-Ryong, *Chôsen gakkô no sengoshi—1945–1972* (Tokyo: Shakai Hyôronsha, 2004), 188–194, 274.

For articles cited from the journal *Korea*, see "Ministry-Run Store Opened," *Korea*, no. 21 (1958): 18–19; "More Foodstuffs and Daily Necessaries," *Korea*, no. 26 (1958): 19–21; "Construction of Pyongyang," *Korea*, no. 26 (1958): 22–23; "Modern Village," *Korea*, no 27 (1958): 30–31; "Abundant Daily Necessities," *Korea*, no. 27 (1958): 14; "Two Families from Japan," *Korea*, no. 27 (1958) 13.

Yi Yang-Soo's comments are from author's interview with Yi Yang-Soo, 2 June 2005; Oh Su-Ryong's comments are from author's interview with Oh Su-Ryong, 20 June 2005.

For development of ethnic schools and financial support for the schools from North Korea, see Kim Deok-Ryong, *Chôsen gakkô no sengoshi—1945–1972* (Tokyo: Shakai Hyôronsha, 2004); see also Kim Chan-Jong, *Chôsen Sôren* (Tokyo: Shinchô Shinsho, 2004), 69–73.

For North Korean government spent 400 million yen, see letter from Testuz to Ruff, 26 April 1961, ICRC Archives, file no. B AG 232 105-031, *Problème du rapatriement des Coréens du Japon, dossier XIX: Généralités pour la periode 1961–1964*, 03.01.1961-14.12.1964, Geneva.

For North Korean Red Cross telegram to ICRC about money transfers to Ômura, see *On the Question of 600,000 Koreans in Japan*, SKDDKJR, 723.1 JA, file number 177, Seoul, p. 469. For Shimazu's telegram to Boissier about money transfers, see Japan Red Cross telegram g471 from Shimazu to Boissier, 3 December 1956, ICRC Archives, file no. B AG 232 105-005.01, Geneva. For evidence to Parliamentary Committees on money transfer, see Yoon Bong-Gyu's evidence to the Foreign Affairs Committee of the Lower House of the Diet, KG, 18 March 1958; evidence of Socialist parliamentarian Tanaka Orinoshin to Accounts Committee of the Diet, KG, 29 October 1958; telegram from Kim Eung Ki to Shimazu, 10 October 1959 ICRC Archives, file no. B AG 232 105-013, *Problème du rapatriement des Coréens du Japon, dossier XI: Généralités pour la période septembre-decembre 1959, deuxième partie*, 11.10.1959-29.12.1959, Geneva; Mechior Borsinger to ICRC, 31 October 1959, ICRC Archives, file no. B AG 232 105-013, Geneva. For Gallopin's comments on propaganda, see Gallopin to Inoue, 16 April 1957, ICRC Archives, file no. B AG 232 105-005.01, Geneva.

CHAPTER 14 - THE DIPLOMATS' DIARIES

For a discussion of North Korean motives for supporting repatriation, see Pak Jeong-Jin, "Kita Chôsen ni totte 'kikoku jigyô' to wa nan datta no ka," in Takasaki and Pak, eds., *Kikoku undô to wa nan datta no ka* (Tokyo: Heibonsha, 2005),180–211.

For Kim Il-Sung's 8 Sept. 1959 speech, see *On the Question of 600,000 Koreans in Japan*, SKDDKJR, 723.1 JA, file number 177, Seoul, p. 419.

For further discussion of Soviet sources on the repatriation, see Tessa Morris-Suzuki, "Buksong saeop gwa talnaeng jeonggi ingweon jeongchi" (Repatriation and the Politics of Humanitarianism in the Cold War and Beyond) *Changjak gwa Bipyeong*, 129, Fall 2005, 97–113, and Tessa Morris-Suzuki, "Defining the Boundaries of the Cold War Nation: 1950s Japan and the Other Within," *Japanese Studies*, 26, no. 3, (December 2006), 303–316.

For Puzanov-Kim discussion on return of sixty students, see Puzanov Diaries, 19 August 1957, JRA, file no. RU Secret 57-2-1-2, Seoul.

For Puzanov attends farewell for Chinese "volunteers," see Puzanov Diaries, 15 March 1958, JRA, file no. RU secret 58, Seoul. For Soviet position on Korean re-unification, see Balász Szalontai, *Kim Il Sung in the Khrushchev Era: Soviet-DPRK Relations and the Roots of North Korean Despotism* (Washington, DC: Woodrow Wilson Center Press, 2005), 157–161.

For North Korea seeks return of ethnic Koreans from China, see Szalontai, *Kim Il Sung in the Khrushchev Era* (Washington, DC: Woodrow Wilson Center Press, 2005), 152. See also Puzanov Diaries, 3 March 1959, JRA , file no. RU-secret 59-2-2, Seoul.

For North Korean messages to Japan about Ômura detainees, see *On the Question of 600,000 Koreans in Japan*, in SKDDKJR, 723.1 JA, file number 177, Seoul,.

For Nam Il's summer vacation, see Puzanov Diaries, 20 May 1958, JRA, file no. RU Secret 58-4, Seoul.

For Kim Il-Sung's conversation with Pelishenko, see "Record of Conversation with Comrade Kim Il-Sung, 14 and 15 July 1958," in Diary of V. I. Pelishenko, 23 July 1958, Foreign Policy Archives of the Russian Federation, archive 0102, collection 14, file 8, folder 95. (I am very grateful to Dr. A. Lankov for drawing my attention to this document.) This document is also cited in Tessa Morris-Suzuki, "Defining the Boundaries of the Cold War Nation: 1950s Japan and the Other Within," *Japanese Studies*, 26, no. 3, (December 2006), 303–316 and Kikuchi Yoshi-aki, "'Kikoku undô' no haigo ni Kita Chôsen no 'kôsaku'," *Yomiuri Weekly*, 16 July 2006, 71–73.

For quotation from *On the Question of 600,000 Koreans in Japan*, see SKDDKJR, 723.1 JA, file number 177, Seoul, p. 414.

For Chinese and Mongolian assistance with repatriation, see Szalontai, *Kim Il Sung in the Khrushchev Era* (Washington, DC: Woodrow Wilson Center Press, 2005), 146; Japan Red Cross telegram to China Red Cross, 28 November 1959, ICRC Archives, file no. B AG 232 105-015.05, *Copies de déclarations officielles, de notes, de télégrammes, pour information transmises par la Croix-Rouge japonaise*, 4.9.1959-26.12.1959, Geneva. For change of personnel at Soviet Embassy, Tokyo, see Inoue to Gallopin, 31 October 1958, ICRC Archives, file no. B AG 232 105-006.04, Geneva. For USSR provides foreign currency, see Record of Conversation with Attache of DPRK Embassy in USSR Kim Don Tek [*sic*], 11 June 1959, JRA, file no. RU-secret 59-1-4, Seoul.

For Kim Il-Sung's thanks to USSR for help with repatriation, see Puzanov Diaries, 16 December 1959, JRA, file no. RU-Secret 59-3-3, Seoul. For Nam Il–Mikoyan conversation, see Record of Conversation of A. I. Mikoyan with Deputy Chairman of the Ministerial Cabinet and Foreign Minister of the DPRK Nam Il, 29 July 1959, JRA, file no. RU Secret 59-1-3, Seoul; also cited in Tessa Morris-Suzuki, "Buksong saeop gwa talnaeng jeonggi ingweon jeongchi" (Repatriation and the Politics of Humanitarianism in the Cold War and Beyond) *Changjak gwa Bipyeong*, 129, Fall 2005, 110.

For North Korea prepares pamphlets to send to UN, see minutes of conversation with Comrade Kwon Son-Man, Attache, DPRK Embassy to USSR, by V. Lisikov,

2nd Secretary, Ministry of Foreign Afairs, 23 October 1958, JRA, file no. RU-secret, 58-1, Seoul.

For Ri Il-Gyeong, head of Propaganda and Agitation Department, see minutes of conversation with Ri Il-Gyeong, Head, Department of Propaganda and Agitation, Central Committee, Korean Workers' Party, by G. Samsonov, First Secretary, Embassy of USSR in DPRK, 15 July 1957, JRA, file no. RU-secret 57-4-1-3, Seoul. Ri's comments about Japan were reported to Ambassador Puzanov by newly appointed Foreign Minister Pak Song-Cheol. See Puzanov Diaries, 18 December, JRA, file no. RU-Secret 59-3-3, Seoul.

CHAPTER 15 - FROM GENEVA TO CALCUTTA

For relations between Inoue and Ri Il-Gyeong, see Angst to ICRC, 11 March 1959, ICRC Archives, file no. B AG 232 105.01, Geneva. For Ri's five children, see Szalontai, *Kim Il Sung in the Khrushchev Era* (Washington, DC: Woodrow Wilson Center Press, 2005), 202.

For Ri Il-Gyeong's opposition to ICRC screening, see Puzanov Diaries, 17 July 1959, JRA, file no. RU-Secret 59-2-4, Seoul; for North Korean views on ICRC involvement, see Puzanov Diaries, 13 March 1959, JRA, file no. RU-Secret 59-2-2, Seoul. For Kim Il-Sung's fear of "reactionary and espionage elements," see "Record of Conversation with Comrade Kim Il-Sung, 14 and 15 July 1958," in Diary of V. I. Pelishenko, 23 July 1958, Foreign Policy Archives of the Russian Federation, archive 0102, collection 14, file 8, folder 95.

For Soviet mediation and prodding, see confidential memo for Boissier and Gallopin, "Point essentials de la conversation avec Mr. Tchikalenko," 5 March 1959, ICRC Archives, file no. B AG 232 105-009 - *Problème du rapatriement des Coréens du Japon, dossier VIII: généralités concernant la période janvier-juin 1959*, 21.01.1959-29.06.1959, Geneva; see also Puzanov Diaries, 14 March 1959, JRA, file no. RU-Secret 59-2-2, Seoul.

On the positions of the Japanese government and Japanese Red Cross, see minutes (procès-verbal) of meeting, ICRC Conseil de Présidence, no. 337, 28 May 1959, ICRC Archives microfilm, p. 3; on conflicts between the position of the Japanese government and the Japan Red Cross Society, see also *Asahi Shimbun*, 28 May 1959. On what mattered to the Japanese government: This became evident in late October 1959, when the government agreed to a compromise set of "supplementary explanations" governing the procedures for repatriation. See chapter 17.

For North Korean proposal on radio broadcast and Ri Il-Gyeong's claim that negotiations were a "success," see Puzanov Diaries, 17 June 1959, JRA, file no. RU-secret 59-2-4, Seoul. For North Korean proposal of 7 June, see Puzanov Diaries, 8 June 1959, JRA, file no. RU-secret, 59-2-4, Seoul; for Gallopin on Japanese "capitulation" to North Korea demands, see minutes of ICRC Plenary Meeting, 3 June 1959, ICRC Archives, file no. B AG 232 105-009, Geneva.

For text of the draft accord, see ICRC Archives, file no. B AG 232 105-007.01, *Plan de l'Accord entre la Société de la Croix-Rouge japonaise et la Société de la Croix-Rouge de la République démocratique populaire de Corée relatif au retour des Coréens qui résident au Japon, signé le 24 juin 1959 à titre provisoire et définitivement à Calcutta le 13 août 1959*, 24.06.1959-13.08.1959, Geneva.

For early March ICRC Plenary Session, see "Comité – Séance plénière du Jeudi 5 mars 1959 à14.h. 30," 5 March 1959, ICRC Archives, file no. B AG 232 105.01, Geneva.

For Presidential Council meeting, see "Conseil de Présidence – Séance du Jeudi 1959, à 14h.30," 25 June 1959, ICRC Archives, file no. B AG 232 105-009, Geneva.

For visits from Kasai, Inoue, Okumura, and Avramov, see "Note d'entretiens," 8 July 1959, ICRC Archives, file no. B AG 232 105-010, *Problème du rapatriement des Coréens du Japon, dossier VIII: Généralités concernant le période juillet-août 1959*, 01.07.1959-28.08.1959, Geneva. For Fujiyama letter, see Fujiyama to Boissier, 15 July 1959, ICRC Archives, file no. B AG 232 105-010, Geneva. For *Chongryun* demonstrations, see Takasaki, "Kikoku mondai no keika to haikei," in Takasaki and Pak eds. *Kikoku undô to wa nan datta no ka* (Tokyo: Heibonsha, 2005), 36.

For Japanese Foreign Ministry Officials meeting with Harry Angst, see Angst to ICRC Geneva, "Repatriation to North Korea," 20 July 1959, ICRC Archives, file no. B AG 232 105-010, Geneva. For problem of finding Swiss nationals who spoke Japanese, see "Rapport du Dr. Junod sur sa mission au Japon et en Corée du Sud, 21 août–27 septembre 1959," 21 August–27 September, ICRC Archives, file no. B AG 232 105-014, *Problème du rapatriement des Coréens du Japon, dossier XII: Rapports de Dr. Junod, délégué, et annexes*, 28.08.1959-06.10.1959, Geneva.

For seven questions sent to Okumura and Inoue, see Part II of memorandum attached to Gallopin letter to Inoue, 24 July 1959, ICRC Archives, file no. B AG 232 105-011.03, *Aide-mémoire du 24 juillet 1959 transmis à la Croix-Rouge japonaise et projets de communication, réponses*, 03.07.1959-12.08.1959, Geneva. For reply to seven questions, see "English translation of the cable received from President Shimazu addressed to President Boissier, ICRC, on July 27th, 1959," attached to Inoue letter to Boissier, 28 July 1959, ICRC Archives, file no. B AG 232 105-011.03, Geneva. For confidential statement on treatment of Koreans in Japan, see "Treatment of Koreans in Japan," 3 August 1959, ICRC Archives, file no. B AG 232 105-011.06, *Notes et procès-verbaux d'entretiens avec Masutaro Inoue, directeur du Département des Affaires etrangères de la Croix-Rouge japonaise, lors de son séjour à Genève*, 10.07.1959-13.08.1959, Geneva. For statement on unemployment insurance and Labor Standards Law, see "Note à l'attention de Monsieur R. Gallopin," from Inoue, 30 July 1959, ICRC Archives, file no. B AG 232 105-011.06, Geneva. For statement on forced labor, see press release, "A brief review of Korean residents in Japan," 11 July 1959, ICRC Archives, file no. B AG 232 105-011.06, Geneva.

For Inoue's report referring to forced labor, see "Repatriation Problem of Certain Koreans Residing in Japan," October 1956, ICRC Archives, file no. B AG 232 105-027, *Documentation concernant le rapatriement des Coréens et les pêcheurs japonais détenues à Pusan.* 10.10.1956–04.03.1959, p. 2, Geneva; see also Shimazu to Boissier, 28 February 1959, ICRC Archives, file no. B AG 232 105-002. For Kasai's "test case," see annex to Kasai letter to Li Byung Nam, 10 December 1957, ICRC Archives, file no. B AG 232 105-003.01, Geneva.

The life stories of returnees suggest the many and complex ways in which forced labor affected Koreans in Japan. For example, Pu Song-Gyu, who left for North Korea with his family on the first repatriation ship, described how he had first come to Japan as a voluntary migrant from Jeju, then moved to Manchuria, from where he was forcibly recruited to work for the Japanese military on Tinian in the South Pacific, being sent back to Japan in the closing stages of the war; see *Asahi Shimbun*, 14 December 1959. Chang Myeong-Su (who organized meetings in the Niigata Red Cross Center at which returnees, on the night before their departure, spoke of their memories of life in Japan) recalls numerous older people who spoke of experiences of forced labor, in which they had experienced "slave-like conditions in coal and ore mines and on dangerous construction sites"; see Chang Myeong-Su, "Kikoku Undô to wa nan data no ka," *Mintô* (December 1989): 150–170, quotation from 152.

On Unemployment Insurance Law, National Health Insurance Act, and National Pension Act, see Ministry of Health and Welfare, *Social Welfare Services in Japan* (Tokyo: Ministry of Health and Welfare, 1960); see also Shin Yeong–Hon, "Zainichi Chôsenjin to shakai hoshô" in Pak Chong-Myeong, ed., *Zainichi Chôsenjin: Rekishi, genjô, tenbô* (Tokyo: Akashi Shoten, 1995) 287–288.

For ICRC's response to accord, see Boissier to Shimazu, 7 August 1959, ICRC Archives, file no. B AG 232 105-011.03, Geneva; Boissier to Gloor, 24 July 1959, ICRC Archives, file no. B AG 232 105-010, Geneva.

For the dog in the night-time, see Arthur Conan Doyle, "Silver Blaze," in *The Memoirs of Sherlock Holmes, The Penguin Complete Sherlock Holmes* (Harmondsworth: Penguin Books, 1981), 347.

CHAPTER 16 - SILENT PARTNERS

Nehru's speech is reproduced in "XIXme Conference Internationale de la Croix-Rouge," *Revue Internationale de la Croix-Rouge*, no. 471 (March 1958): 98–103.

For Kasai on responsibility for accord, see Angst to ICRC, 22 July 1959, ICRC Archives, file no. B AG 232 105-010, Geneva.

For emigration of Jews from the USSR, see memorandum of conversation, Bilateral Issues Discussed between Secretary of State and Soviet Foreign Minister Gromyko, 26 September 1959, Thomson-Gale Declassified Documents Reference System, document number CK100179855.

For U.S. knowledge of the propaganda campaign directed at *Zainichi* Koreans, see "Notes for Confidential use of ICRC," 19 June 1959, ICRC Archives, file no. B AG 232 105-009, Geneva.

For Villard's phone call to Boissier, see Boissier, Procès-verbal de telephone, 2 March 1959, ICRC Archives B AG 232 105-009, Geneva. For Villard's face-to-face meeting with ICRC, see Borsinger, Procès-Verbal d'entretien, "Concernant le problème des Coréens au Japan," 18 March 1959, ICRC Archives, file no. B AG 232 105-009, Geneva. For Christian groups' involvement and Rev. Hallam Shorrock, representative of the World Council of Churches in South Korea, who played a particularly active role in trying to encourage various governments and organizations involved to rethink the repatriation plan, see Hallam C. Shorrock Jr., *An Analysis and Appraisal of the Problem of Koreans in Japan and the Role of the International Committee of the Red Cross and Other Agencies in the Solution*, 1 July 1959, ICRC Archives, file no. B AG 232 105-011.02, *Rapports du M. Junod, délégué au Japon*, 26.08.1959-06.10.1959, Geneva.

For position of the American Red Cross on the repatriation, see "Synopsis of State and Intelligence Material Communicated to the President, June 24 thru 26 1959," in Thomson-Gale Declassified Documents Reference System, doc. no. CK3100317878.

For Villard on "inadequate" proposed agreement, see "Note de dossier" by R. Gallopin, 12 June 1959, ICRC Archives, file no. B AG 232 105-009, Geneva.

For Ambassador MacArthur's comments on Kishi and repatriation, see "Synopsis of State and Intelligence material reported to the President, June 24 thru 26, 1959," Thomson-Gale Declassified Documents Reference System, doc. no. CK3100105127.

For John S. D. Eisenhower memo on repatriation, see "Staff Notes 5/1/59," 1 May 1959, in Thomson-Gale Declassified Documents Reference System, doc. no. CK3100256085.

For in the "last resort" the ICRC should "announce its decision in principle," see "Aide-Mémoire remis par M. Villard, représentant des USA à Genève, à M. Boissier, le 4 août 1959, à propos de la signature de l'Accord entre la Croix-Rouge japonaise et la Croix-Rouge Nord Coréenne portant sur le rapatriement des Coréens au Japon," ICRC Archives, file no. B AG 232 105-010, Geneva.

For U.S. concerns about Kishi's future and Japan's political orientation, see for example, National Intelligence Estimate no. 41-58, "Probable Developments in Japan's International Orientation," 23 December 1958, reproduced in Madeline Chi, Louis J. Smith, and Robert J. McMahon, eds., *Foreign Relations of the United States 1958–1960*, microfiche supplement to vols. XVII–XVIII (Indonesia, Japan, Korea), document no. 478, Washington, Department of State, 1994, (hereafter FRUS supplement XVII–XVIII); see also letter from Hugh S. Cumming to the Acting Secretary of State, "Parliamentary Crisis in Japan," 12 November 1958, FRUS XVIII, reproduced as document no. 477, p. 871. For U.S. government documents repeatedly stressed the importance of repatriation in winning voted support for the Kishi regime—particularly since a parliamentary election took place in June 1959, in the middle of the Geneva negotiations, see for example memorandum of conversation, Call by Korean Foreign Minister Cho, 29 May 1959, FRUS supplement XVII–XVIII, reproduced as document no. 766.

For Eisenhower's comments on "wrong direction," see memorandum of conversation, President's Far Eastern Trip, 20 June 1960, FRUS XVIII, reproduced as document no. 323, p. 671.

For "best chance to settle this matter," see Department of State, memorandum of conversation, "Call by Korean Foreign Minister Cho," 29 May 1959, supplement to FRUS vols. XVII–XVIII, reproduced as document no. 766.

For Syngman Rhee seen as an embarrassment, see telegram from Parsons, FE, State Department to Ambassador, Seoul, 24 August 1959, reproduced as document no. 795, supplement to FRUS vols. XVII–XVIII; memo from Bane to Parsons, 8 December 1959, supplement to FRUS vols. XVII–XVIII, reproduced as document no. 819; telegram from Gilstrap, U.S. Embassy Seoul to State Department, 16 October 1959, supplement to FRUS vols. XVII–XVIII, reproduced as document no. 809.

For State Department background paper on repatriation, see "The Korean Minority in Japan and the Repatriation Problem," report attached to confidential memo from Parsons to Herter, "Korean Repatriation Problem," 10 July 1959, DOS, FE Files Lot 61 D6, "Japan-ROK Repatriation Dispute," FRUS supplement XVII–XVIII, reproduced as document no. 786. For Parsons' "helpful suggestion" to Asakai, see memorandum of conversation, "(1) Courtesy Call (2) Asakai's Visit to Japan (3) Geneva Talks," 9 July 1959, FRUS supplement XVII–XVIII, document no. 488.

For South Korean Foreign Ministry's "positive program," see Synopsis of State and intelligence material reported to President Eisenhower, 2–6 July 1959, in Thomson-Gale Declassified Documents Reference System, doc. no. CK3100317878.

For Herter's letter to Syngman Rhee, see Secretary of State Herter, letter to President Rhee, 24 September 1959, FRUS supplement XVII–XVIII, reproduced as document no. 803.

For Huh-Eisenhower discussion, see memorandum of conversation, President's Far Eastern Trip, 20 June 1960, FRUS XVIII, document no. 323, pp. 670–671.

For MacArthur and Fujiyama's discussion about discrimination against *Zainichi* Koreans, and MacArthur's comments on "face-saving document," see memorandum of conversation between Foreign Minister Fujiyama, Ambassador Douglas MacArthur II and others, 22 August 1959, in NARA, section RG95, CFDF 1955-1959, box 2722, document no. 694.958/8-2859, Washington D.C.

For State Department meeting with Kishi, Fujiyama, and others, see Department of State memorandum of conversation, "Problems Relating to the Republic of Korea," 19 January 1960, FRUS XVIII, document no. 142, p. 275.

CHAPTER 17 - A GUIDE FOR MR. RETURNEE

For repatriation Coordination Committee established, see Kôseishô, *Hikiage to engo sanjûnen no ayumi*, 1978, extract reproduced in Kim and Takayanagi, *Kita Chôsen kikoku jigyô kankei shiryôshû* (Tokyo: Shinkansha, 1995), 304–305.

For 3,655 "Red Cross Windows," see Otto Lehner, "ICRC Special Mission in Japan – Information and Instructions for ICRC Representatives," 17 September 1959, ICRC Archives, file no. B AG 232 105-012, *Problème du rapatriement des Coréens du Japon, dossier XI: Généralités pour la période septembre-decembre 1959, première partie*, 1.9.1959-10.10.1959, Geneva.

For *Chongryun* procedures for processing *Zainichi* Koreans, see Borsinger to ICRC, "Conversation with Mr. Masutaro Inoue, International Relations Director, JRCS," 31 October 1959, ICRC Archives, file no. B AG 232 105-013, Geneva.

For North Korean "Returnees Welcoming Committee," see Takasaki, "Kikoku Mondai no Keika to Haikei," in Takasaki and Pak, eds., *Kikoku undô to wa nan datta no ka* (Tokyo: Heibonsha, 2005), 25; for North Korean information campaign about repatriation, see *Chôsen Sôren*, 5 October 1959. For Soviet Union prepares naval escort, see Puzanov Diaries, 8 December 1959, JRA, file no. RU–Secret 59-3-3, Seoul.

For Marcel Junod's wartime visit to Japan, see Marcel Junod, *Warriors without Weapons*, trans. Edward Fitzgerald (London: Jonathan Cape, 1951), 272–307. For Junod arrives in Japan 23 August 1959 and attends meeting of Repatriation Coordination Committee, see "Rapport du Dr. Junod sur sa mission au Japon et en Corée du Sud – 21 Août – 27 Septembre 1959," ICRC Archives, file no. B AG 232 105-014, Geneva. For "Red Cross Windows" staffed by local government officials, see memo from Melchior Borsinger, "A l'attention du Monsieur le Délégué, Chef de Mission spéciale au Japon," 30 October 1959, ICRC Archives, file no. B AG 232 105-024, *Documents relatifs au rapatriement des Coréens du Japon rédiges par Melchior Borsinger, délégué, et Jacques Chenvière, Vice-Président*, 29.06.1959-04.11.1959, Geneva.

For *A Guide for Mr. Returnee* given to Ambassador MacArthur, see "Rapport du Dr. Junod sur sa mission au Japon et en Corée du Sud – 21 Août – 27 Septembre 1959," ICRC Archives, file no. B AG 232 105-014, Geneva. For text of *A Guide for Mr. Returnee*, see ICRC Archives, file no. B AG 232 015-014, Geneva. For ICRC concerns about content of *Guide*, see "Conseil de Présidence – Séance du Jeudi 17 Septembre 1959 à 14 hr 30," ICRC Archives, file no. B AG 105-015, *Problème du rapatriement des Coréens du Japon, dossier XIII: Les premiers départs vers la République démocratique populaire de Corée*, 03.09.1959-28.01.1960, Geneva.

For just 432 people signed up, see Note no. 38 to ICRC Geneva, "Rapport sur l'enregistrement des Coréens qui désirent se rendre en République Démocratique de Corée," 24 December 1959, ICRC Archives, file no. B AG 232 105 013, p. 2, Geneva.

For North Korean protest about Japan Red Cross refusal to transfer funds, see telegram from Kim Eung Ki to Shimazu, 10 October 1959, ICRC Archives, file no. B AG 232 105-013, Geneva.

For supplementary negotiations worked out by Foreign Ministry and Hoashi Kei, see Borsinger to ICRC, "Concerning Meeting with M. Miaki, Gaimucho, [sic] Asian Department, MM. Kasai and Inoue JRCS and, for the ICRC, Mr. Lehner, Hoffmann, Gouy and Borsinger," 31 October 1959, ICRC Archives, file no. B AG

232 105-013, Geneva; see also "Supplementary Explanations on Certain Aspects of Actual Operation of Repatriation Work," ICRC Archives, file no. B AG 232 105-013, Geneva.

For sample question to returnees, see "Supplementary Explanations on Certain Aspects of Actual Operation of Repatriation Work," ICRC Archives, file no. B AG 232 105-013, Geneva; see also "Kikan gyômu jisshi ni atte no sochi," in Nihon Sekikjûjisha, ed., *Nihon Sekijûjisha shashikô*, vol. 7 (Tokyo: Nihon Sekijûjisha, 1986), 207–209, quotation from 208. It should be noted that the Japanese version of this question differs somewhat from the English translation provided to the ICRC. The Japanese could more precisely be translated as: "We are giving you your exit permit. You fully understood this message and have not changed your mind—right?" For removal of doors to "special rooms," see Borsinger to ICRC, 31 October 1959, ICRC Archives, file no. B AG 232 105-013, Geneva.

For 24 October meeting between Inoue and Lehner et al., see Borsinger to ICRC, "Conversation with Mr. Masutaro Inoue, International Relations Director, JRCS," 31 October 1959, ICRC Archives, file no. B AG 232 105-013, Geneva. For meeting of Lehner and others with police, see Borsinger, highly confidential minutes to ICRC, "Meeting at JRCS Headquarters between representatives of the Japanese National Police Agency, the JRCS and ICRC," 31 October 1959, ICRC Archives, file no. B AG 232 105-013, Geneva. The central role of *Chongryun* in the registration process is also stressed in other documents, for example Note no. 38 to ICRC Geneva, "Rapport sur l'enregistrement des Coréens," 24 December 1959, ICRC Archives, file no. B AG 232 105 013, Geneva.

For impossible for ICRC to withdraw from action, see "Conseil de Présidence – Séance du Jeudi 17 septembre 1949 à 14 hr 30, ICRC Archives, file no. B AG 232 105-015, Geneva. For instructions to delegates, see Lehner, "ICRC Special Mission in Japan – Information and Instructions for ICRC Representatives," 17 September 1959, ICRC Archives, file no. B AG 232 105-012, Geneva.

For a list of ICRC delegates in Japan, see Nihon Sekijûjisha, ed., *Nihon Sekijûjisha shashikô*, vol. 7 (Tokyo: Nihon Sekijûjisha, 1986), 207. For restrictive conditions faced by ICRC delegates, see Otto Lehner, "ICRC Special Mission in Japan – Information and Instructions for ICRC Representatives," 17 September 1959, ICRC Archives, file no. B AG 232 105-012, Geneva. For "Russians or Americans," see Durand to ICRC, 14 March 1960, ICRC Archives, file no. B AG 232 105-015, Geneva. For lack of access to the Guide Book, see André Durand, "Aide Mémoire: Rapatriement des Coréens du Japon" 23 June 1960, ICRC Archives, file no. B AG 232 105-017, *Problème du rapatriement des Coréens du Japon, dossier XIII: généralités concernant l'anneé 1960, deuxième partie*, 12.04.1960-12.12.1960, p. 17, Geneva.

For *Chongryun* boycott lifted, see George Hoffmann to ICRC, "Weekly Report for the Period from 2nd November till 7th November 1959," ICRC Archives, file no. B AG 232 105-013, Geneva. For Japan Red Cross wants to send as many repatriates as possible, see telegram from Japancross to Koreacross, 9 November 1959, ICRC Archives, file no. B AG 232 105-015.05, *Copies de déclarations officielles, de notes, de télégrammes, pour information transmises par la Croix-Rouge japonaise,* 04.09.1959-26.12.1959, Geneva.

For Ri Il-Gyeong now happy, see Puzanov Diaries, 18 December 1959, JRA, file no. RU-secret 59-3-3, Seoul.

For Shimazu's visits to Niigata, see Shimazu Tadatsugu, *Jindô no hata no moto ni* (Tokyo, Kodansha, 1965), 246–249.

CHAPTER 18 - TOWARD THE PROMISED LAND

The account of Yi Yang-Soo's experiences in this chapter are based on interview with Yi Yang-Soo, 2 June 2005; see also "Aru oyako no sengo," *Kyodo Tsûshin*, 7 August, 10 August, 13 August, and 14 August 2003; Yang-Su Lee, "The Repatriation of Koreans from Japan to North Korea," *Life and Human Rights*, no. 4 (1997): 10–25; Yi Yang-Soo, "Honrô sareta jinsei ni shûshifu o utsu!" *Kurio*, nos. 5–7, 1987–1988.

The account of "Yamada Kumiko's" experiences is based on interviews with "Yamada Kumiko," 26 May 2005 and 3 June 2005.

For Zeller's report on repatriation process, see M. Zeller, report to Durand, 23 January 1961, ICRC Archives, file no. B AG 232 105-031, Geneva.

For information from Public Security Investigation Bureau, see "Re-Call on Messrs. Satoshi Kurisaka, Chief, Nobuo Miyamoto, Section 2 – Koreans, of the Public Peace Investigation Bureau, Hyogo District, 24 August 1960," attached to Zeller to Durand, 4 September 1960, ICRC Archives, file no. B AG 232 105-017, *Problème du rapatriement des Coréens du Japon, dossier XIV: Généralités concernant l'année 1960, deuxième partie,* 12.04.1960-12.12.1960, Geneva. See also memo on meeting between the Red Cross and the Japanese Government about the diminution in the number of candidates for repatriation, 27 January 1961, ICRC Archives, file no. B AG 232 105-031, *Problème du rapatriement des Coréens du Japon, dossier XIX: Généralités pour la période 1961–1964,* 03.01.1961-14.12.1964, Geneva.

For U.S. pressure to complete the repatriation and terminate the accord and the Japanese response, see telegram from the Embassy in Japan to the Department of State, 22 July 1960, in FRUS XVIII, document no. 194, p. 389. For Japanese Red Cross urges a speed up of repatriation, see Kasai to Boissier, 7 December 1960, ICRC Archives, file no. B AG 232 105-017, Geneva.

Inoue's talk to U.S. servicemen is quoted in Maunoir to Durand, "Rapatriement des Coréens du Japon," 16 February 1960, ICRC Archives, file no. B AG 232 105-016, *Problème du rapatriement des Coréens du Japon, dossier XIV: Généralités concernant l'année 1960, première partie,* 05.01.1960-08.04.1960, Geneva.

For compromise figure of 1,200, see letter from Kasai to Boissier, 7 December 1960, ICRC Archives, file no. B AG 232 105-017, Geneva.

For Immigration Control Bureau's report on Yi and his mother, see Immigration Control Bureau, Ministry of Justice, "Monthly Report on the Repatriation to

North Korea," no. 18, June 30 1961, ICRC Archives, file no. B AG 232 105-030.01, *Monthly Reports on the Repatriation to North Korea*, 31.03.1961-31.12.1964, Geneva. For ICRC Report on the same subject, see Fred Bieri, Note no. 409 to ICRC, Geneva, "Report Regarding the 65th Ship," ICRC Archives, file no. B AG 232 105-028.02, *Rapports sur les convois*, 17.01.1961-28.12.1964, Geneva.

The account of Oh Su-Ryong's experiences in this chapter is based on interview with Oh Su-Ryong, 20 June 2005.

CHAPTER 19 - RETURN TO NOWHERE

Oh Su-Ryong's experiences based on interview with Oh Su-Ryong, 20 June 2005. "Yamada Kumiko's" experiences based on interviews with "Yamada Kumiko," 26 May 2005 and 3 June 2005.

For returnee's letter, see annex to letter from Durand to ICRC, 19 October 1960, ICRC Archives, file no. B AG 232 105-017, Geneva.

For Inoue's reponse to appeal on freedom of movement, see letter from Testuz to Maunoir, 22 July 1963, ICRC Archives, file no. B AG 232 105-028.04, *Problème du libre passage entre la Corée-du-Nord et le Japon*, 05.06.1963-28.12.1964, Geneva. For government "wishes to get rid of as many Koreans as possible," see letter from Maunoir to Testuz, 6 February 1964, ICRC archives, file no. B AG 105-028.04, Geneva. For asylum seeker in Cambodia, see Kim Yeong-Dal and Takayanagi Toshio, eds., *Kita Chôsen kikoku jigyô kankei shiryô* (Tokyo: Shinkansha, 1994), 344.

For the end of the Calcutta Accord and the signing of the Moscow Agreement, see Takasaki, "Kikoku mondai no keika to haikei," in Takasaki Sôji and Pak Jeong-Jin, eds., *Kikoku undô to wa nan datta no ka* (Tokyo: Heibonsha, 2005), 49–50.

Remark by Hungarian diplomat is quoted in Balàsz Szalontai, *Kim Il Sung in the Khrushchev Era: Soviet-DPRK Relations and the Roots of North Korean Despotism* (Washington, DC: Woodrow Wilson Center Press, 2005), 153.

On stereotypes of and prejudice toward returnees from Japan, see Bradley K. Martin, *Under the Loving Care of the Fatherly Leader: North Korea and the Kim Dynasty* (New York: St. Martin's Press, 2004), 228-229, 584; see also Ishimaru Jirô, *Kita Chôsen nanmin* (Tokyo: Kôdansha, 2002), 153–175. For other discussions of the experience of returnees in North Korea, see Satô Hisashi, "Kikusha no sono ato," in Takasaki Sôji and Pak Jeong-Jin, eds., *Kikoku undô to wa nan datta no ka* (Tokyo: Heibonsha, 2005), 93–120; Wada Haruki, "Kikoku undô wa nan datta no ka" Part 2, *Ronza* (May 2004) 132–143.

For returnee arrested as a "spy," see Cheong Gi-Hae, *Kikokusen* (Tokyo: Bungei Shunjûsha, 1997), particularly 132–141. For Kang Cheol-Hwan's experiences, see Kang Chol-Hwan and Pierre Rigoulot, *Aquariums of Pyongyang: Ten Years in the North Korean Gulag*, trans. Yair Reiner (New York: Basic Books, 2001), 6. On North Korean punishment zones, see also Heo Man-Ho, "North Korean Human Rights in Cooperative-Antagonistic Relations: Intervention and Education," in

National Human Rights Commission of the Republic of Korea, ed., *North Korean Human Rights: Trends and Issues* (Seoul: National Human Rights Commission of the Republic of Korea, 2005), 12–40. On the internment of returnees, see also Ishimaru Jirô, *Kita Chôsen nanmin* (Tokyo: Kôdansha, 2002); Ahn Hyok, "I Met Korean Repatriates and Their Japanese Wives in the North Korean Concentration Camp," in *Life and Human Rights* (the journal of the Society to Help Returnees to North Korea, English edition), no. 4 (1997): 26–31;

For the execution of Ri Il-Gyeong, see Balàsz Szalontai, *Kim Il Sung in the Khrushchev Era: Soviet-DPRK Relations and the Roots of North Korean Despotism* (Washington, DC: Woodrow Wilson Center Press, 2005), 202.

"Taniguchi Hiroko's" experiences based on interview with "Taniguchi Hiroko," 10 June 2005.

CHAPTER 20 - THE WILLOW TREES OF NIIGATA

Hokari Minoru's book is *Radikaru ôraru hisutori* (Tokyo: Ochanomizu Shobô, 2004).

The passage quoted is from Minoru Hokari, "The Living Earth: The World of the Aborigines," trans. Uchida Kyoko, *Conversations* 6, no. 2 (Summer 2006): 51, originally published as "Seimei afureru daichi: Aborijini no sekai" (serial column), *Niigata Nippô*, 2003.

INDEX

ABOUT THE AUTHOR

Tessa Morris-Suzuki was born in England and lived and worked in Japan before migrating to Australia in 1981. She is currently professor of Japanese history in the Research School of Pacific and Asian Studies at the Australian National University, where her research focuses on Japan's frontiers and minority communities and on questions of historical memory in East Asia. Her previous books include *Re-Inventing Japan: Time, Space, Nation* (1998) and *The Past Within Us: Media, Memory, History* (2005).